THE ILLUSTRATED GUIDE
GARDEN TREES

An A–Z guide to choosing the best trees for your garden, with 230 stunning photographs

How to select trees for colour, height and seasonal variation and for different kinds of location, soil and aspect, with expert tips on cultivation, pruning and propagation

MIKE BUFFIN

southwater

This edition is published by Southwater, an imprint of
Anness Publishing Ltd, Hermes House,
88–89 Blackfriars Road, London SE1 8HA
tel. 020 7401 2077; fax 020 7633 9499

www.southwaterbooks.com; www.annesspublishing.com

If you like the images in this book and would like to investigate
using them for publishing, promotions or advertising, please visit
our website www.practicalpictures.com for more information.

UK agent: The Manning Partnership Ltd
tel. 01225 478444; fax 01225 478440;
sales@manning-partnership.co.uk

UK distributor: Grantham Book Services Ltd
tel. 01476 541080; fax 01476 541061;
orders@gbs.tbs-ltd.co.uk

North American agent/distributor: National Book Network
tel. 301 459 3366; fax 301 429 5746; www.nbnbooks.com

Australian agent/distributor: Pan Macmillan Australia
tel. 1300 135 113; fax 1300 135 103;
customer.service@macmillan.com.au

New Zealand agent/distributor: David Bateman Ltd
tel. (09) 415 7664; fax (09) 415 8892

ETHICAL TRADING POLICY
At Anness Publishing we believe that business should be
conducted in an ethical and ecologically sustainable way,
with respect for the environment and a proper regard to
the replacement of the natural resources we employ.

As a publisher, we use a lot of wood pulp to make high-quality
paper for printing, and that wood commonly comes from spruce
trees. We are therefore currently growing more than 500,000
trees in two Scottish forest plantations near Aberdeen – Berrymoss
(130 hectares/320 acres) and West Touxhill (125 hectares/
305 acres). The forests we manage contain twice the number
of trees employed each year in paper-making for our books.

Because of this ongoing ecological investment programme,
you, as our customer, can have the pleasure and reassurance of
knowing that a tree is being cultivated on your behalf to naturally
replace the materials used to make the book you are holding.

Our forestry programme is run in accordance with the
UK Woodland Assurance Scheme (UKWAS) and will be certified
by the internationally recognized Forest Stewardship Council
(FSC). The FSC is a non-government organization dedicated
to promoting responsible management of the world's forests.
Certification ensures forests are managed in an environmentally
sustainable and socially responsible way. For further information
about this scheme, go to www.annesspublishing.com/trees

Previously published as part of a larger volume,
The Gardener's Guide to Planting and Growing Trees

Publisher: Joanna Lorenz
Senior Managing Editor: Conor Kilgallon
Editors: Clare Hill and Lucy Doncaster
Copy Editor: Lydia Darbyshire
Designer: Mike Morey
Production Controller: Don Campaniello

ACKNOWLEDGEMENTS
The publishers would like to thank Peter Anderson for his work
on the original photography.
Unless listed below, photographs are © Anness Publishing Ltd.
t = top; b = bottom; l = left; r = right; c = centre.
Garden World Images: 14br (Bot. Images Inc.); 21br (K.
Jayaram); 46t (P. Lane); 47tr (Bot. Images Inc.); 50bl (Bot.
Images Inc.); 51t (M. Keal); 54t (G. Harland); 61bl (L. Stock);
61tr; 63tr; 67tr; 70br (J. Swithinbank); 74br (T. McGlinchey);
76b (L.Claeys-Bouuaert); 83tr (Bot. Images Inc.).

Front cover, clockwise from top left: *Stewartia pseudocamellia*;
Pyrus communis 'Williams Bon Chrétien'; *Citrus limon*; *Prunus* cv.
Front cover flap, from left: *Betula pendula*; *Arbutus unedo* 'Elfin
King'. **Back cover, clockwise from top left:** *Acer palmatum* cv.;
Juniperus chinensis; *Morus alba* 'Pendula'; *Magnolia stellata*; *Pterocarya
stenoptera*; *Crataegus laevigata* 'Punicea'. **Back cover flap:** *Thuja plicata*;
Cornus officinalis. **Page 1, clockwise from top left:** *Malus ×
schiedeckeri* 'Hillieri'; *Olea europea*; *Plumeria alba*; *Artocarpus altilis*.
Page 2, from top left: *Chamaerops humilis*; *Abies bracteata*;
Acer rubrum 'Columnare'; *Magnolia campbellii* subsp. *mollicomata*
'Lanarth'. **Page 3, from top left:** *Malus* 'Evereste'; *Acer japonicum*
'Aconitifolium'; *Aesculus × carnea*; *Liriodendron tulipifera*.

Contents

Introduction	4	Citrus	30	Livistona	53	Pseudotsuga	75
How to use		Cladrastis	32	Maackia	54	Psidium	75
the directory	5	Cornus	32	Magnolia	54	Pterocarya	76
		Corylus	34	Malus	57	Punica	76
THE DIRECTORY:		Cotinus	34	Malus sylvestris		Pyrus	76
		Crataegus	35	var. domestica	58	Quercus	77
Abies	6	Cryptomeria	36	Maytenus	60	Rhamnus	80
Acacia	6	Cunninghamia	36	Melia	60	Robinia	80
Acer	7	X Cupressocyparis	36	Metasequoia	60	Roystonea	81
Aesculus	13	Cupressus	37	Metrosideros	60	Sabal	81
Agathis	14	Davidia	37	Michelia	61	Salix	82
Ailanthus	14	Dillenia	38	Morus	61	Sassafras	83
Albizia	15	Diospyros	38	Myrtus	62	Schefflera	83
Aleurites	15	Embothrium	39	Nothofagus	62	Sciadopitys	83
Alnus	15	Eriobotrya	39	Nyssa	62	Sequoia	84
Amelanchier	16	Eucalyptus	40	Olea	62	Sequoiadendron	84
Araucaria	16	Eucryphia	41	Oxydendron	63	Sophora	84
Arbutus	17	Fagus	42	Parrotia	63	Sorbus	84
Artocarpus	18	Ficus	42	Paulownia	64	Spathodea	86
Banksia	18	Fitzroya	43	Phellodendron	64	Staphylea	86
Bauhinia	18	Fortunella	43	Phoenix	64	Stewartia	87
Betula	19	Fraxinus	44	Picea	64	Styrax	87
Bismarckia	20	Ginkgo	44	Pinus	65	Syzygium	88
Brachychiton	21	Gleditsia	45	Pistacia	67	Tabebuia	88
Butia	21	Grevillea	45	Pittosporum	67	Taxodium	88
Brownea	21	Halesia	46	Platanus	68	Taxus	89
Calliandra	22	Ilex	46	Plumeria	68	Tecoma	90
Callistemon	22	Jacaranda	47	Podocarpus	68	Thuja	90
Calocedrus	23	Juglans	48	Populus	69	Thujopsis	90
Calophyllum	23	Juniperus	48	Portlandia	70	Tilia	91
Carpinus	23	Koelreuteria	49	Protea	70	Trachycarpus	91
Carya	24	Laburnum	49	Prumnopitys	70	Tsuga	92
Caryota	24	Lagerstroemia	50	Prunus	71	Ulmus	92
Cassia	25	Larix	50	Prunus armeniaca	72	Washingtonia	93
Castanea	25	Laurus	51	Prunus avium	73	Zelkova	93
Catalpa	26	Licuala	51	Prunis cerasus	73		
Cedrus	26	Ligustrum	52	Prunus domestica	74		
Cercidiphyllum	27	Liquidambar	52	Prunus dulcis	74	Index	94
Cercis	28	Lithocarpus	53	Prunus institia	74	US plant hardiness	
Chamaecyparis	29	Liriodendron	53	Pseudolarix	75	zones	96
Chamaerops	30						

Introduction

This beautifully illustrated book is a celebration of garden trees in all their forms, from hardy evergreens and deciduous broadleaves, to desert survivors and tropical palms. Containing more than 140 of the most common garden trees found around the world, it is designed to help you to identify and choose the best trees for your needs.

The number of trees available is constantly expanding, and it is obviously impossible to keep pace with every new introduction. Instead, the book aims to bring together tried and tested trees, which have already proved their value in gardens and can be expected to perform reliably for many years to come alongside newer introductions that are likely to appear on the market.

This *Nyssa sylvatica* (tupelo) is hardy, but needs protection from cold, drying winds.

Hardiness

All the trees in this book have been assessed for their hardiness and, for the US, the range of zones where they can be grown outdoors is given. Most, apart from some tropical species, can be grown outdoors in most temperate areas, and can withstand lows of -15°C/5°F.

Trees described as "half hardy" will need some form of protection from the coldest weather, either by growing them in a warm, sheltered spot (for instance in the lee of a sunny wall) or by protecting them in winter by erecting a protective shield made from plastic and horticultural fleece. However, severe lows in themselves are less damaging than cold, drying winds, which strip the trees of moisture.

The benefits of trees

Trees play a vital role in the environment, releasing oxygen into the atmosphere through the process of photosynthesis, as well as cleaning our air by filtering out pollutants. In addition to this, they can be used to provide security, privacy and shade in our gardens and to reduce the level of traffic noise.

A major benefit of trees is their value to wildlife. Whenever we plant a new tree we will attract birds, animals and insects into our garden. In addition, because trees create shade and shelter for other plants, our garden is able to develop into a richer and more sustainable habitat. The increased biodiversity will benefit the wider environment, as well as helping to ensure garden pests are kept in check by predators.

Trees are also the natural habitat of birds and a variety of wild animals, which use the trees as a permanent or temporary home or as a shelter during bad weather.

The colour and shape of foliage are among the many factors to consider when choosing a tree for your garden, such as that of *Acer palmatum* 'Osakazuki' shown here.

Choosing a tree

Whether you want a tree purely for its aesthetic qualities, or for a more practical reason, there is a tree to meet every requirement.

In order to help you decide which tree is best for your garden, this comprehensive directory contains a detailed description of the aesthetic qualities of each species, including seasonal variations and any interesting or desirable features, such as shape, colour, flowering habits, fruits, leaves and bark. Important practical information regarding each tree's potential height and spread is also given, as well as the growing requirements of each genus and advice on how to care for it, to ensure every tree fulfils its fabulous potential.

Packed with information and beautifully illustrated with stunning colour photographs, this authoritative volume contains everything you need to know to choose the best tree for your garden.

How to use the directory

Within the directory, trees are arranged alphabetically, by genus. Each main entry features a general introduction to that genus, plus specific useful information such as tips on cultivation, propagation and pruning. This is followed by a selection of trees from that genus, also arranged alphabetically according to their most widely accepted names. One of these entries might be a species, a hybrid (or group of hybrids), a variety, form or cultivar. Each is given a useful description that may include a description of its foliage or flowers and its height and spread, as well as its degree of hardiness.

Fagus sylvatica 'Dawyck Purple'

Caption
The full botanical name of the tree in question is given with each photograph.

Photograph
Most entries feature a full-colour photograph that makes identification easy.

Genus name
This is the internationally accepted botanical name for a group of related plant species.

Common name
This popular, non-scientific name applies to the whole of the plant genus.

Cultivation
This section gives the level of sun or shade that the plants described in the selection either require or tolerate, advice on the best type of soil in which they should be grown, and any other helpful tips that might be appropriate.

Propagation
This section gives useful information on how and when to increase the plant – from seed, by dividing plants or by taking various types of cutting.

Individual plant entry
This starts with the current botanical name of the plant in bold, and this can refer to a species, subspecies, hybrid, variant or cultivar. If a synonym (syn.) is given, this provides the alternative name(s) for a plant. A common name may be given after the botanical name.

Plant description
This gives a description of the plant, along with any other information that may be helpful and relevant.

FAGUS
Beech

The ten species of deciduous trees in the genus are found in temperate areas throughout the northern hemisphere. They are grown for their elegant habit and their autumn colour.
Cultivation Grow in moisture-retentive but well-drained soil in sun or semi-shade. Purple-leaved forms give best colour in full sun; yellow-leaved forms should be planted in semi-shade.
Pruning Early formative pruning should produce a clear, straight trunk and a balanced crown. Remove dead, dying, diseased or crossing branches.
Propagation Collect and sow seed in autumn. Put in an unheated glasshouse or cold frame until germination occurs. Winter grafting of ornamental European beech cultivars on to seed-raised European beech is the best way of propagating different forms.

F. grandifolia
American beech

A majestic, spreading tree, this specimen will require space around it as it is likely to grow as wide as it is tall. The attractive dark green leaves, up to 15cm (6in) long, are oval and toothed and turn golden-bronze in autumn. H and S 15–20m (50–65ft).
Aspect Full sun or semi-shade.
Hardiness ✿✿✿ Zones 4–9.

Genus introduction
This provides a general introduction to the genus and may state the number of species within that genus. Other information featured here may include general advice on usage, preferred conditions, and plant care, as well as subspecies, hybrids (indicated by an x symbol in the name), varieties and cultivars (featuring names in single quotes) that are available.

Pruning information
This section gives the type and frequency of pruning that the tree requires, and what it should aim to achieve.

Size information
The average expected height and spread of a genus or individual plant is frequently given (as H and S), although ultimate sizes and growth rates may vary a great deal depending on location and conditions. Metric measurements always precede imperial ones.

Plant hardiness
A symbol indicating hardiness, or minimum temperature requirement, is given at the end of this section, as well as the hardiness zone or range of zones.

In Europe the symbols apply, as follows:
✿✿✿ Fully hardy, down to -15ºC (5ºF)
✿✿ Frost hardy, down to -5ºC (23ºF)
✿ Half hardy, down to 0ºC (32ºF)
For more tender plants, a minimum temperature is given, rather than a symbol.

In the United States, the zones apply, and these are shown on the map on page 96.

ABIES
Silver fir

These evergreen conifers are native to mountainous areas of Europe, North America, Asia and North Africa. There are about 50 species, from which a number of cultivars have been hybridized. They make good specimen trees and can also be used in windbreaks.

Cultivation Grow in fertile, moisture-retentive but well-drained, neutral to acidic soil in full sun. Protect young plants from cold winter winds.

Pruning Firs require very little in the way of regular pruning. However, while young they will benefit from occasional pruning to develop clear leaders while tipping back side shoots to encourage bushy growth.

Propagation Propagation is by seed for the species and it should be collected while the cones are still fresh. Cultivars are propagated by winter indoor grafting on to seedling grown rootstocks.

A. alba
European silver fir, common silver fir

The species is a conical tree with long, slightly drooping branches. The small, needle-like leaves are attached to the branches in Vs. They are dark green above and silvery beneath. The brown, resinous cones are upright with the scales arching slightly backwards, and they fall apart by late autumn. A fast-growing tree, it is occasionally susceptible to damage by frosts in late spring. H 40m (130ft), S 20m (65ft).
Aspect Prefers full sun, but is more shade tolerant than most other firs.
Hardiness ❀❀❀ Zones 4–6.

A. bracteata
Santa Lucia fir, bristlecone fir

A fast-growing, very beautiful conifer, this has narrow, dark green needles up to 5cm (2in) long, borne almost flat against the stems and with two distinct white bands along the underside. The straw-coloured buds are pointed. The spiky, egg-shaped cones turn brown with age. This is an adaptable but large conifer, which will grow on a wide range of soils. H 35m (115ft), S 6m (20ft).
Aspect Full sun.
Hardiness ❀❀❀ Zone 7.

A. concolor
White fir, Colorado white fir

A beautiful, strongly conical conifer, this has blue-green needles, up to 6cm (2½in) long, which lie forwards and upwards along the stem. If branches are left unpruned they will arch and sweep down to the ground. It is a widely planted tree and is adaptable to both heat and cold. H 25–40m (80–130ft), S 5–7m (16–23ft).
Named varieties The cultivar 'Candicans' is an initially narrow-growing form that spreads with age. The foliage is a ghostly pale blue-grey.

Trees in the Lowiana Group (Pacific white fir) are seed-raised forms with short branches that produce a narrow, conical shape. The greenish-grey needles are arranged in V-shaped bands along the stems.
Aspect Full sun.
Hardiness ❀❀❀ Zones 4–7.

A. firma
Japanese fir, momi fir

This large, quick-growing conifer will reach its potential height in its natural habitat in Japan, where it grows in fertile, moist soils in areas of high rainfall. However, in most gardens it will be much smaller. It is a beautiful tree with stiff, almost spiky needles and a branching, almost fern-like canopy. H 20–40m (65–130ft), S 6–10m (20–33ft).
Aspect Full sun.
Hardiness ❀❀❀ Zones 6–9.

A. nebrodensis
Sicily fir

This reasonably small conifer has a flattish top and beautiful cones. The needles are dark green and arranged in a V shape around the stems. It is one of the most beautiful of garden-sized conifers and will do well in shallow, free-draining soil. H 10m (33ft), S 5m (16ft).
Aspect Full sun.
Hardiness ❀❀❀ Zone 6.

A. pinsapo
Spanish fir, hedgehog fir

This distinctive, drought-tolerant fir has clusters of stout, blue-green needles, up to 2cm (¾in) long, arranged in a spiral around each shoot. It does best in free-draining, alkaline soil. H 25m (80ft), S 8m (26ft).
Named varieties The slower growing cultivar 'Aurea' has beautiful gold-coloured needles that turn blue-green in summer. It does not have such a neat habit of growth as the species.
Aspect Full sun to light shade.
Hardiness ❀❀❀ Zone 6.

ACACIA
Wattle

This is a very large genus of 1,100 or more species of ornamental deciduous and evergreen trees.

Abies alba

They are native to Australia, southern Africa and Central and South America, and they are tolerant of poor soils and drought.

They are grown for their dense clusters of often scented, bright yellow flowers. Some species have alternate, fern-like leaves; other species bear phyllodes (flattened leaf stalks), which look and function like leaf blades. The dark green phyllodes are narrow, and during droughts they often fall to enable the plant to conserve water, while the stems and branches alone produce the tree's energy.

Some species are hardier than others and can be grown with minimal winter protection in temperate areas; in warmer climates some species may be invasive.

Cultivation Grow in free-draining, neutral to acidic soil in full sun.
Pruning Formative pruning should aim to produce a clear trunk and a balanced crown. Occasional pruning is required to remove any dead, dying, diseased or crossing branches.
Propagation Seed is the easiest method of propagation and should be collected when fresh, soaked in warm water for 24 hours and sown into a free-draining compost

Abies bracteata

in a container greenhouse and kept frost-free until ready to plant out.

A. auriculaeformis
Black wattle

This attractive and quick-growing tree has brownish-silver bark. In winter and early spring it bears dense spikes of yellow flowers. These are followed by dark brown fruits shaped like curled pea pods. H 30m (100ft), S 20m (65ft).
Aspect Full sun.
Hardiness ❋ Zones 10–12.

A. baileyana
Cootamundra wattle

A fast-growing, strongly arching, small evergreen tree, this is grown for its small clusters of scented, golden-yellow flowers that appear in late winter. The attractive, fern-like foliage has a silvery sheen. H and S 8m (26ft).
Named varieties The cultivar 'Purpurea' has stunning purple foliage and yellow flowers.
Aspect Full sun.
Hardiness ❋ Zones 9–11.

A. confusa
False koa

This beautiful small tree has long, pointed, dark green phyllodes. In winter and early spring it bears profuse and dense clusters of bright yellow flowers amid the foliage. H and S 15m (50ft).
Aspect Full sun.
Hardiness ❋ Zones 9–12.

Acacia dealbata

A. dealbata
Mimosa, silver wattle

A widely grown, fast-growing evergreen tree, the mimosa has slender, silver-green foliage. Abundant clusters of fragrant, bright yellow flowers are produced in late winter and early spring. In a favourable climate it will develop into an open-headed tree. H and S 15m (50ft).
Aspect Full sun.
Hardiness ❋ Zones 8–10.

A. longifolia
Sydney golden wattle

This beautiful but invasive tree is one of the most lime-tolerant of the wattles. In early spring abundant clusters of highly scented, bright yellow flowers are borne alongside the long, dark green leaves. H and S 8m (26ft).
Aspect Full sun.
Hardiness ❋ Zones 9–11.

A. melanoxylon
Blackwood wattle

A broadly spreading, evergreen tree, the species has angular stems and blue-green foliage. It bears clusters of small, creamy-yellow flowers in early spring. H 25m (80ft), S 12m (40ft).
Aspect Full sun.
Hardiness ❋ Zones 9–11.

A. pravissima
Oven's wattle

The small, triangular phyllodes of this deciduous species are dark green. It is an open-headed tree with slightly weeping branches, bearing fragrant, bright yellow flowers in late winter. It is one of the hardiest of the wattles, but it will require protection when young in temperate areas. H and S 8m (26ft).
Aspect Full sun.
Hardiness ❋ Zones 8–11.

ACER
Maple

About 150 species of maples grow in temperate regions of the world. They are usually deciduous trees, but a number of evergreen forms exist. They are easily distinguished by their opposite leaves and winged fruits (commonly known as keys). The wings allow the seeds to be widely

Abies pinsapo

distributed by the wind, so they germinate away from the parent tree and do not compete with it.

Many maples have fine flowers but their chief characteristics are their palmate (hand-shaped) leaves (often brilliantly coloured in autumn), bark and elegant habit.
Cultivation Most maples prefer an open, sunny location in fertile, moisture-retentive soil, but this is a large group of trees, and the individual requirements of the species may differ, as noted below.
Pruning Generally, maples require little pruning apart from the removal of dead, diseased, dying or crossing branches, which should be removed during winter or summer. Reverted green shoots of variegated leaf forms should be removed as soon as they appear.
Propagation Some species can be propagated by fresh seed, which germinates readily. Propagate

cultivars by winter indoor grafting or budding. Take softwood cuttings in late summer, allow them to root and do not pot them on until the following summer.

A. buergerianum
Trident maple, three-toothed maple

Native to China and Japan, this species is grown in hot areas instead of *A. palmatum*, which is less tolerant of high summer temperatures. It is a small to medium-sized tree with red to orange autumn colour. It does best in moist, slightly acidic soil, and grows well in either sun or shade. It is often grown as a multi-stemmed specimen. H and S 15m (50ft), but H up to 30m (100ft) in its natural habitat.
Aspect Full sun or semi-shade.
Hardiness ❋❋❋ Zones 5–9.

Acer X *conspicuum* 'Phoenix'

A. campestre
Field maple, hedge maple

The species, native to Europe and North Africa, is a dainty tree with a rounded habit. The dark green, palmate leaves, up to 6cm (2½in) long, are red-purple when they first emerge. When grown in moist, acidic soil, autumn colours can range from dark red or purple through to orange-red; otherwise, the leaves turn butter yellow.

The leaves and corky branches weep a milky sap if broken or cut. It is a highly adaptable tree, which is often found growing in hedgerows on shallow, free-draining, alkaline soils. It can tolerate regular, close clipping and makes an attractive hedge. H and S 15m (50ft).

Named varieties 'Carnival' is a striking Dutch cultivar with leaves broadly edged in white.

'Elsrijk', another Dutch selection, has a narrow habit and makes a good street tree.

'Postelense' is a small, mop-headed tree with leaves that are golden-yellow as they emerge but fade to light green in summer. It is excellent for a small garden.

'Queen Elizabeth' is a widely grown selection with a narrow habit and good autumn colour, but it is susceptible to mildew in cooler climates.

'Streetwise' is a narrow-growing form with red keys and butter yellow autumn colour.
Aspect Full sun or semi-shade.
Hardiness ❁❁❁ Zones 4–8.

A. cappadocicum
Cappadocian maple, Caucasian maple

This spreading tree has five- to seven-lobed leaves, up to 10cm (4in) long, which turn yellow in autumn. Native to the Caucasus, the Himalayas and western China, it is an adaptable, quick-growing tree that will tolerate a wide range of soils and habitats, including alkaline soils. H 20m (65ft), S 15m (50ft).

Named varieties 'Aureum' is a slower growing form. The leaves are red when they first emerge but turn yellow and remain long into summer, when they become lime green, finally turning yellow again before they fall. This is best planted in semi-shade because the foliage will scorch in full sun. H 15m (50ft), S 10m (33ft).

'Rubrum' is more vigorous than 'Aureum' but is just as beautiful. The emerging leaves are bronze-red and remain red-tinted long into summer, before turning yellow in autumn. This is one of the most widely grown forms.
Aspect Full sun or semi-shade.
Hardiness ❁❁❁ Zone Min. 6.

A. X conspicuum

The hybrids in this group include crosses between *A. pensylvanicum* and *A. davidii*. They are grown for their spectacular snakebark trunks and beautiful autumn colours. They require neutral to acidic soil and cool summers.
Named varieties 'Elephant's Ear' has large, unlobed leaves, which turn bright yellow in autumn and, once fallen, reveal purplish stems and white-striped bark.

'Phoenix' is perhaps the best of the group; it is a quick-growing tree with stark white stripes up its green trunk. Striking bright red winter shoots are complemented by vibrant yellow autumn colour.

'Silver Cardinal' has attractive variegated foliage.

'Silver Vein' is a small tree similar to *A. pensylvanicum*, but its arching branches are more like *A. davidii*. Its stems are heavily striped and the leaves are glowing butter yellow in autumn. H 10m (33ft), S 5m (16ft).
Aspect Full sun or semi-shade.
Hardiness ❁❁❁ Zone Min. 6.

A. davidii
Père David's maple, snakebark maple

This is one of the most useful of the snakebark maples. It was named after the French missionary Jean-Pierre-Armand David, who discovered this delightful tree in China in 1869. It has glossy, dark green leaves, up to 15cm (6in) long, which turn red, yellow and orange in autumn.

It is a woodland tree, preferring a cool root run in slightly acidic soil and thriving under the shade of other more dominant trees. Occasional spring frost damage may occur, and it is intolerant of high temperatures. H and S 15m (50ft).

Named varieties 'Ernest Wilson' is perhaps the best of the available cultivars. More compact than the species, it has arching branches and pale green leaves, which turn vibrant orange and yellow in autumn. H 8m (26ft), S 10m (33ft).

'George Forrest', another fine selection, is more widely grown than any of the other forms. It has a widely spreading habit and dark green leaves, up to 20cm (8in) long, and red stalks. The autumn colour is less intense than the species and tends to be slightly disappointing.

Acer 'Ginger Bread'

The Dutch cultivar 'Karmen' is best grown as a small, multi-stemmed tree and pruned to maintain this habit. Such treatment will encourage deeply striped bark that is flushed with dark purple, which makes this a favourite landscape tree for winter bark. The young leaves are bronze, turning yellow-orange in autumn.

The Dutch cultivar 'Serpentine' has an upright habit and is the best choice for winter stem effects, having purple shoots and wonderful striations on the bark. The leaves, up to 10cm (4in) long, colour well in autumn.
Aspect Full sun or semi-shade.
Hardiness ❋❋❋ Zone Min. 6.

A. x *freemanii*
Freeman's maple, hybrid red maple
This is a distinctive group of named forms that are hybrids between *A. rubrum* and *A. saccharinum*. First raised in 1933, its characteristics are intermediate between both parents, and it will grow in the same conditions as both. It is a quick-growing, upright tree, which spreads with age. The leaves are dark green, with a deeply cut shape, and produce superb autumn colour.

Widely planted in North America, it is less well known in Europe. A number of heat- and

Acer griseum

cold-tolerant forms have been developed from natural stands where the parent species have hybridized. H 25m (80ft), S 5m (16ft).
Named varieties The first form to be sold, 'Armstrong', has now been superceded by superior forms. 'Autumn Blaze' is a broad, dense, oval-shaped tree with brilliant and long-lasting red and orange autumn colour.

'Celebration' is a more compact form with strongly upright branches and deeply cut leaves that turn golden-red in autumn.

'Morgan' is both vigorous and fast-growing, with an attractive open habit and large, deeply lobed leaves that turn brilliant red-purple, scarlet and orange-yellow in autumn.
Aspect Full sun or semi-shade.
Hardiness ❋❋❋ Zones 4–7.

A. 'Ginger Bread'
This interesting hybrid between *A. griseum* and *A. maximowiczianum* (syn. *A. nikoense*; Nikko maple) was introduced in the USA in 1995 and is becoming more popular. The bark is intermediate between both parents but less fluted than *A. griseum*. It is quicker growing and more heat and cold tolerant than either parent. It has exceptional red autumn colour. H and S 10–15m (33–50ft).
Aspect Full sun or semi-shade.
Hardiness ❋❋❋ Zones 5–7 (poss. 8).

A. griseum
Paperbark maple, Chinese paperbark maple
This medium-sized tree is a delightful year-round garden tree. Native to China, it has cinnamon-coloured, flaking bark and beautiful autumn colour, although this can vary as it is mainly seed propagated. The leaves, up to 10cm (4in) long, are trifoliate (having three leaflets). They are dark green above and silver-blue beneath. It will grow in a range of conditions, including acidic and alkaline soils, as long as they are deep and humus rich. H and S 10–15m (33–50ft).
Aspect Full sun or semi-shade.
Hardiness ❋❋❋ Zones 5–7 (poss. 8).

Acer japonicum 'Vitifolium'

A. grosseri var. hersii
(syn. *A. davidii* subsp. *grosseri*, *A. grosseri*, *A. hersii*)
Hersii maple
This is perhaps the most beautiful of the snakebark maples. It is a small tree from northern China with stunning marbled bark and shallowly lobed leaves, which colour well in autumn. H 8m (25ft), S 10m (30ft).
Aspect Semi-shade.
Hardiness ❋❋❋ Zone 6.

A. japonicum
Full moon maple, Japanese maple
This species of maple is native to Japan. There are numerous cultivars, all of which will thrive in moist, slightly acidic, free-draining soil. They are best grown in the shade of other trees where they can be protected from cold winds, especially in spring when the delicate new leaves are emerging. H and S 10m (33ft).
Named varieties Among the cultivars is 'Aconitifolium' (syn. 'Filicifolium', 'Laciniatum'), a superb form with typical lime green, deeply cut foliage, which turn ruby red in autumn. H 5m (16ft), S 6m (20ft).

'Vitifolium' has broadly fan-shaped leaves, with up to 12 lobes, which are up to 8cm (3in) long. They turn yellow and orange-red in autumn.
Aspect Full sun or semi-shade.
Hardiness ❋❋❋ Zones 5–7 (but not heat tolerant in the southern USA).

Acer japonicum 'Aconitifolium'

A. macrophyllum
Oregon maple, big-leaf maple
This spreading tree with coarse leaves is suitable only for large gardens or open parkland. The deeply lobed leaves, up to 25cm (10in) across, are glossy, dark green, and if removed in summer they weep a milky sap. Autumn colours are yellow, orange and orange-brown. H 25m (80ft), S 20m (65ft).
Aspect Full sun or semi-shade.
Hardiness ❀❀❀ Zone 5–7 (poss. 9 in milder regions).

Acer palmatum

A. negundo
Box elder, ash-leaved maple
This is a tough but quick-growing maple, which is heat tolerant, very cold hardy and adaptable to a range of soil conditions. The light green leaves, up to 20cm (8in) long, turn yellow in autumn. It is a small to medium-sized garden tree with attractive, tassel-like, green-yellow flowers. H 20m (65ft), S 10m (33ft).
Named varieties 'Flamingo' is the most widely grown cultivar. New leaves are edged with salmon-pink, which fades to a white variegation in summer. Intense leaf colour appears on trees that are coppiced every two years.
'Kelly's Gold', which originated in New Zealand, has yellow-green leaves that rarely scorch in the sun.
'Winter Lightning' is a green-leaved form with stunning, vivid yellow-white winter stems. It is best grown as a coppiced tree.
Aspect Full sun or semi-shade.
Hardiness ❀❀❀ Zones 3–9.

A. palmatum
Japanese maple
The trees in this group are probably the most widely planted of the maples, because of their extraordinary range of shape, size and colour. The larger forms will tolerate alkaline soils and are more resistant to wind damage. Nevertheless, they require moist, free-draining soil and protection from cold spring winds. H 15m (50ft), S 10m (33ft).
Named varieties 'Bloodgood' is a widely grown cultivar with deeply cut, dark reddish-purple leaves, which turn crimson in autumn and contrast with the iridescent bright crimson, winged fruits. H and S 5m (16ft).
'Chitoseyama' is a graceful maple with deeply cut, green leaves that turn shades of purple-red in autumn. It eventually becomes a mound-like small tree with strongly arching branches. H 1.8m (6ft), S 3m (10ft).
A. palmatum var. *dissectum* 'Crimson Queen' has very finely cut, purple leaves that retain their colour long into summer before turning dark scarlet in autumn. H 3m (10ft), S 4m (12ft).
The strongly growing *A. palmatum* var. *dissectum* 'Garnet' has deeply cut, purple leaves that turn red-purple in autumn.
A. palmatum var. *dissectum* 'Inaba-shidare' is a distinctive form with large, finely divided foliage that is purple throughout the growing season and turns crimson in autumn.
'Ōsakazuki' is one of the most widely grown cultivars because of its amazing scarlet autumn colour. The leaves are green in spring and summer. H and S 6m (20ft).

Acer palmatum 'Ōsakazuki'

'Sango-kaku' (syn. 'Senkaki'; coral bark maple) has red young branches, which contrast with the small, butter yellow autumn leaves. It is one of the smallest of the green-leaved forms of *A. palmatum*. H 6m (20ft), S 5m (16ft).
Aspect Best in semi-shade.
Hardiness ❀❀❀ Zones 5–8.

A. pensylvanicum
Striped maple, moosewood, snakebark maple
This small, shade-loving tree is often grown as a multi-stemmed tree. Another of the snakebark maples, its trunk is pale green with white stripes that are more conspicuous on younger branches. The bright green leaves, up to 20cm (8in) long, turn butter yellow in autumn. H 8m (26ft), S 5m (16ft).
Aspect Best in semi-shade.
Hardiness ❀❀❀ Zones 3–7.

A. platanoides
Norway maple
The species is an adaptable, fast-growing tree, tolerant of atmospheric pollution and poor soils, and often used as a pioneer species. It bleeds if cut in summer, like *A. macrophyllum*. H 25m (80ft), S 15m (50ft).
Named varieties Among the many cultivars is 'Cleveland', a broadly upright but spreading form with gorgeous yellow autumn colour.

Widely planted as a street tree, 'Crimson King' has dark maroon, palmate leaves that darken to almost purple-red by midsummer. It grows poorly in extreme summer heat and is slightly slower growing than some of the other purple-leaved forms.

'Drummondii' is a wonderful form with light green leaves edged with white. Susceptible to reversion, it needs constant pruning to remove any plain green leaves. H and S 10–12m (33–40ft).

'Erectum' is a strongly growing, upright form, similar in some ways to *A. saccharum* subsp. *nigrum* 'Monumentale'.

'Emerald Lustre' is very quick growing when young and matures into a round-headed tree. The leaves are reddish-green initially, puckered along the edges, but fade to dark green in late summer.

'Palmatifidum' (syn. 'Lorbergii') has deeply lobed, long, pointed leaves that are attractive early in the year and again when they turn yellow-orange in autumn. It is a wide, spreading tree.

'Schwedleri', a parent of many purple-leaved cultivars, is grown for its purple foliage, which is even more stunning if the tree is pollarded and pruned hard every second year.
Aspect Full sun or semi-shade.
Hardiness ❋❋❋ Zones 4–7.

A. pseudoplatanus
Sycamore, plane tree maple, great maple

This large tree, native to Europe and south-western Asia, is tolerant of a wide range of growing conditions and highly tolerant of exposed locations, making it especially useful for seaside planting. H 25–30m (80–100ft), S 15–25m (50–80ft).
Named varieties
'Brilliantissimum' is a delightful small garden tree with salmon-pink leaves in spring, turning pale yellow and finally green. H 6m (20ft), S 8m (26ft).

A. pseudoplatanus f. *erythrocarpum* is a green-leaved form with vivid red winged fruits that develop through late summer and last long into winter.

Introduced from New Zealand, *A. pseudoplatanus* Purpureum Group encompasses all green-leaved forms that have purple undersides, most of which are seedling selections.

The leaves of *A. pseudoplatanus* f. *variegatum* 'Esk Sunset' are pink at first, turning green mottled with pink, white and grey-green as they age. H and S 10m (33ft).
Aspect Full sun or semi-shade.
Hardiness ❋❋❋ Zones 4–7 (but will not perform well in warmer areas of the southern USA).

Acer platanoides

A. pycnanthum
Japanese red maple

Although it is widely planted in its native Japan as a street tree because it is heat tolerant and drought resistant, this medium-sized tree is little grown elsewhere. It bears its blooms in spring. It has bright green foliage, which turns crimson and yellow in autumn. It is best grown in a free-draining, acidic soil. H 15m (50ft), S 10m (33ft).
Aspect Full sun or semi-shade.
Hardiness ❋❋❋ Zone 6.

A. rubrum
Red maple, scarlet maple, swamp maple

A large tree from eastern North America, *A. rubrum* produces scarlet autumn colour when it is grown in neutral to acidic soil. It will grow well in chalk soils, but the autumn colour is often poor. The dark green leaves, up to 10cm (4in) long, have three to five lobes, the central one being longer than the others. Red flowers are produced in spring. H 25m (80ft), S 15m (50ft).
Named varieties Several cultivars have been developed for heat and cold tolerance. 'Armstrong', a fast-growing, upright form, has deeply cut leaves and vivid autumn tints.

'Columnare' is narrow, almost pillar-like and produces fantastic autumn colour. H 25m (80ft), S 3m (10ft).

'October Glory', a widely planted form of US origin, has long-lasting, red autumn colour.

'Red Sunset' produces red-orange colour early in autumn; it has a pyramidal habit, ageing to a round-headed tree.

'Schlesingeri' is usually the first red maple to colour in autumn, showing scarlet mixed with the patchwork of the green leaves that have yet to turn. The colour lasts over a long period in autumn.
Aspect Full sun.
Hardiness ❋❋❋ Zones 3–9.

Acer pseudoplatanus

Acer rubrum 'Columnare'

A. rufinerve
Red-vein maple, grey-budded snakebark maple
This small to medium-sized tree is similar in many respects to *A. pensylvanicum*, although its leaves are smaller, up to 12cm (5in) long, and turn a lovely red and orange-yellow in autumn. It prefers cool, moist, acidic soil. H and S 10m (33ft).
Named varieties 'Erythrocladum' is a slow-growing tree with pale yellow new shoots in summer, which intensify in colour as temperatures fall. They eventually turn red by winter.

   'Hatsuyuki' (syn. 'Albolimbatum', 'Albomarginatum') is an interesting form with mottled and variegated leaves, which are splashed with white. It has incredibly vibrant autumn colour.
Aspect Full sun or semi-shade.
Hardiness ❀❀❀ Zones 5–7.

A. saccharinum
(syn. *A. dasycarpum*)
Silver maple
This large, stately tree has five-lobed leaves, up to 20cm (8in) long, that are pale green above and silver-white beneath, turning bright yellow in autumn. It is a fast-growing, heat-tolerant tree that can adapt to both moist, fertile soils and nutrient-poor, drier soils. H 30m (100ft), S 20m (65ft).
Aspect Full sun.
Hardiness ❀❀❀ Zones 3–9.

A. saccharum
Sugar maple, rock maple
The species, native to eastern North America, is a large ornamental tree that is also cultivated for the production of maple syrup. It is widely grown in North America for its long-lasting autumn colours, which

Acer saccharum

are vivid orange, scarlet, crimson and gold. It does best in fertile, neutral to acidic, free-draining soil. H 30m (100ft), S 20m (65ft).
Named varieties Among the cultivars 'Adirondak' is a strongly growing, upright form with five widely lobed leaves. It has orange autumn colour and shows good drought resistance.

   'Arrowhead', a tight growing form with a distinct central leader, has dark green leaves that turn orange in autumn. H 20m (65ft), S 8m (26ft).

   'Crescendo' is probably the best form for both heat and drought tolerance. It has dark green leaves, which turn yellow in autumn.

   A. saccharum subsp. *nigrum* 'Monumentale' (syn. *A. saccharum* 'Temple's Upright') is often confused with 'Newton Sentry', but it has a strong central leader and beautiful autumn colour. H 20m (65ft), S 5m (16ft).

   A. saccharum subsp. *nigrum* 'Newton Sentry' (syn. *A. saccharum* 'Columnare') is a strongly growing, upright form with vivid autumn colour but without a distinct central leader. H 10m (33ft), S 2.4m (8ft).

   'Sweet Shadow' has finely cut, dark green foliage, which produces vivid yellow-orange autumn

colour. It is vase-shaped and very cold tolerant.
Aspect Full sun.
Hardiness ❀❀❀ Zones 4–8.

A. sterculiaceum
(syn. *A. villosum*)
Himalayan maple
The species has large, rather architectural, palmate leaves that are pale green in summer, turning orange in autumn. It looks striking in spring with its large, pendulous flowers. A broadly

Acer x *conspicuum* 'Silver Cardinal'

Acer 'White Tigress'

Aesculus × carnea

Pruning Requires little regular pruning apart from the removal of dead, dying, diseased or crossing branches, which are best removed during summer when the tree is in full leaf.

Propagation Species of horse chestnuts and buckeyes can be produced by seeds, which should be sown as soon as they ripen and fall from the tree. Cultivars are propagated by grafting on to seedling chestnuts or buckeyes and propagated as winter indoor grafts. It can also be successfully chip- or T-budded during summer.

A. × carnea
Red horse chestnut

A hybrid between *A. hippocastanum* and *A. pavia*, this slow-growing tree has a compact habit and red flowers. The palmate leaves are dark green and up to 25cm (10in) long. It is widely used in avenues for street planting. H and S 20m (65ft).

Named varieties Among the cultivars 'Briotii' is grown for its darker red flowers and more compact growth.

'Plantierensis' is a sterile form that bears no fruit, and so is often used in street planting. It has pale pink flowers and is closer in habit and growth to *A. hippocastanum*. Aspect Full sun.
Hardiness ✹✹✹ Zones 5–7.

A. hippocastanum
Horse chestnut

The species, which is native to south-eastern Europe, is ultimately a large, broadly spreading and showy spring-flowering tree. The palmate leaves, up to 30cm (12in) long, are attached to the petiole (leaf stalk) at the base and turn brown and yellow in autumn.

Aesculus indica

The showy white flowers appear in spring and are borne in large, upright panicles. Each flower has a yellow and red blotch. It will grow in a range of soil types in sun. H and S 30m (100ft).

Named cultivars 'Baumannii' (syn. 'Flore Pleno') is a sterile form with big, double, white flowers.

The slow-growing 'Hampton Court Gold' has yellow leaves in spring that fade to pale yellow-green. The foliage often scorches in strong sunlight, so this cultivar is best grown in light shade.

'Pyramidalis' has a more upright habit and is suitable for smaller gardens where space is restricted. Aspect Full sun or semi-shade.
Hardiness ✹✹✹ Zones 4–8.

A. indica
Indian horse chestnut

This medium to large tree may be distinguished from *A. hippocastanum* by its finer leaves and narrower clusters of flowers. These are borne in late spring and are whitish-pink, blotched yellow and red. The flowers are followed by the typical chestnut seedcases, but these are small and spineless. It does best in moist, deep, fertile soil, which may be alkaline or acidic. H and S 30m (100ft). Aspect Full sun.
Hardiness ✹✹✹ Zone 7.

spreading tree, it is especially suitable for milder maritime climates, thriving in moist, free-draining soil. H and S 10 (33ft). Aspect Full sun or semi-shade. Hardiness ✹✹ Zone 8.

A. 'White Tigress'

Another snakebark maple of uncertain parentage, this may be a hybrid of *A. tegmentosum* and *A. davidii*. It is a graceful, small tree with a multi-stemmed habit and blue-green and white striped bark. The smallish leaves turn golden-yellow in autumn. It requires neutral to acidic soil and cool summer temperatures. H 10m (33ft), S 5m (16ft). Aspect Full sun or semi-shade. Hardiness ✹✹✹ Zones 5–7.

AESCULUS

Horse chestnut, buckeye

The 15 species of deciduous trees in this genus are found in woodlands in Europe, North America and eastern Asia. They have opposite leaves and are grown for their flower panicles in late spring to early summer, as well as for their distinctive fruits. They make fine specimens in large gardens.

Cultivation Grow in deep, fertile, moisture-retentive soil in sun or semi-shade.

Aesculus hippocastanum

Aleurites moluccana

A. x *neglecta* 'Erythroblastos'
Sunrise horse chestnut
This is an ideal chestnut for a small garden. It is also one of the showiest because in spring the emerging leaves are salmon-pink. The foliage turns pale yellow by summer, then green. New growth may be damaged by frosts in late spring, so it does best if grown in fertile soil in semi-shade or sheltered by other trees. H 6m (20ft), S 3m (10ft).
Aspect Semi-shade.
Hardiness ✳✳✳ Zone 7.

A. turbinata
Japanese horse chestnut
The flowers of this species are similar to those of *A. hippocastanum* but often appear a few weeks later. They are white, stained yellow with a red spot, and are borne in cylindrical panicles. The leaves, up to 40cm (16in) long, are heavily veined and turn yellow-brown in autumn. A large tree, widely used in parkland or avenue planting, it is easy to grow in any free-draining soil. H 20m (65ft), S 12m (40ft).
Aspect Full sun.
Hardiness ✳✳✳ Zones 5–7.

AGATHIS
Kauri pine, dammar pine
The genus contains 13 species of evergreen, coniferous trees that are native to the southern hemisphere. They are large trees with exposed trunks and upswept branches. The foliage is dark green and quite thick, rather than needle-like. The cones are extremely large. Kauris are slow-growing but ultimately large trees, which can live for more than 1,000 years.
Cultivation Grow in deep, free-draining, fertile soil in sun or semi-shade.
Pruning Formative pruning should aim to encourage a clear trunk and a balanced crown, while tipping the lateral branches of young trees will encourage a denser crown.
Propagation Seed is the easiest method of propagation and should be collected when fresh and be sown into a container in a heated glasshouse in a frost-free and humid environment until germination occurs. Softwood cuttings will also root during summer if the cutting base is dipped in a rooting hormone and placed in a glasshouse in a humid environment until rooting occurs.

A. australis
Kauri pine
A widely planted avenue tree, these are used extensively where large evergreen trees are required in tropical climates. They have a distinctive outline with a clear trunk and upright, tufted branches. Young trees need to be protected from strong winds. H 25m (80ft), S 5m (16ft).
Aspect Full sun.
Hardiness ✳ Zones 9–11.

A. robusta
Queensland kauri, smooth-bark kauri
This slow-growing tree tolerates temperatures below freezing for very short periods. It is a widely planted coastal tree, and drought tolerant, so it is widely planted in exposed locations. H 50m (165ft), S 10m (33ft).
Aspect Full sun.
Hardiness ✳ Zones 9–11.

AILANTHUS
The genus contains five species of deciduous shrubs and spreading trees, which are native to Australia and South-east Asia. They are fast-growing plants and will grow in poor soils, which is why they are often used as pioneer trees. They also tolerate pollution. Male and female flowers are borne on separate trees in long racemes, but it is the female flowers that develop into long, flat, greenish-red seeds that persist long into winter.
Cultivation Grow in fertile, deep and well-drained soil in sun or semi-shade.
Pruning Formative pruning should aim to encourage a clear trunk and a balanced crown, with occasional pruning to remove dead, dying, diseased or crossing branches when the tree is in full leaf.
Propagation Fresh seed germinates readily if it is sown in a container in a unheated glasshouse or cold frame. Alternatively, you can dig up root suckers in winter and pot them up.

A. altissima
(syn. A. glandulosa)
Tree of heaven
This broadly columnar tree is the most widely planted species in the genus. It grows very quickly, and often produces root suckers, which can prove to be somewhat troublesome.

Female forms produce masses of seeds, so it is not surprising that in some parts of the world this tree is a weed. Male forms do not pose this problem, but the seeds are one of the attractive features of the tree. This is one of the most adaptable trees for difficult locations, especially on very poor or polluted soils. H 25m (80ft), S 12–15m (40–50ft).
Named varieties The cultivar 'Pendula' is identical in many respects to the species in growth and overall height, except that it has long foliage, which droops heavily to produce a graceful weeping effect.
Aspect Full sun or semi-shade.
Hardiness ✳✳✳ Zones 4–8 (although may not be adaptable to tropical climates).

Ailanthus altissima

ALBIZIA
Silk tree
The genus contains about 150 species of deciduous trees and shrubs from Asia, South and Central America and Australia. They are grown for their delicate foliage and mimosa-like flowers.
Cultivation Grow in fertile, well-drained soil in full sun or semi-shade.
Pruning Formative pruning should encourage a clear trunk and a balanced crown. Prune occasionally to remove dead, dying, diseased or crossing branches.
Propagation Sow fresh seed in a pot in a humid and frost-free heated glasshouse.

A. julibrissin
(syn. *Acacia julibrissin*)
Silk tree
This tree is well adapted to nutrient-poor, dry soils. Dark green fern-like leaves turn pale yellow in autumn. Clusters of greenish-yellow flowers appear in summer, followed by flat, brown pods in autumn. It can be grown in protected locations in temperate areas. H and S 10m (33ft).
Named varieties *A. julibrissin* f. *rosea* is a widely grown form with pale pink flowers.
Aspect Full sun or semi-shade.
Hardiness ❂❂ Zones 7–10.

ALEURITES
The six species in the genus are evergreen trees that are native to tropical and subtropical areas of China, Indonesia and the western Pacific. They are tender trees that grow well in warm areas but should otherwise be grown under glass.
Cultivation Grow in moisture-retentive but well-drained, neutral to acidic soil. They prefer full sun but will tolerate semi-shade.
Pruning Formative pruning should aim to encourage a clear trunk and a balanced crown.
Propagation Sow fresh seed in a pot in a humid and frost-free heated glasshouse until germination occurs. Root hardwood cuttings by dipping in a rooting hormone. Keep in a humid, frost-free environment.

A. moluccana
Candlenut
This attractive, often multi-stemmed tree from South-east Asia produces maple like new leaves that are strongly felted and white. These coincide with clusters of small, white flowers. From a distance the tree looks as if it has been touched by frost. This species is more tolerant of alkaline soils than others in the genus, and it is also resistant to drought and salt spray. H 20m (65ft), S 10m (33ft).
Aspect Full sun.
Hardiness (Min. 7°C/45°F) Zone 11.

ALNUS
Alder
The genus contains some 35 species of fast-growing, deciduous trees and shrubs. In spring, male and female catkins are borne on the same plant.
Cultivation Most species prefer damp soil, which does not need to be especially fertile, but individual preferences are noted below.
Pruning Little pruning is required apart from the removal of dead, dying, diseased or crossing branches, or pruning to encourage a clear leader. Many alders respond favourably to coppicing or pollarding. This should be undertaken during winter, with trees being pollarded or coppiced every three years.
Propagation Most alders can easily be grown from seed, as long as it is sown quickly once ripe. Cultivars can be grown from

Alnus cordata

softwood cuttings during summer or from hardwood cuttings during winter. Ornamental forms are also produced from winter indoor grafting or chip- and T-budding during summer.

A. cordata
Italian alder
A fast-growing, conical tree native to Italy and Corsica, this is one of the alders that will tolerate free-draining soil. It has a neat habit and glossy, dark green leaves that grow up to 10cm (4in) long. Yellow catkins appear in late winter and early spring, followed by dark green fruits, which mature to dark brown. It is often grown as a windbreak. H 25–30m (80–100ft), S 10m (33ft).
Aspect Full sun.
Hardiness ❂❂❂ Zones 4–7.

A. glutinosa
Common alder
This species thrives in damp conditions, although when under stress it is susceptible to root rot. The dark green leaves, up to 10cm (4in) long, are sticky in spring. Yellow catkins are borne in late winter to early spring. H 25m (80ft), S 10m (33ft).
Named varieties 'Aurea' has yellow leaves in spring and summer and a more compact habit. H 12m (40ft), S 5m (16ft).
   'Imperialis' has deeply cut leaves and is the most decorative of the alders.
   'Pyramidalis' is a conical form with a tight habit and strong central leader. H 15m (50ft), S 5m (16ft).
Aspect Full sun.
Hardiness ❂❂❂ Zones 4–7.

Albizia julibrissin

Alnus glutinosa 'Laciniata'

A. incana
Grey alder

The hardiest and most cold-tolerant of the alders, *A. incana*, which is native to Europe, is more compact than either *A. cordata* or *A. glutinosa*. The yellow-brown catkins appear in late winter to early spring, before the leaves, up to 10cm (4in) long, which are dark green above and covered with white hairs beneath. It will grow in free-draining soil. H 20m (65ft), S 10m (33ft).
Named varieties The cultivar 'Pendula' is a small weeping tree. H 10m (33ft), S 6m (20ft).
   'Ramulis Coccineis' is a beautiful small tree. In spring the shoots are tinged with pinkish-red and the leaves are yellow. The catkins are orange-yellow. H 10m (33ft), S 5m (16ft).
Aspect Full sun.
Hardiness ❀❀❀ Zones 2–6.

AMELANCHIER
Juneberry, snowy mespilus, shadbush

Most of the 25 deciduous species in the genus are small to medium-sized shrubs, but there are a few small trees, which are grown for their spring to early summer flowers and vibrant autumn colours. If left unpruned they will be shrub-like, but with regular formative pruning a tree-like habit can be achieved.
Cultivation Grow in fertile, moisture-retentive but well-drained, acidic or alkaline soil in full sun or semi-shade.

Pruning Some species are best grown as multi-stemmed trees with the lower sections of the trunks kept clear of branches. However, a few can be easily trained as small garden trees with a single trunk and balanced crown. Occasional pruning is required to remove diseased, damaged or crossing branches.
Propagation Seed germinates if collected fresh and sown in an unheated glasshouse or cold frame until germination occurs. Semi-ripe cutting are taken in late summer, dipped in a rooting hormone, and placed in a humid environment until rooting occurs.

A. × grandiflora

This hybrid of *A. arborea* and *A. laevis* is a shrubby plant with a spreading habit. The young leaves, up to 8cm (3in) long, are bronze, turning green and, in autumn, red and orange. Racemes of white flowers are borne in spring and are followed by black berries. H 8m (26ft), S 10m (33ft).
Named varieties The best cultivar is 'Ballerina' (sometimes classified as a clone of *A. laevis*), which is a beautiful garden tree with masses of small, rose-like, white flowers in early spring, coinciding with the emerging leaves, which are small, pointed and toothed, bronze-green when young and turning red-purple in autumn. H and S 6m (20ft).
Aspect Full sun or semi-shade.
Hardiness ❀❀❀ Zones 4–7.

A. laevis
Allegheny serviceberry

This small tree or, more often, large shrub, will be covered with masses of white flowers, which contrast with the pinkish new foliage. Autumn colour is spectacular: the leaves, up to 6cm (2½in) long, turn yellow, orange and purple-red. H 8–12m (26–40ft), S 8m (26ft).
Aspect Full sun or semi-shade.
Hardiness ❀❀❀ Zones 4–8.

A. lamarckii

In spring this broadly spreading tree, which is naturalized in Europe but of uncertain origin, produces an explosion of tiny white flowers from beneath the bronzy-coppery-red new foliage. In early autumn the leaves produce a range of fiery tints before they fall. H 10m (33ft), S 12m (40ft).
Aspect: Full sun or semi-shade.
Hardiness ❀❀❀ Zones 4–7.

ARAUCARIA

The genus of evergreen, coniferous trees contains about 18 species, which are found in Australia, Oceania and South America. Only one species, *A. araucana*, is hardy and makes a handsome specimen tree.
Cultivation Outdoors, grow in moisture-retentive but well-drained soil. All young plants should be protected from cold winter winds.

Araucaria araucana

Amelanchier lamarckii

Pruning Formative pruning should aim to encourage a clear trunk and a balanced crown, while tipping the lateral branches of young trees will encourage a denser crown. Occasional pruning is required for the removal of dead, dying, diseased or crossing branches.

Propagation Seed is the easiest method of propagation and should be collected when fresh and be sown into a container in a heated glasshouse in a frost-free and humid environment until germination occurs.

A. araucana
(syn. A. imbricata)
Monkey puzzle, Chilean pine
This large tree has whorled and spiky foliage and long, rather lax branches. In mild areas all the lower branches remain attached, but elsewhere the lower branches are soon lost and the tree assumes the distinctive umbrella-like shape. It is an adaptable tree that is tolerant of salt spray. It does best in fertile, moisture-retentive but well-drained soil with some protection from cold winds. H 25m (80ft), S 10m (33ft).
Aspect: Full sun.
Hardiness ✸✸✸ Zone 8.

A. heterophylla
(syn. A. excelsa)
Norfolk Island pine
A distinctive and widely grown conifer in warmer climates, the species is tolerant of salt spray and heat and is often planted in coastal locations to help stabilize sandy soils. The foliage takes the form of upswept, V-shaped fans, which spiral around the branches while the trunk is left almost bare. Despite their potential size, young plants are popular houseplants in temperate areas. H 60m (200ft), S 30m (100ft).
Aspect Full sun to light shade.
Hardiness ✸ Zones 9–11.

ARBUTUS
Strawberry tree, Madroño
The genus contains about 14 species of ornamental, small-leaved, evergreen trees, which are grown for their highly polished bark, heather-like flowers and small, hard strawberry-like (but unpalatable) fruits, which ripen in autumn. The bark is particularly attractive in winter. The flowers are quite showy and are produced from late summer to autumn.

Although some species are relatively tender when they are young, once they mature they are all relatively hardy, and all will tolerate coastal planting.
Cultivation Grow in fertile, well-drained soil; A. andrachne, A. x andrachnoides and A. unedo will tolerate alkaline soil, but A. menziesii prefers acidic conditions.
Pruning Remove dead, dying, diseased or crossing branches. Lower branches should be removed so their ornamental bark can be seen. Occasionally the crown of Arbutus unedo may require thinning. This is best done during late spring or early summer.

Arbutus unedo 'Elfin King'

Propagation Strawberry trees can be propagated by seed, which should be sown into acidic compost. Semi-ripe cuttings can be taken in late summer, dipped in a rooting hormone and then placed in a humid environment to root. Arbutus 'Marina' is produced by winter indoor grafting on to Arbutus unedo rootstock.

A. andrachne
Grecian strawberry tree
Native to south-eastern Europe, this is a small, round-headed tree with glossy, dark green leaves. Creamy-white flowers are borne on short stalks in late spring and are followed by orange-red fruits. The rough bark is orange-brown but flakes to reveal attractive bright orange underbark. H and S 10m (33ft).
Aspect Full sun or semi-shade.
Hardiness ✸✸ Zone 8.

A. x andrachnoides
This interesting tree is a hybrid between A. andrachne and A. unedo. It has reddish-brown, flaking bark that peels in long strips. It develops into a small, round-headed tree with glossy, mid-green leaves, up to 10cm (4in) long. The small white flowers are not usually followed by fruit. H and S 10m (33ft).
Aspect Full sun or semi-shade.
Hardiness ✸✸✸ Zone 8.

A. 'Marina'
Although the parentage of this cultivar is unknown, it is probably a hybrid between A. x andrachnoides and A. canariensis (Canary Island strawberry tree). Its endearing features are its shiny, cinnamon-coloured, flaking bark, the white, pink-flushed autumn flowers and the masses of small strawberry fruits that ripen alongside the flowers. It grows into a small, wide-spreading, round-headed tree. H and S 10m (33ft).
Aspect Full sun or semi-shade.
Hardiness ✸✸✸ Zone 8.

A. unedo
Strawberry tree
This broad-headed tree is also the hardiest and is most tolerant of salt spray. It grows wild in exposed coastal locations throughout Europe and Asia Minor, and it is sometimes known as the Killarney strawberry tree.

In autumn it bears small clusters of white flowers, which ripen alongside the fruit that develop from the previous year's flowers. The large fruit is initially orange, turning orange-red, and sometimes grows up to 2.5cm (1in) across. Its bark is dark brown and does not flake or shed. 'Elfin King' is a compact growing form. H and S 10m (33ft).
Aspect Full sun or semi-shade.
Hardiness ✸✸✸ Zone 6.

Arbutus 'Marina'

Banksia spinulosa

ARTOCARPUS
Breadfruit

This is a genus of about 50 evergreen and deciduous trees found in the tropics. The best-known species, *A. altilis,* is the breadfruit sought by Captain Bligh on the ill-fated voyage from Tahiti on HMS *Bounty.*

Cultivation These trees need tropical conditions: reliably warm weather and plentiful moisture.

Pruning Formative pruning should aim to encourage a clear trunk and a balanced crown, while tipping the lateral branches of young trees will encourage a denser crown. Occasional pruning is required for the removal of dead, dying, diseased or crossing branches.

Propagation Breadfruit can easily be propagated by bending lower branches down and layering them

Artocarpus altilis

in situ or from root cuttings taken during the dormant season and potted up and placed in a frost-free, humid environment until shoots develop.

A. altilis
(syn. *A. communis*)
Breadfruit

This broadly spreading tree has evergreen leaves resembling those of *Monstera deliciosa* (Swiss cheese plant) but with white veins across the surface of the leaves. The rounded, pear-like, light green fruits ripen in summer. They have a white, fleshy, potato-like centre that must be boiled or baked prior to eating. H and S 20m (65ft). Aspect Full sun or semi-shade. Hardiness (Min. 5°C/41°F) Zones 10–11.

BANKSIA

The genus contains about 70 species of highly ornamental evergreen shrubs and small trees, which rank alongside the South African proteas in their beauty. Banksias are native to Australia and New Guinea. They vary in height but are often large, multi-stemmed trees. Like other members of the *Proteaceae* family (including *Protea, Grevillea* and *Leucadendron*), banksias are intolerant of phosphate, so take care with fertilizers.

Cultivation In the wild, banksias grow in nutrient-poor, moist to dry, sandy soil. A few can grow in dry, warm temperate areas, but they dislike damp winters.

Pruning Formative pruning should aim to encourage a clear trunk and a balanced crown. Tipping the lateral branches on young trees encourages a dense crown. Occasional pruning is required for the removal of dead, dying, diseased or crossing branches.

Propagation In the wild, fire is required for the 'cones' to open and release the seeds. The easiest way to replicate these conditions and force the seeds to germinate is to place the seeds in a shallow container, cover with boiling water and leave to soak overnight. Alternatively, place the seeds on a baking tin (pan) in the oven at 200°C (400°F) for 10 minutes. Allow them to cool before sowing in an acidic potting medium in a frost-free and humid environment.

B. baxteri

This small tree has light green, angular leaves, up to 17cm (7in) long, which sometimes turn reddish. The large, creamy-yellow, protea-like flowerheads are produced in reasonable numbers in late summer and autumn. It is an unusual tree that is certain to turn heads when in flower. H and S 3m (10ft).
Aspect Full sun.
Hardiness ❃ Zone 9 (will require winter protection).

B. coccinea
Scarlet banksia

The dark green leaves of this small tree are toothed and silver on the underside. Columns, up to 8cm (3in) long, of spiky scarlet flowers are produced throughout spring and summer. This is a tree that requires winter protection. H 8m (26ft), S 4m (12ft).
Aspect Full sun.
Hardiness ❃ Zone 9.

B. integrifolia
Coast banksia

Erect columns of spiky, bright yellow flowers are borne on the tree in summer and autumn. The dark green leaves are notched at the tip and a beautiful silver underneath. It is tolerant of free-draining, sandy, acidic soil. H 7m (23ft), S 3m (10ft).
Aspect Full sun.
Hardiness ❃ Zones 10–11.

B. menziesii
Firewood banksia

An attractive, small tree that flowers over a long period from summer to autumn. It produces spiky columns of reddish flowers that fade to orange, occasionally pinkish and then bronze-brown. The stout foliage is covered with reddish hairs at first, but as the leaves mature they turn dark grey-green. Requires winter protection. H 15m (50ft), S 10m (33ft).
Aspect Full sun.
Hardiness (Min. 3–5°C/37–41°F) Zone 9.

B. serrata
Saw banksia

This banksia has extremely dramatic foliage. The long leaves, which have strongly toothed edges, are reddish-grey at first but turn glossy, dark green. The flowers are yellowish-grey and orange-yellow on the inside, and they are borne in late summer and autumn. It is a relatively fast-growing tree but it requires winter protection.
H 20m (65ft), S 8m (26ft).
Aspect Full sun.
Hardiness ❃ Zone 9.

BAUHINIA
Mountain ebony, orchid ebony

There are between 250 and 300 species of evergreen or deciduous trees and shrubs in the genus, which are grown mainly for their orchid-like flowers. They are not reliably hardy but may be grown in a glasshouse environment.

Cultivation Outside, grow in fertile, moisture-retentive, well-drained alkaline soil in full sun.

Pruning Formative pruning should aim to encourage a clear trunk and a balanced crown, while tipping the lateral branches of young trees will encourage a denser crown. Occasional pruning is required for the removal of dead, dying, diseased or crossing branches.

Propagation Seed is the easiest method of propagation. Collect fresh seed and sow in a pot in a heated glasshouse in a frost-free and humid environment until germination occurs. Softwood tip cuttings can also be rooted during late spring and early summer.

Bauhinia x blakeana

Dip in rooting hormone and place in a frost-free, humid environment until they root.

B. x *blakeana*
Hong Kong orchid tree
This stunning evergreen hybrid between *B. variegata* and *B. purpurea* originated in China. The round-headed trees are quick-growing but sterile, and so do not bear fruit. The fragrant flowers are maroon-pink and broadly striped with white through the centre. H 12m (40ft), S 10m (33ft).
Aspect Full sun.
Hardiness (Min. 7°C/45°F) Zones 10–12.

B. *purpurea*
Fall orchid tree
The narrowly cut petals, which make the flowers appear more ruffled than those of other species in the genus, are purple-pink streaked with white. H 12m (40ft), S 10m (33ft).
Aspect Full sun.
Hardiness (Min. 7°C/45°F) Zones 10–12.

B. *variegata*
Poor man's orchid
The heart-shaped leaves of this wide-spreading, loose-crowned, deciduous tree consist of two lobes and have veins radiating from the stalk to the tip. The large flowers, a bit like a honeysuckle, are dark magenta, streaked with white. They appear over a period from summer to autumn. The pea-like seedpods are bright red. H 12m (40ft), S 10m (33ft).
Named varieties *B. variegata* var. *alba* is a stunning form with elegant white flowers. It has a similar habit to the species but is somewhat shy to flower.
Aspect Full sun.
Hardiness ❀ Zones 10–12.

BETULA
Birch
The 60 or so species of deciduous trees and shrubs in the genus are found throughout the northern hemisphere. Male and female catkins are borne on the same plant in spring. Many species have attractive bark and are planted for their autumn colour and graceful habit of growth.
Cultivation Grow in deep, moisture-retentive but well-drained soil in full sun or semi-shade.

Betula albosinensis var. *septentrionalis*

Pruning Most birch require little pruning apart from the removal of dead, dying, diseased or crossing branches. Lower branches may be removed so their ornamental bark can be seen. This is best done during late spring or early summer; if undertaken too early in spring the cut surfaces will 'bleed' profusely.
Propagation Birch are most widely propagated by seed or winter indoor grafting. Sow ripe seed in a pot and place in an unheated glasshouse or cold frame until germinated. Most forms with ornamental bark are produced by winter indoor grafting on to *Betula pendula* rootstock. The forms of *Betula nigra* are widely produced by softwood cuttings during summer.

B. *albosinensis*
Chinese red birch
This graceful and elegant tree has finely toothed leaves, up to 8cm (3in) long, which turn yellow in autumn. It has coppery-pink peeling bark. It will grow well in most soils, but prefers damp conditions. H 25m (80ft), S 10m (33ft).
Named varieties Some consider *B. albosinensis* var. *septentrionalis* as the best form of the species. It has pink and pale grey flaking bark that turns darker in winter. The winter shoots are reddish-brown. The branches weep slightly and produce a beautiful outline in spring and summer.
Aspect Full sun or semi-shade.
Hardiness ❀❀❀ Zones 5–6.

B. *alleghaniensis*
(syn. B. lutea)
Yellow birch
A fast-growing and ultimately large tree from North America, the species has golden-brown flaking bark. In autumn the leaves turn yellow. The stems smell of wintergreen if the bark is rubbed or the leaves are crushed. It is a shade-tolerant birch that does best in fertile, free-draining soil. H 30m (100ft), S 15m (50ft).
Aspect Full sun or semi-shade.
Hardiness ❀❀❀ Zone 3.

Betula alleghaniensis

Betula pendula

B. ermanii
Erman's birch, Russian rock birch, gold birch

This ultimately large and spreading pyramidal tree is grown for its creamy-white bark, which peels in long strips to reveal creamy-pink underbark. The dark green leaves, up to 10cm (4in) long, turn yellow in autumn, and slender, long catkins are borne in spring. It is an excellent year-round tree for fertile, free-draining, neutral to acidic soils. H 25m (80ft), S 20m (65ft).
Named varieties There are several cultivars, including 'Grayswood Hill', which has exceptionally beautiful white bark.

'Hakkoda Orange', which originated in a batch of seed from Japan, has attractive flaking orange bark.
Aspect Full sun or semi-shade.
Hardiness ❀❀❀ Zones 5–6.

B. 'Hergest'

Sometimes sold as a cultivar of *B. albosinensis*, this is a fast-growing form with salmon-pink and whitish flaking bark. H 25m (80ft), S 10m (33ft).
Aspect Full sun or semi-shade.
Hardiness ❀❀❀ Zones 5–6.

B. lenta
Cherry birch, sweet birch

This species is similar in many respects to *B. alleghaniensis*. It is native to the east of the USA, where it is found in fertile woodlands. Young leaves and the bark smell and taste of wintergreen when crushed or rubbed. The yellow-green leaves, up to 10cm (4in) long, turn yellow in autumn. It grows well on neutral, moisture-retentive, fertile soil. H 25m (80ft), S 12m (40ft).
Aspect Full sun or semi-shade.
Hardiness ❀❀❀ Zone 3.

B. nigra
Black birch, river birch

This species from North America is distinguished from other birches by its purplish-orange shaggy bark, which looks as if sheets of paper have been stuck to the trunk. It is a slender tree with slightly weeping branches, and the glossy leaves, up to 8cm (3in) long, turn yellow in autumn. It is tolerant of wet sites

Betula ermanii 'Grayswood Hill'

but does as well in free-draining soil. H and S 30m (100ft).
Named varieties The cultivar 'Cascade Falls' has a strongly weeping form, similar to, but more graceful than, that of *B. pendula* 'Youngii'; it is probably the best weeping birch currently available.

The most widely planted cultivar, 'Heritage', has whitish-pink flaking bark and a good pyramidal habit. It is equally beautiful whether trained as a single-stemmed, upright tree or as a multi-stemmed bushy tree.

'Dura-Heat', a US selection, is more heat-tolerant than 'Heritage' and has glossier leaves and whiter bark.
Aspect Full sun or semi-shade.
Hardiness ❀❀❀ Zones 3–9.

B. papyrifera
Paper birch, canoe birch

This fast-growing, cold-tolerant birch from North America has whitish peeling bark. The dark green leaves, up to 10cm (4in) long, turn orange-yellow in autumn. This tree will not do well in shallow, free-draining, strongly alkaline soil. H 30m (100ft), S 15m (50ft).
Named varieties The cold-tolerant cultivar 'Saint George' is grown for its white bark and dark brown branches.

'Vancouver' has duller, pinkish-brown and white bark and a lovely orange autumn colour.
Aspect Full sun or semi-shade.
Hardiness ❀❀❀ Zones 2–7.

B. pendula
Silver birch

The silver birch, which is native to Europe, is widely grown for its whitish bark, which turns black at the base as the tree matures. It has mid-green leaves, up to 6cm (2in) long, which turn yellow in autumn, and yellow-brown catkins in early spring. The species is more tolerant of drier conditions than many other birches and will do well in shallow, free-draining, alkaline soil. H 30m (100ft), S 10m (33ft).
Named varieties 'Golden Cloud' is a pretty form with vivid yellow leaves that turn yellow-green in summer. H 6m (20ft), S 5m (16ft).

'Obelisk' is an upright form with a strong main leader and twisted, upswept branches.

The graceful 'Purpurea' has purplish bark and leaves; the latter turn yellow in autumn. It is slower growing than many other forms of the silver birch. H 10m (33ft), S 3m (10ft).

'Youngii' (Young's weeping birch) is a small, graceful weeping tree, which requires regular pruning to maintain its attractive shape. H 8ft (26ft), S 5ft (16ft).
Aspect Full sun or semi-shade.
Hardiness ❀❀❀ Zones 2–7.

B. utilis var. jacquemontii
Himalayan birch

The species is usually represented in gardens by this naturally occurring form, which is one of the most widely planted garden trees, grown for its stunning white bark, long, dangling catkins in spring and yellow autumn leaf colour. A broadly conical tree, it is fast-growing when first planted. It does best in fertile, moist, neutral to acidic soil. H 25m (80ft), S 10m (33ft).
Named varieties Among the cultivars of *B. utilis* var. *jacquemontii*, the Dutch selection 'Doorenbos' has whitish bark that peels to reveal an orange underbark.

'Grayswood Ghost' has stunning white bark and very long catkins and is quick to establish.

The quick-growing 'Jermyns' has extremely long catkins, which are up to 15cm (6in) long, and beautiful bark. It is ultimately a tall, broadly spreading birch.

'Silver Shadow' is the smallest birch of this group, has the starkest white bark, and is one of the best for general planting.

B. utilis 'Ramdana River' is an exquisite form with white, pink-tinged bark and glossy green leaves in summer.
Aspect Full sun or semi-shade.
Hardiness ❀❀❀ Zones 5–6.

BISMARCKIA

The bismarckia palm is only found on the island of Madagascar where it flourishes in open grassland and grows quickly. It is one of the most ornamental palms, with beautiful bluish-tinted foliage, and is widely

Bismarckia nobilis

planted. As a landscape palm, it has many uses and can be planted as a specimen or in groups.
Cultivation Although they will grow in poor, dry conditions, these palms will grow more quickly in fertile, free-draining soil. They will not survive temperatures below 15°C (59°F), although those with the most intense blue-coloured leaves are the most hardy.
Pruning Like most palms, little pruning is required apart from the removal of dead leaves and spent flower clusters in early summer.
Propagation Seed should be collected when fresh and sown into a pot in a heated glasshouse in a humid environment at 29°C (84°F) until germination occurs.

B. nobilis
Noble palm
This palm, which is native to Madagascar, has silver-grey, fan-shaped leaves, which can be over 3m (10ft) across. The palmate fans are upright and angled in a different direction above the main trunk. The trunk itself is brown and slightly matted. Female plants

bear clusters of fleshy brown fruits.
H 12m (40ft), S 6m (20ft).
Aspect Full sun.
Hardiness ❋ Zones 9–11.

BRACHYCHITON
Bottletree, kurrajong
There are some 30 species of evergreen and deciduous trees in the genus, native to Australia and Papua New Guinea. They are tender plants, which can be grown as specimens in mild areas but otherwise are grown under glass.
Cultivation Outdoors, grow in fertile, free-draining, neutral to acidic soil in full sun.
Pruning Formative pruning should encourage a clear trunk and a balanced crown. Tipping the lateral branches will encourage a denser crown. Occasional pruning is required to remove dead, diseased or crossing branches.
Propagation Collect seeds when fresh and sow in a pot in a heated glasshouse in a frost-free and humid environment until germination occurs. Semi-ripe cuttings can be taken in late summer. Place in a frost-free, humid environment until rooted.

B. acerifolius
(syn. *Sterculia acerifolia*)
Flame tree, flame kurrajong
In warm areas this Australian species is a widely grown street tree. In spring, masses of small, bell-shaped, scarlet flowers cover the upswept branches and give the effect of vivid autumn colour. This large tree stores water in its thick trunk during droughts.
H 40m (130ft), S 20m (65ft).
Aspect Full sun.
Hardiness (Min. 10°C/50°F)
Zones 9–11.

BROWNEA
The genus of about 25 species of evergreen trees and shrubs is native to tropical South America. These plants are tender and need restrictive pruning if grown under glass in temperate areas.
Cultivation Outdoors, grow in moisture-retentive but well-drained, neutral to acidic soil in semi-shade.
Pruning Formative pruning should aim to encourage a clear trunk and a balanced crown. Tipping the lateral branches of young trees will encourage a denser crown. Occasional pruning is required to remove dead, dying, diseased or crossing branches.
Propagation Sow fresh seed in a heated glasshouse until germination occurs. Semi-ripe cuttings can be rooted in late summer. Dip in a rooting hormone and place in a frost-free, humid environment until they root.

B. macrophylla
Panama flame tree
In summer this tree bears stunning scarlet flowers with stamens pointing in every direction. The new leaves are flushed with pink, turning dark green as they mature. Seeds are borne in long, dark brown pods.
H and S 20m (65ft).
Aspect Light to semi-shade.
Hardiness ❋ Zones 10–12.

BUTIA
Yatay palm, jelly palm
The 12 species come from cool areas of South America, where they develop into tall, straight-stemmed palms. They can be grown as houseplants when they are young. x *Butiagrus nabonnandii* is a hybrid between *B. capitata* and *Syagrus romanzoffiana* (queen palm), and it is one of the hardiest and most tropical-looking of the V-leaved palms. It has the graceful habit of *B. capitata* and the quality of *S. romanzoffiana*.
Cultivation This tree will grow in any free-draining but fertile soil. It thrives in full sun but will tolerate light, dappled shade.
Pruning Jelly palms require little annual pruning apart from the removal of the dead fronds and fruit spikes as and when needed.
Propagation Fresh seed germinates readily if it is planted in loam-based potting compost, in a frost-free humid environment with temperatures around 29°C (84°F).

Brownea grandiceps

Butia capitata

B. capitata
(syn. *Cocos capitata*)
Pindo palm, jelly palm
This slow-growing palm has distinctive, strongly arching, V-shaped, silver-green fronds. Brown, dead leaves hang from the trunk, and are best removed to reveal the wide-based trunk. The leaves can measure up to 3m (10ft) long. In summer it bears panicles of yellow flowers. H 6m (20ft), S 3m (10ft).
Aspect Full sun.
Hardiness (Min. 5–10°C/41–50°F) Zones 8–11.

Callistemon citrinus

CALLIANDRA
Powder puff tree
There are over 200 species of evergreen shrubs, trees and perennials in the genus. They are native to tropical and subtropical areas in India, Africa and Central and South America. Although they will withstand temperatures of -3°C (27°F), in temperate areas they are grown as conservatory plants.
Cultivation Outdoors, grow in fertile, well-drained soil in full sun.
Pruning Formative pruning should aim to encourage a clear trunk and a balanced crown. Occasional pruning is required for the removal of dead, dying, diseased or crossing branches.
Propagation Sow fresh seed in a heated glasshouse until germination occurs. Softwood tip cuttings can be rooted during late spring and early summer. Dip in a rooting hormone and place in a frost-free, humid environment until they root.

C. haematocephala
(syn. *C. inaequilatera*)
This small, broadly spreading tree bears pompons of silky, dark rosy-red flowers on short days, mainly in the late autumn and winter. The glossy, dark green leaves, up to 45cm (18in) long, are fern-like. H 6m (20ft), S 4m (12ft).
Aspect Full sun.
Hardiness (Min. 13°C/55°F) Zones 9–12.

C. tweedii
Mexican flame bush
This small tree has whitish-yellow flowers over a long period from winter to late spring. The leaves, up to 15cm (6in) long, are mid-green. It is more tolerant of drought than other species. H 5m (16ft), S 1.8m (6ft).
Aspect Full sun.
Hardiness (Min. 13°C/55°F) Zones 9–12.

CALLISTEMON
Bottlebrush
The 25 species of bottlebrush are native to Australia, where they are found in reliably moist soil. These evergreen trees are recognizable from the spikes of colourful flowers. Although the majority are shrubs, many attain sufficient height to make beautiful landscape trees.
Cultivation Outdoors, grow in moisture-retentive but well-drained, neutral to acidic soil in full sun.
Pruning Formative pruning should aim to encourage a clear trunk and a balanced crown. Tipping the lateral branches of young trees will encourage a denser crown. Remove dead, dying, diseased or crossed branches.
Propagation Sow fresh seed in a heated glasshouse in a frost-free and humid environment until germination occurs. Semi-ripe cuttings can be rooted in late summer. Dip in a rooting hormone and place in a frost-free, humid environment until rooted.

C. citrinus
Crimson bottlebrush
This tree has brown flaking bark and, in spring and summer, dense clusters of scarlet flowers. It is a widely planted species, often best grown as a multi-stemmed small tree. Requires winter protection. H 10m (33ft), S 8m (26ft).
Aspect Full sun.
Hardiness ❋ Zones 8–11.

C. salignus
Willow bottlebrush, white bottlebrush
A small tree with white, papery bark, this bottlebrush has willow-like leaves and masses of bright red flowers, which are borne at the ends of the stems from late spring to midsummer. Although

Calliandra haematocephala

Calocedrus decurrens

the red-flowering form is most often seen, there are also forms with pink and whitish-green flowers. Requires winter protection. H 15m (50ft), S 5m (16ft). Aspect Full sun. Hardiness ✿ Zones 8–11.

C. viminalis
Weeping bottlebrush
This highly variable species usually has large scarlet flowers in clusters at the end of the stems. However, white, pink and mauve forms have also been introduced. It has a strongly weeping habit and coppery new growth in spring. H and S 8m (26ft). Aspect Full sun. Hardiness ✿ Zones 9–11.

C. viridiflorus
Green bottlebrush
The hardiest of the bottlebrushes, this makes a large shrub or small tree. It has dark green leaves, up to 3cm (1½in) long, and pale yellow-green flowers in mid- to late summer. New growth is flushed pink. Requires winter protection. H and S 10m (33ft). Aspect Full sun. Hardiness ✿✿ Zones 8–11.

CALOCEDRUS
Incense cedar
The three species of evergreen conifer in the genus come from North America and South-east Asia. They can be grown as specimen trees.
Cultivation Grow in any moisture-retentive but well-drained, fertile soil in sun or semi-shade.
Pruning Formative pruning should aim to produce a clear trunk and a balanced crown. Tipping the lateral branches of young trees will encourage a denser crown. Prune to remove dead, dying, diseased or crossing branches.
Propagation Sow fresh seed in a pot in an unheated glasshouse or cold frame until germination occurs. Semi-ripe and softwood cuttings can be rooted in summer.

C. decurrens
(syn. *Heyderia decurrens, Libocedrus decurrens*)
Incense cedar
This beautiful, tightly conical, columnar tree is usually available in the form 'Fastigiata' or 'Columnaris', and plants may not be so named. (The true species will be more open and less columnar in habit.) It produces flat sprays of dense foliage, similar to a cypress, but with a strongly corrugated bark. H 20m (65ft), S 1.8m (6ft).
Aspect Full sun.
Hardiness ✿✿✿ Zone 7.

CALOPHYLLUM
The genus contains over 180 species of evergreen trees and shrubs, but only a few are cultivated.
Cultivation Grow in humus-rich, moisture-retentive soil in full sun.
Pruning Formative pruning should aim to encourage a clear trunk and a balanced crown. Tipping the lateral branches of young trees will encourage a denser crown. Remove dead, dying, diseased or crossing branches.
Propagation Sow fresh seed in a heated glasshouse in a frost-free and humid environment until germination occurs.

C. inophyllum
Alexandrian laurel, Indian laurel, laurelwood
This large tree has leathery, oval leaves, up to 20cm (8in) long. The fragrant, waxy, creamy-white blooms are borne in dense clusters above the foliage. The flowers, which appear late in the day and fade by the following morning, appear in late spring and summer, followed by blue-green, golf-ball-sized fruits, which ripen o brown. H 35m (115ft), S 20m (65ft).
Aspect Full sun to semi-shade.
Hardiness (Min. 8°C/46°F) Zones 10–11.

CARPINUS
Hornbeam
The 40 or so species of hornbeam are deciduous trees found in Europe, North America and Asia. They are useful for hedging or as specimen trees, providing good autumn colour, an attractive habit and catkins in spring.
Cultivation Grow in moisture-retentive but well-drained soil in sun or semi-shade (but see species requirements).
Pruning Most hornbeams require little pruning apart from the removal of dead, dying, diseased or crossing branches. The habit of many of the hornbeams is usually slightly untidy and so it is difficult to prune for shape without removing too many branches. Any pruning is best done during early summer and care is needed.
Propagation Sow fresh seed in a container and place outside in an unheated glasshouse or cold frame until germination occurs. Some forms can be grown from softwood cuttings during summer, or grafted on to the common hornbeam during winter.

Carpinus betulus

Carya illinoinensis

C. betulus
Common hornbeam
The species is widely planted as a medium-sized to large specimen tree. It has fluted grey bark and leaves similar to *Fagus sylvatica*

Carya ovata

(common beech). In spring it bears both male and female catkins on the same tree, followed in autumn by clusters of green fruits that turn yellow-brown as they age. These plants tolerate close pruning and are shade tolerant. They make attractive hedges. H and S 30m (100ft). Named varieties 'Frans Fontaine' has a narrow habit, similar to that of *Cupressus sempervirens* (Italian cypress), rarely exceeding 6m (20ft) across, and it is useful where space is limited.
Aspect Full sun or semi-shade.
Hardiness ❀❀❀ Zones 4–7.

C. caroliniana
American hornbeam
This small, graceful tree has spreading, slightly upturned branches. The blue-green leaves, up to 12cm (5in) long, turn vivid shades of yellow and orange-red in autumn, especially when the tree is growing in moist, fertile, alkaline soil. H and S 10–12m (33–40ft).
Aspect Full sun or semi-shade.
Hardiness ❀❀❀ Zones 3–9.

CARYA
Hickory
Found in woodland in North America and eastern Asia, the 25 or so species are deciduous trees that are grown for their very attractive foliage. Both male and female produce catkins, which are borne on the same plant in late spring. All the species have alternate, pinnate leaves. They are long-lived trees that require plenty of space for their questing roots. However, they can be slow to establish and do not transplant well so are best planted as container-grown saplings.
Cultivation Grow in deep, fertile, moisture-retentive but well-drained soil in sun or semi-shade.
Pruning Hickories require little pruning apart from the removal of dead, dying, diseased or crossing branches. They do require formative pruning to encourage a nice straight trunk and an even balanced crown. Any pruning is best done during early summer when the tree is in full leaf.
Propagation Hickories are widely grown from seed, which should be sown when fresh and placed in an unheated glasshouse or cold frame to germinate. Seedlings are best planted in their eventual location as they can take a considerable amount of time to establish and do not transplant well. Selected forms can also be grown from softwood cuttings during the summer, or grafted on to seedling hickories during the winter.

C. cordiformis
Bitternut, bitternut hickory, swamp hickory
Like most hickories, this is a large tree with a broadly spreading habit. The mid-green leaves, up to 25cm (10in) long, turn golden-yellow in autumn. H 30m (100ft), S 15m (50ft).
Aspect Full sun or semi-shade.
Hardiness ❀❀❀ Zones 4–9.

Caryota mitis

C. illinoinensis
Pecan
The mid-green, pinnate leaves, up to 50cm (20in) long, of this quick-growing tree have 11–17 leaflets along the main leaf stem and turn yellow in autumn. The nuts, up to 6cm (2½in) long, are edible in warm areas. H 30m (100ft), S 15m (50ft).
Aspect Full sun.
Hardiness ❀❀❀ Zones 5–9.

C. ovata
Shagbark hickory
This broadly conical tree has distinctive grey bark, which forms large, detached curls as the tree matures. The leaves, up to 30cm (12in) long, have five slender leaflets. These are mid-green, turning golden-brown and yellow in autumn. The spent bark is widely used in the production of hickory flakes for barbecues or smoking meat. The small nuts, produced in their thousands in autumn, are edible. H 30m (100ft), S 15m (50ft).
Aspect Full sun or semi-shade.
Hardiness ❀❀❀ Zones 4–8.

CARYOTA
Fishtail palm
These upright palms are native to South-east Asia, India, Australia and the Solomon Islands. In temperate areas small plants are often grown as houseplants, but in tropical zones they make handsome specimen trees.
Cultivation Outdoors, grow in deep, humus-rich, moisture-retentive but well-drained soil. Shelter from the midday sun.

Castanea sativa

Pruning Fishtail palms require little annual pruning, apart from the cosmetic removal of the dead fronds and fruit spikes during late spring or early summer.

Propagation Fresh seed germinates readily if planted in loam-based potting compost, in a humid glasshouse with temperatures around 29°C (84°F).

C. mitis
Burmese fishtail palm, clustered fishtail palm

This is a densely clumping palm. It is monocarpic: after the flower spikes are produced and the fruits ripen, the top growth dies. However, because it produces suckers, the whole plant does not die. The pinnate leaves consist of small, angular, opposite leaflets with serrated edges. In summer, cream-coloured flowers are borne in panicles, up to 30cm (12in) long. H 6m (20ft), S 4m (12ft). **Aspect** Full sun to semi-shade. **Hardiness** (Min. 15°C/59°F) Zones 10–11.

CASSIA
Shower tree

This large genus contains over 500 species, comprising evergreen or deciduous trees and shrubs. Many of the species have been reclassified into the genus *Senna*. **Cultivation** Outdoors, grow in fertile, deep, moisture-retentive soil in full sun. **Pruning** Formative pruning should encourage a clear trunk and a balanced crown. Prune only occasionally to remove dead, dying, diseased or crossing branches.

Propagation Seed is the easiest method of propagation and should be collected when fresh, soaked in water and sown into a pot in a heated glasshouse in a frost-free and humid environment until germination occurs.

C. fistula
Golden shower tree, Indian laburnum, pudding pipe tree

This semi-evergreen, medium-sized tree has a slightly arching habit. The pinnate leaves, up to 60cm (24in) long, consist of 6–16 bright green leaflets. From late spring to early summer it has hanging clusters of golden, pea-like flowers. The flowers are followed by large, brown, cylindrical pods. H 20m (65ft), S 15m (50ft). **Aspect** Full sun. **Hardiness** (Min. 15°C/59°F) Zones 10–12.

C. javanica
Pink shower tree, rainbow shower tree

In spring, this broadly spreading, deciduous tree with spiny branches and trunk bears long, rigid clusters of rose-pink, fading to whitish pink, flowers. H and S 25m (80ft). **Aspect** Full sun. **Hardiness** (Min. 16°C/61°F) Zones 10–12.

CASTANEA
Sweet chestnut

The 12 or so species of long-lived deciduous trees in the genus are found in Europe, North America, Asia and northern Africa. They have handsome foliage and sometimes edible nuts. In summer catkins bear fragrant flowers. **Cultivation** Grow in deep, fertile, free-draining soil that is on the acid side of neutral.

Pruning Remove dead, dying, diseased or crossing branches. Formative pruning encourages a straight trunk and evenly balanced crown. Remove suckers when they appear, as well as reverted shoots on the variegated leaf forms. Prune during early summer when the tree is in full leaf. **Propagation** Fresh seed should be sown in an unheated glasshouse or cold frame until it germinates.

C. dentata
American sweet chestnut

This majestic tree is susceptible to chestnut blight. The long, tapered, toothed leaves, up to 25cm (10in) long, are mid-green, turning golden-brown in autumn. Edible fruits appear in autumn. H 30m (100ft), S 25m (80ft). **Aspect** Full sun or semi-shade. **Hardiness** ❀❀❀ Zones 4–8.

Castanea dentata

Castanea sativa

Cedrus atlantica

C. sativa
Sweet chestnut, Spanish chestnut
This ornamental tree is widely grown in Europe for its edible fruits and its timber. It is a broadly spreading tree. Mature specimens are easily identified by the spirally patterned bark. The glossy, mid-green leaves, up to 20cm (8in) long, are slender, with distinctive bristles along the margins. In autumn they turn brown. H 30m (100ft), S 25m (80ft).
Named varieties The cultivar 'Albomarginata' (syn. 'Argenteomarginata') has beautiful dark green, white-edged leaves. The spines on the fruits are also variegated white. This form tends to revert and so needs occasional pruning to remove any all-green shoots. It is slightly less vigorous

than the species.
Aspect Full sun or semi-shade.
Hardiness ✿✿✿ Zones 5–8.

CATALPA
The 11 species of deciduous trees in the genus are native to eastern Asia and North America. They are grown for their large leaves and bell-shaped flowers, which are followed by the distinctive hanging fruits. Most catalpas are susceptible to damage from late spring frosts, but they are tolerant of heat and are particularly suitable for courtyards.
Cultivation Grow in fertile, moisture-retentive but well-drained soil in full sun. Protect from strong, cold winds.
Pruning Bean trees require little pruning apart from the removal of dead, dying, diseased or crossing branches. Formative pruning is important when young as it will encourage a straight trunk and an evenly balanced crown. Suckers should be removed from the trunks as they appear, as should any reverted shoots on the variegated leaf forms. Pruning is best done during early summer when the tree is in full leaf.
Propagation The most widely used methods of propagation are softwood cuttings during the summer and hardwood cuttings during the winter. Softwood cuttings should be placed in a humid environment and the leaves should be cut in half to reduce

water loss. Hardwood cuttings can be rooted in the garden where they are to grow.

C. bignonioides
Indian bean tree, southern catalpa
In summer, this tree bears large, white, bell-shaped flowers with yellow and purple markings. These are followed by large, bean-like fruits, which hang down from the branches in autumn and persist long into winter. The mid-green leaves, up to 25cm (10in) long, are heart-shaped and turn yellow in autumn. Leaves and young shoots are prone to frost damage. H and S 15m (50ft).
Named varieties The golden form, 'Aurea', is a fast-growing tree, with vibrant yellow leaves in early summer that fade to pale green in late autumn. It can be grown as a coppiced tree and will produce massive leaves. H and S 10m (33ft).
   'Variegata' has beautiful green, yellow and white variegated and mottled leaves, which gradually fade to pale green in summer.
Aspect Full sun or semi-shade.
Hardiness ✿✿✿ Zones 5–9.

C. x erubescens
The hybrid form arising from a cross between *C. bignonioides* and *C. ovata* is usually represented in gardens by 'J.C. Teas' (syn. 'Hybrida'). Its flowers are similar to those of *C. bignonioides* but they are smaller and more numerous.

The young leaves are tinged with purple. 'Purpurea' is grown for its dark purple new leaves, which become dark green by summer, but the shoots remain purple. When it is coppiced, the leaves retain their purple colour longer into summer. H 15m (50ft), S 10–15m (33–50ft).
Aspect Full sun or semi-shade.
Hardiness ✿✿✿ Zones 5–9.

C. ovata
Yellow catalpa
This slow-growing tree produces large panicles of small white flowers, blotched with yellow and red, in midsummer. The pale green leaves, up to 25cm (10in) long, are slightly lobed and turn yellow in autumn. H 15m (50ft), S 10m (33ft).
Aspect Full sun or semi-shade.
Hardiness ✿✿✿ Zones 5–8.

CEDRUS
Cedar
The four species of delightful evergreen conifers in the genus are native to the Mediterranean and Himalayas. These large, imposing trees are best grown as specimen trees in spacious gardens so that their handsome shape can be admired.
Cultivation Grow in any well-drained, fairly fertile soil in a sunny, open position.
Pruning Formative pruning should aim to produce a clear trunk and a balanced crown. Tipping the

Catalpa bignonioides

Cedrus deodara

Cedrus deodara 'Aurea'

Cercidiphyllum japonicum f. pendulum

lateral branches on young trees encourages a denser crown. Prune to remove dead, dying, diseased or crossing branches.
Propagation Sow fresh seed in a pot in an unheated glasshouse or cold frame until germination occurs. Selected forms can be winter grafted on to seedling-raised rootstocks.

C. atlantica
(syn. C. libani subsp. atlantica)
Atlas cedar
This is an initially fast-growing, upright tree, which spreads as it matures. The green to grey-green needles are arranged in whorls at the tips of small stems, which are arranged along the branches. It is a widely planted conifer in parks and large estates. H 40m (130ft), S 10–20m (33–65ft).
Named varieties Trees in Glauca Group (blue cedar) are beautiful and widely grown selections. They have electric blue foliage, which is silver-white at first, and upswept branches, which give this stately tree its spiky, shaggy appearance.
Aspect Full sun.
Hardiness ❋❋❋ Zone 7.

C. deodara
Deodar, deodar cedar
This is grown for its long, pendulous foliage and conical habit. Although it is often planted in suburban gardens, it is not really suitable for such small spaces as it is ultimately a very large tree indeed. It is reasonably cold hardy and drought tolerant. H 50m (160ft), S 20m (65ft).

Named varieties The slow-growing 'Aurea' (golden deodar) is a beautiful and more compact form with glorious gold-coloured needles in spring that fade to greenish-yellow by summer.
'Cream Puff', also a slow-growing variety, has white-tipped green needles.
'Shalimar' is widely grown in the USA for its superior cold hardiness, attractive blue-green foliage and strongly arching habit.
Aspect Full sun.
Hardiness ❋❋❋ Zones 7–9.

C. libani
Cedar of Lebanon
This is the most easily identifiable cedar, with its straight trunk and majestic layers of branches. Widely cultivated throughout the world, it can be seen in many large, landscaped gardens. In exposed positions it will not achieve its full potential height. H 40m (130ft), S 20m (65ft).
Aspect Full sun.
Hardiness ❋❋❋ Zones 5–9.

CERCIDIPHYLLUM
Katsura
This genus of deciduous trees is native to China and Japan, where it is found in woodland. It is grown for its beautiful autumn colour.
Cultivation Grow in deep, fertile, moisture-retentive but well-drained, neutral to acidic soil. New growth may be damaged by late spring frosts, so plant in a sheltered position.

Pruning Katsura trees require little pruning apart from the removal of dead, dying, diseased or crossing branches. Formative pruning is important when young as it will encourage a straight trunk and an even balanced crown.
Propagation The most widely used method of propagation is by taking softwood cuttings during the summer. These should be placed in a humid environment until rooted and then hardened off carefully. Seed is also widely used. The weeping forms are produced by indoor grafting in the winter months and are grafted high up on standard grown rootstocks.

C. japonicum
Katsura tree
This wonderful tree has delicate, heart-shaped leaves, which are tinged with bronze-pink in spring and which turn orange-yellow, occasionally pink, in autumn. As the leaves fall in autumn and rot on the ground, they smell of burnt sugar or cotton candy. Small red flowers appear before the leaves emerge. It generally develops an attractive multi-stemmed habit, but can be trained as a standard with a central leader. H 20–30m (65–100ft), S 15–25m (50–80ft).
Named varieties The slow-growing *C. japonicum* f. *pendulum* (syn. *C. magnificum* f. *pendulum*) has long, weeping branches covered with small, heart-shaped leaves in summer. These are flushed with bronze in spring and turn vivid orange-yellow in autumn. It has a beautiful intricate, weeping silhouette against the winter sky. H and S 10m (33ft).

Cercidiphyllum japonicum f. pendulum

Chamaecyparis lawsoniana

C. japonicum f. *pendulum* 'Amazing Grace' is a superior weeping form with orange-yellow autumn colour.

C. japonicum 'Strawberry', a striking, slow-growing, pyramidal form, has blue-green, heart-shaped leaves, which turn gold and rose in autumn.

The leaves of 'Tidal Wave' turn yellow in autumn.
Aspect Full sun or semi-shade.
Hardiness ❀❀❀ Zones 4–8.

CERCIS

The six species of deciduous trees in this genus are native to North America, Asia and southern Europe. They are grown for their spring flowers, which are borne before the leaves appear.
Cultivation Grow in deep, fertile, moisture-retentive but well-drained soil in sun or semi-shade. Established plants do not respond well to being transplanted.
Pruning Redbuds and Judas trees require little pruning apart from removing dead, dying, diseased or crossing branches. Formative

pruning when young encourages an even and well-balanced crown. Redbuds are prone to anthracnose and any diseased branches should be removed back to healthy wood.
Propagation Redbuds are difficult to propagate as the seed coat requires special treatment so that water can penetrate it. To expose the pale seed the end of the hard seed coat can be rubbed away using a fine sandpaper, or a thin sliver of the seed coating can be removed using a sharp knife. Alternatively, cover the seed with boiling water and leave to soak for 12 hours before sowing as normal.

C. canadensis
Eastern redbud, redbud
This shrub or multi-stemmed small tree flowers in late spring. The pea-like flowers, which may be red, purplish, pink or white, are borne on the bare stems before the heart-shaped leaves appear. The young leaves are bronze and turn yellow in autumn. It prefers warmer areas than *C. siliquastrum*. H and S 10m (33ft).

Named varieties 'Forest Pansy' has beautiful purple, heart-shaped leaves in summer and orange and yellow autumn colour. The smallish pink flowers are almost overwhelmed by the intense leaf colour. H and S 10m (33ft).

'Royal White' is the first of the white forms to bloom in spring and has the largest flowers.

'Silver Cloud' has leaves that are mottled with white, silver and green and small pale pink flowers. It needs a semi-shaded position.

The mound-forming *C. canadensis* var. *texensis* 'Traveller' has rose-pink flowers and copper-red new leaves, which turn green in summer. H and S 1.8m (6ft).
Aspect Full sun or semi-shade.
Hardiness ❀❀❀ Zones 3–9.

C. chinensis
Chinese redbud
This large shrub or small, multi-stemmed tree bears dark pink flowers before the glossy, mid-green leaves appear. H 6m (20ft), S 5m (16ft).
Named varieties The Chinese redbud is often represented in gardens by the cultivar 'Avondale',

a dark pink flowering form from New Zealand. It is shrubbier than the species. H and S 3m (10ft).
Aspect Full sun or semi-shade.
Hardiness ❀❀❀ Zones 3–9.

C. siliquastrum
Judas tree
The common name alludes to the fact that this tree, which is native to south-eastern Europe and south-western Asia, is said to have been the tree from which Judas Iscariot hanged himself. It is a small, widely spreading tree, which thrives in poor, free-draining soil, including alkaline soil. The heart-shaped, blue-green leaves follow the dense clusters of dark purple flowers, which are borne in late spring, and small pods follow the flowers. H and S 10m (33ft).
Named varieties *C. siliquastrum* f. *albida* (syn. 'Alba') is grown for its white flowers and attractive pale green leaves.

The excellent 'Bodnant' is grown for its very dark purple flowers, which are produced on even young plants.
Aspect Full sun.
Hardiness ❀❀❀ Zones 7–8.

Chamaecyparis nootkatensis

CHAMAECYPARIS
False cypress, cypress

The seven species in the genus used to be classified as *Cupressus* (cypress), but they differ from the true cypress in that they have rather flattened sprays of foliage. They are evergreen conifers, native to Japan, Taiwan and North America. They make excellent specimen trees and are also often used as hedging, although, as with most other conifers, they will not re-shoot from old wood. The heights indicated here are the likely maximum size of garden-grown plants; in the wild species often grow taller.

Cultivation Grow in fertile, moisture-retentive but well-drained, neutral to slightly acidic soil in full sun. These are not as tolerant of very high temperatures as some other conifers.

Pruning Formative pruning should aim to produce a straight trunk with well-spaced branches and a balanced crown. Tipping back side shoots when young will encourage bushy growth.

Propagation Sow fresh seed in an unheated glasshouse or cold frame until germination occurs. Semi-ripe and softwood cuttings can be rooted during summer and placed in a humid environment until rooting occurs.

C. lawsoniana
Lawson cypress

This fast-growing, conical conifer from North America has bright green foliage in fan-shaped sprays and rather drooping branches. The species has given rise to dozens of cultivars, incredibly varied in size, shape and colour, and these are more often seen than the species. H 40–50m (130–165ft), S 5m (16ft).

Named varieties Of the cultivars, 'Alumii' is a reliable and widely grown form that has a tight, narrow habit and blue-green foliage. The colour intensifies in bright sunlight. H 15–25m (50–80ft).

'Ellwood's Pillar' has feathery, bluish leaves in a tight, upright column. H 10–15m (33–50ft).

The more compact 'Fletcheri' often develops into a multi-stemmed small tree with a round but still columnar habit. It is a pretty tree, with feathery, blue-green foliage. H 5–6m (16–20ft).

'Intertexta', a distinctive tall tree, has semi-pendulous branches clothed in long, weeping, fan-like leaves that produce a shaggy effect from a distance. The foliage is grey-green.

'Pelt's Blue' (syn. 'Van Pelt's Blue') is one of the best blue-leaved varieties currently available. H 4m (12ft), S 1.8m (6ft).

The fastigiate 'Wisselii' has slightly weeping branches of fern-like, blue-green foliage. It is easy to identify in spring when the leaves are covered with masses of tiny, purple-red male cones, which, if knocked, release plumes of bright yellow pollen. H 10m (33ft), S 1.8m (6ft).

Aspect Full sun or semi-shade.
Hardiness ✳✳✳ Zones 5–7.

C. nootkatensis
Nootka cypress

This beautiful, dark green conifer, which originates from the western USA, does best in regions with relatively even temperatures throughout the growing season. It is widely grown for its semi-pendulous habit and brown, flaking bark. The foliage is dark green. It is one of the parents of x *Cupressocyparis leylandii* (Leyland cypress). H 30m (100ft), S 8m (28ft).

Named varieties The cultivar 'Pendula' is one of the most beautiful of the hardy weeping conifers. It develops into a mass of widely arching branches, the light catching the angled stems and producing a lovely contrast between pale and dark foliage.

Aspect Full sun or semi-shade.
Hardiness ✳✳✳ Zones 4–7.

C. obtusa
Hinoki cypress

This Japanese conifer has attractive, flaking strips of brownish-red bark. The spray-like green leaves are arranged in flat layers along the stems, producing an arching effect. This is not a particularly drought-tolerant tree, although it will grow in sandy soils. There is an array of different forms, and these vary in height, shape and colour. H 20–30m

Chamaecyparis obtusa

(65–100ft), S 6m (20ft).
Aspect Full sun or semi-shade.
Hardiness ✳✳✳ Zones 5–8.

C. pisifera
Sawara cypress

Native to Japan, this is a fairly broad, attractive garden conifer with reddish bark, which peels in long threads. The bright green needles are flattish and fern-like in shape and have small Xs on the underside. Although the canopy looks rather sparse from a distance, this gives a cloud-like appearance to the foliage. This is a hardy conifer, with good heat and cold tolerance. It will thrive in any moist, deep, fertile, free-draining soil. H 20–35m (65–115ft), S 5m (16ft).

Named varieties The round-headed cultivar 'Filifera Aurea' has fern-like, bright yellow foliage and long, fine, whippy tips, which give a shaggy, fluffy appearance. H 8–12m (25–40ft).

Aspect Full sun or semi-shade.
Hardiness ✳✳✳ Zones 4–7.

Chamaerops humilis

CHAMAEROPS
Dwarf fan palm, European fan palm

This monotypic genus is native to Mediterranean countries. It is one of only two palms (the other is *Phoenix theophrasti*) native to Europe. It is usually grown as a houseplant or in a conservatory in cooler climes, but in milder areas it can be used as a small specimen tree.

Cultivation Outdoors, grow in fertile, well-drained soil in full sun. This palm is drought tolerant.

Pruning Like most palms, little pruning is required apart from removing dead leaves and spent flower clusters in early summer.

Propagation Seed is the easiest method of propagation. Sow fresh seed in a pot in a heated glasshouse in a humid environment at 29°C (84°F) until it has germinated.

C. humilis

This attractive palm develops a single trunk, although mature plants can sucker, forming clumps up to 6m (20ft) across. The pinnate, fan-shaped, blue-green leaves can get up to 1m (3ft) long, and the stems are armed with forward-pointing, usually black thorns. H 3–4m (10–12ft), S 1.8m (6ft).

Named varieties *C. humilis* var. *argentea* (syn. *C. humilis* var. *cerifera*) is similar to the species in most aspects, but the leaves are narrower and a wonderful silver-green colour, with vicious black thorns. It is slower growing and may be hardier than the species.

The cultivar 'Vulcano' has lovely silver-green leaves and a compact habit. It is ideal for growing in a container.
Aspect Full sun.
Hardiness ❋ Zones 8–11.

CITRUS

The genus, which includes oranges, lemons, limes and grapefruits, contains about 16 species of evergreen, often spiny shrubs and small trees. These plants have been cultivated for many centuries in China, Japan and Europe. They are frost tender, and in cooler climates are often grown in large containers so that they can be given the protection of a greenhouse or conservatory during the winter but moved outside for the summer months.

In Europe in the 1600s and 1700s, large, glass-fronted buildings were constructed to house the ever-increasing range of citrus fruits that were arriving from the East. These were known as orangeries. Some were unheated and were used to protect the plants in winter, while others were heated so that growth could be accelerated to produce earlier crops.

The dimensions given below are for plants growing outdoors all year round. Container-grown plants will be significantly smaller. This tree needs shelter.

Cultivation All species require plenty of light and a minimum winter temperature of 5°C (41°F). During the growing season give container-grown plants a balanced NPK fertilizer that also contains trace elements. Pot on every two to three years, using an ericaceous compost, and top dress in other years. Outdoors, grow in moisture-retentive but well-drained, neutral to acidic soil.

Pruning Formative pruning should aim to encourage a clear trunk and a balanced crown. Tipping the lateral branches on young trees will encourage a denser crown. Long, whippy growth is produced during spring and summer and this should be reduced so that a balanced, round-headed crown is produced. Prune to remove dead, dying, diseased, or crossing branches.

Propagation: Most citrus fruits are produced by T-budding, done during the winter when the seedling rootstock is dormant. Limes, oranges, grapefruits and kumquats are used in tropical climates, whereas the trifoliate Japanese orange (*Poncirus trifoliata*) is more widely used in more temperate locations. Many oranges and limes will come true from seed and can be propagated this way, but require an even temperature of above 25°C (77°F) to germinate.
Aspect: Full sun.
Hardiness (Min. 3–5°C/37–41°F) Zones 8–9.

C. aurantiifolia
Lime

The species is native to tropical Asia, where its fruits are produced for pickling and making juice. This is perhaps the least ornamental tree of this group. It is a dense, spiny plant, with masses of criss-crossing branches, which make it useful as a hedge or screen. The green fruits follow the waxy, white flowers. Limes can

Citrus aurantium

Citrus aurantifolia

be grown from seed because this a true species and not a natural or complex hybrid, like many of the other citrus plants. H 5m (16ft) S 1.8m (6ft).
Aspect Full sun.
Hardiness (Min. 3–5°C/37–41°F) Zones 10–12.

C. aurantium
Seville orange, bitter orange, bigarade
This small tree from South-east Asia is widely grown in Spain for its fruit, which is used in marmalade. Mature trees have oval, mid-green leaves, up to 10cm (4in) long. The scented white flowers are followed by flat-topped, thick-skinned fruits. When grown in containers, plants need restrictive pruning. H 10m (33ft), S 6m (20ft).
Aspect Full sun.
Hardiness (Min. 3–5°C/37–41°F) Zones 8–9.

C. limon
Lemon
This small, spiny, broadly spreading tree has been widely grown around the Mediterranean Sea since about 1200, when it was introduced from Asia. The creamy-white, scented flowers are produced in clusters in late spring and summer, followed by the fruits, which ripen by the autumn. H 7m (23ft), S 3m (10ft).
Named varieties There are several cultivars, providing a range of plant size as well as different fruit sizes and colours. They include 'Imperial', which produces very large fruits, and 'Menton', which is believed to be more tolerant of the cold and bears large fruits.

'Quatre Saisons' is widely grown for the quality and reliability of its fruits. It is also known as the 'Eureka' lemon.
'Variegata' has attractive leaves with yellow edges and silver-grey blotches. The fruits are mottled green and yellow.
'Villa Franca' bears large quantities of medium-sized fruits and is almost thornless.
Aspect Full sun.
Hardiness (Min. 3–5°C/37–41°F) Zones 8–9.

C. medica
Citron
This large, spiny shrub or small tree, which originated in south-west Asia, bears purple-tinged, white flowers and broad, dark green leaves, up to 18cm (7in) long. The large, heavy fruits, up to 30cm (12in) long, resemble knobbly lemons. It is slightly hardier than most types of citrus and will survive short periods below -5°C (23°F). H 5m (16ft), S 3m (10ft).
Named varieties The cultivar 'Ethrog' is the most widely available of the forms of citron. It bears fragrant fruits the same size as lemons.
Aspect Full sun.
Hardiness (Min. 3–5°C/37–41°F) Zones 8–9.

C. 'Meyer'
(syn. C. limon 'Meyer', C. x meyeri 'Meyer')
Meyer's lemon
This may be a hybrid of *C. limon* and *C. sinensis*. It is a small tree with glossy green leaves. The fragrant white flowers are followed by fruit that looks like a lemon in shape but is the colour of *C. sinensis*. This is one of the hardier of the citrus trees and will withstand short periods of temperatures around -5°C (23°F). H 3m (10ft), S 1.5m (5ft).
Aspect Full sun.
Hardiness (Min. 3–5°C/37–41°F) Zones 8–9.

C. x paradisi
Grapefruit
This is grown commercially in Israel, Turkey, California and Florida, where summer temperatures are sufficiently

high to ripen the fruits. Although the origin of the grapefruit is unknown, it may be a hybrid between *C. maxima* (pummelo) and *C. sinensis*. It is a round-headed tree with sparse, spiny leaves, flowering in spring and summer and fruiting in the autumn. H and S 7m (23ft).
Named varieties Orange-fruiting forms include the white-fleshed 'Golden Special' and 'Oro Blanco' and the seedless 'Marsh'.
Red-fruiting forms include 'Red Blush' and 'Star Ruby'.
Aspect Full sun.
Hardiness (Min. 3–5°C/37–41°F) Zones 8–9.

C. 'Ponderosa'
(syn. C. limon 'Ponderosa')
Giant American wonder lemon
This dwarf lemon is ideally suited to being grown in a container, when it will fruit and flower regularly. H and S 3m (10ft).
Aspect Full sun.
Hardiness (Min. 3–5°C/37–41°F) Zones 8–9.

C. reticulata
Clementine, mandarin, satsuma, tangerine
These ornamental, compact trees produce glossy, dark green leaves, up to 4cm (1½in) long, and an abundance of sweetly scented white flowers in short racemes in spring and early summer. The yellow-orange fruits are about 8cm (3in) across and are borne from autumn to spring. The skin or rind of these fruits detaches easily from the flesh within, and they are popular because they are so easy to peel, as well as being juicy and tasty and a good source of vitamin C. Due to their ultimate size, they make excellent specimens for growing in containers. H 4m (12ft), S 1.8m (6ft).
Named varieties Many forms have been developed, including 'Clementine', 'Cleopatra', 'Dancy' and 'Kinnow'.
Aspect Full sun.
Hardiness (Min. 3–5°C/37–41°F) Zones 8–9.

Citrus limon

Citrus limon

Citrus sinensis

C. sinensis
Sweet orange
This may be a natural hybrid between *C. maxima* (pummelo) and *C. reticulata*. It has long been cultivated and is widely grown in frost-free climates where summer temperatures are high enough to ripen the fruits. If it is grown in a climate with insufficient summer sun, the fruits may not turn the usual orange colour, but remain a greenish-yellow, although the flesh inside will be sweet and juicy. These are large, spiny trees, with glossy, dark green leaves and fragrant white flowers. H 12m (40ft), S 4m (12ft).
Named varieties Numerous cultivars have been developed for their flavour, colour and size of fruit. They include 'Shamouti' (syn. 'Jaffa', a popular seedless form), 'Valencia', 'Murcia' and 'Washington'.
  Blood fruit forms include 'Malta', 'Moro' and 'Ruby'.
Aspect Full sun.
Hardiness (Min. 3–5°C/37–41°F) Zones 8–9.

C. x tangelo
Ugli fruit
This hybrid between *C. x paradisi* and *C. sinensis* bears fruit that is considerably larger than an orange but not quite as large as a grapefruit. The dark green leaves are longer and more pointed than those of *C. sinensis*. White flowers are followed by the reddish or yellow fruits. H 5m (16ft), S 1.8m (6ft).
Named varieties This fruit was originally hybridized in the USA and there are numerous forms grown today, including 'Minneola'.
Aspect Full sun.
Hardiness (Min. 3–5°C/37–41°F) Zones 8–9.

C. unshiu
(syn. *C. reticulata* Satsuma Group)
This Japanese tangerine is grown for its masses of small, deliciously sweet and easy-to-peel fruits. It is a dense small tree, which produces creamy-white, highly scented flowers in spring, followed by the bright orange fruits. H and S 3m (10ft).

Aspect Full sun.
Hardiness (Min. 3–5°C/37–41°F) Zones 8–9.

CLADRASTIS
This small genus contains five species of deciduous trees from China, Japan and North America. They are grown for their early summer flowers, which are borne only on mature wood, and their good autumn colour.
Cultivation Grow in well-drained but moisture-retentive soil in sun. Protect from strong, cold winds.
Pruning Little pruning is necessary, apart from the removal of dead, dying, diseased or crossing branches.
Propagation This is by seed, which should be collected as soon as it falls. The seed coat should be rubbed with sandpaper to allow water to enter the seed and then soaked for 24 hours. Sow into containers, and place in an unheated glasshouse or cold frame until it germinates. Root cuttings can also be taken in early winter. The pink flowering forms are self-fertile and should come true from seed, otherwise they are indoor grafted during the winter.

C. kentukea
(syn. *C. lutea*)
Yellow wood
In summer this beautiful, medium-sized tree, which is native to the south-east of the USA, bears long, wisteria-like panicles of fragrant white flowers. In autumn the leaves turn a vibrant golden-yellow. H 12–15m (40–50ft), S 10m (33ft).
Named varieties 'Perkins Pink' (syn. 'Rosea') has pale pink-white flowers, with the leaves turning yellow in autumn.
Aspect Full sun or semi-shade.
Hardiness ❁❁❁ Zones 4–8.

C. sinensis
Chinese yellow wood
Although this species is rarely seen in gardens, it is just as beautiful as *C. kentukea*. It flowers in mid- to late summer, producing long panicles of white, pink-tinged blooms. H 10m (33ft), S 15m (50ft).
Aspect Full sun or semi-shade.
Hardiness ❁❁❁ Zones 5–8.

CORNUS
Dogwood, flowering dogwood, American boxwood
Although there are only about 45 species of mostly deciduous trees and shrubs in the genus, many cultivars and hybrids have been developed. They are grown for their attractive habit, for their flowers (sometimes with showy bracts) and for their autumn colour and colourful bark.
Cultivation Most dogwoods tolerate any fairly fertile, moisture-retentive but well-drained soil and are not fussy about the position. Grow flowering forms (such as *C. florida*, *C. nuttallii* and their hybrids) in fertile, well-drained but moisture-retentive, neutral to acidic soil in sun or semi-shade.
Pruning Little pruning is required apart from the removal of dead, dying, diseased or crossing branches. The cornelian dogwood and its relatives are difficult to prune due to their dense branch habit, and so are best left to their own devices.
Propagation Seed should be collected as soon as it falls, and soaked for 24 hours. Sow in containers and place in an unheated glasshouse or cold frame until germination. Softwood and hardwood cuttings are used, as is indoor grafting during the winter.

C. 'Aurora'
This is a Stellar hybrid, one of a series of dogwoods that originated in the USA as controlled crosses between *C. nuttallii*, *C. florida* and *C. kousa*. The hybrids, which have characteristics of all the parents, seem to be resistant to anthracnose, the devastating dogwood disease. They are widely planted in the USA and are becoming more available in Europe. This is a vigorous form with an upright habit and numerous flowers with large, creamy-white bracts. H and S to 6m (20ft).
Aspect Full sun or semi-shade.
Hardiness ❁❁❁ Zones 5–8.

C. 'Celestial'
This is a Stellar hybrid (see *C.* 'Aurora'). It is a vigorous, strongly upright form, similar to *C. kousa*,

with smallish, green-white flowers that mature to white. H and S to 6m (20ft).
Aspect Full sun or semi-shade.
Hardiness ❀❀❀ Zones 5–8.

C. 'Constellation'

This is a Stellar hybrid (see C. 'Aurora'). This develops into a large tree, spreading widely as it ages, with white bracts. It is spectacular to see, both up close and from a distance. H and S to 6m (20ft).
Aspect Full sun or semi-shade.
Hardiness ❀❀❀ Zones 5–8.

C. controversa
Table dogwood

This superbly architectural deciduous tree is native to China and Japan. It is grown for its tiered branches. In summer the branch tips are covered in dense clusters of small, creamy-white flowers, which are followed by small black fruit. The narrowly oval leaves, up to 15cm (6in) long, are glossy, dark green and often turn purple in autumn. H 15–20m (50–65ft), S 15m (50ft).
Named varieties The cultivar 'Black Stem' is a vigorous form, grown for its dark purple stems and crimson autumn foliage.

'Variegata' is a beautiful but slow-growing tree. The leaves are broadly edged with creamy-white, and the stems are reddish.
Aspect Full sun or semi-shade.
Hardiness ❀❀❀ Zones 4–7.

Cladrastis kentukea

C. 'Eddie's White Wonder'

This spectacular hybrid between C. nuttallii and C. florida is one of the best of the flowering dogwoods. It develops into a large shrub or small tree. In late spring tiny, purplish-green flowers are surrounded by large, creamy-white, overlapping bracts. The leaves turn brilliant orange-red in autumn. It needs acidic soil. H and S 12m (40ft).
Aspect Full sun or semi-shade.
Hardiness ❀❀❀ Zone 6.

C. florida
Flowering dogwood, eastern dogwood

This small flowering tree is native to the east of North America. It is grown for its tight clusters of tiny green flowers, which are surrounded by four beautiful pink or white bracts. These are followed by attractive red berries in autumn, when the leaves turn purple, orange and yellow. It is tolerant of most soil types. H 12m (40ft), S 10m (33ft).
Named varieties Several cultivars with especially large, colourful bracts have been developed. 'Cherokee Chief' has very dark pink bracts and beautiful autumn colour.

'Cloud Nine', which is one of the most cold-hardy forms, has flowers with large, white, overlapping bracts.

'Daybreak' (syn. C. florida 'Cherokee Daybreak') has large white bracts and leaves edged with

Cornus kousa

yellow-green. These become green and slightly pink flushed in summer and vibrant pink and red in autumn.

The compact 'Rainbow' is grown for its yellow-margined leaves, turning dark red and purple with scarlet margins in autumn. H 3m (10ft), S 2.4m (8ft).
Aspect Full sun or semi-shade.
Hardiness ❀❀❀ Zone 5.

C. kousa
Kousa dogwood

This is a small, conical tree. It is grown for its green flowerheads, which are surrounded by four pink or white bracts that are produced over several weeks in summer; its strawberry-like fruits; its purple-red autumn colour; and its flaking bark. H 15m (50ft), S 10m (33ft).
Named varieties There are several excellent cultivars to choose from. 'Blue Shadow' has lovely blue-green leaves, which turn reddish in autumn. The bracts are white, occasionally with a second flush in autumn.

C. kousa var. chinensis is more upright and open and has larger leaves than other species. The bracts, up to 5cm (2in) long, are initially creamy-white, fading to white and then reddish-pink.

C. kousa var. chinensis 'China Girl' is a vigorous form with masses of white bracts, even on young plants.

The more compact C. kousa var. chinensis 'Milky Way' has plenty of white bracts, which are followed by plentiful fruits.

'National' is an upright form with large white bracts and very large fruits.

'Satomi' has salmon-pink bracts and dark red-purple autumn colour.

'Temple Jewel' has gold, light pink and light green young foliage, which turns green with age, and white bracts.

The leaves of the rather shrubby 'Wolf Eyes' are boldly variegated with white and turn brilliant pink and red in autumn. The bracts are white.
Aspect Full sun or semi-shade.
Hardiness ❀❀❀ Zones 5–8.

Cornus officinalis

C. mas
Cornelian cherry

The species, which is a large shrub or spreading small tree, is native to central and south-eastern Europe. It is especially attractive in late winter, when clusters of small, bright yellow flowers are borne on the bare stems. The bright red fruits that follow are edible. The paired leaves are dark green with strongly marked veins and turn purple in autumn. 'Golden Glory' is similar to the species but has larger leaves and flowers. H and S 5–8m (16–26ft).
Aspect Full sun.
Hardiness ❀❀❀ Zones 4–7.

C. nuttallii
Pacific dogwood, western dogwood

This is one of the larger dogwoods, developing into a large, majestic, deciduous tree. In late spring small purple and green flowers appear, and these are surrounded by four to six large white or pink-tinged bracts. In autumn the leaves turn yellow and red. It does best where temperatures do not get too hot in summer and where there are high levels of rainfall. H 25m (80ft), S 15m (50ft).
Named varieties 'Colrigo Giant' is a vigorous form with large, creamy-white bracts, sometimes with a second flush of flowers in autumn.
'North Star', another vigorous form, has large white bracts and purplish leaves, turning purple-red in autumn.
Aspect Full sun.
Hardiness ❀❀ Zones 7–9.

C. officinalis

This vigorous, spreading, deciduous shrub or small tree has a rather open habit. In early spring, before the leaves appear, it produces clusters of yellow flowers, which are followed by bright red fruits. The dark green leaves turn red-purple in autumn. H and S 5m (16ft).
Aspect Full sun.
Hardiness ❀❀❀ Zones 5–8.

C. 'Porlock'

This small, spreading, semi-evergreen or deciduous tree is a hybrid between C. capitata and C. kousa. Masses of showy white bracts are produced in summer and slowly turn pinkish-red. These are followed by plentiful strawberry-like fruits. H and S 15m (50ft).
Aspect Full sun to semi-shade.
Hardiness ❀❀❀ Zones 7–8.

C. 'Ruth Ellen'

This is a Stellar hybrid (see C. 'Aurora'). It is similar to C. florida but is lower-growing and has a spreading habit. It flowers in early spring. H and S to 6m (20ft).
Aspect Full sun to semi-shade.
Hardiness ❀❀❀ Zones 5–8.

C. 'Stellar Pink'

This is a Stellar hybrid (see C. 'Aurora'). It is a spreading, shrubby plant with soft pink bracts. H and S to 6m (20ft).
Aspect Full sun to semi-shade.
Hardiness ❀❀❀ Zones 5–8.

CORYLUS
Hazel

These deciduous trees come from northern temperate regions and are grown for their attractive catkins and edible nuts. The best known is C. avellana, of which there are several cultivars.
Cultivation Grow in moisture-retentive but well-drained soil in sun or semi-shade. They do well on chalky soil.
Pruning Little pruning is required apart from the removal of dead, dying, diseased or crossing branches. Formative pruning should be used to encourage the horizontal branch effect of the Turkish filbert, so any shoots growing directly up into the crown should be removed.
Propagation Seed should be collected as soon as it falls and sown into containers in an unheated glasshouse or cold frame until germination occurs. Take softwood cuttings during summer and root in a humid environment. Hardwood cuttings can be taken in winter.

C. colurna
Turkish hazel

This quick-growing, attractive, conical tree has a strong architectural habit and is suitable for use in a large garden. The coarse, dark green leaves, up to 12cm (5in) long, are shallowly lobed and turn yellow in autumn. The trunk and stems sometimes show corky growth. In spring large, pendent catkins are produced and occasionally large, fringed cobnuts also. H 20–25m (65–80ft), S 15m (50ft).
Aspect Full sun or semi-shade.
Hardiness ❀❀❀ Zones 4–7.

COTINUS
Smoke tree

The two species of deciduous trees and shrubs in the genus are found in temperate areas of the northern hemisphere. They are grown for their colourful foliage and plumes of tiny flowers, which give the plants their common name.
Cultivation Grow in fertile, moisture-retentive but well-drained soil in sun or semi-shade. Purple-leaved forms do best in full sun.
Pruning Smoke trees grow very quickly when young and produce very long, whippy shoots that require shortening so that a more tree-like habit can be developed.

Corylus avellana

Cornus 'Porlock'

These shoots should be shortened in late spring or early summer. Little other pruning is normally required, apart from the removal of any dead, dying, diseased or crossing branches.

Propagation Softwood cuttings can be taken during summer, then dipped in a rooting hormone and rooted in a humid environment.

C. 'Flame'
(syn. *C. coggygria* 'Flame')
This hybrid between *C. obovatus* and *C. coggygria* (smoke bush, Venetian sumach) has some of the height of the former and the leaf size of the latter. In summer it produces airy plumes of tiny purple flowers; in autumn the light green leaves, up to 10cm (4in) long, turn vibrant orange and yellow. H and S 6–10m (20–33ft).
Aspect Full sun or semi-shade.
Hardiness ✿✿✿ Zones 4–8.

C. obovatus
(syn. *C. americanus, Rhus cotinoides*)
American smoke tree, chittamwood
This little-grown species is a striking tree, which is native to the south-eastern USA. The large leaves, up to 12cm (5in) long, are pinkish-bronze in colour as they emerge in spring and turn vivid orange, purple and red in autumn. In summer, large plumes of pink-grey flowers are borne. It is best grown in a sheltered location. H and S 12m (40ft)
Aspect Full sun or semi-shade.
Hardiness ✿✿✿ Zones 4–8.

CRATAEGUS
Hawthorn
This large genus of some 200 species contains deciduous, semi-evergreen and evergreen trees and shrubs, which may be spiny. They usually have good autumn colour. The pink or white flowers are followed by fleshy fruits.
Cultivation Grow in well-drained soil in sun or semi-shade. They will not tolerate waterlogged soil.
Pruning Fire blight can be a problem, so infected material should be removed and destroyed as soon as it appears.
Propagation Seed is widely used and should be collected in autumn before the birds strip the trees. The flesh should be removed by soaking in water. Once all the pulp is removed, the seed can be sown in an unheated glasshouse or cold frame until it germinates. Cultivars are propagated by winter grafting or summer budding on to seed-raised hawthorn and haw rootstocks.

C. coccinea
(syn. *C. pedicellata*)
This spreading deciduous tree has thorny branches and stems. White flowers, produced in late spring, are followed by bright red, pear-shaped, edible berries. H and S 6m (20ft).
Aspect Full sun or semi-shade.
Hardiness ✿✿✿ Zones 5–7.

C. crus-galli
Cockspur thorn
This is a very hardy, small, round-headed, deciduous tree. The

Crataegus laevigata 'Punicea'

glossy green leaves, up to 10cm (4in) long, are a foil for the masses of white flowers borne in early summer. The bright red fruits that follow in autumn persist into winter. The leaves create a vibrant patchwork of bright orange, yellow and red in autumn. Branches and stems are armoured with large, 8cm- (3in-) long thorns. H 8m (26ft), S 10m (33ft).
Aspect Full sun or semi-shade.
Hardiness ✿✿✿ Zones 4–7.

C. flava
Yellow haw
This deciduous shrub or small tree, which deserves to be more widely grown, has dark green leaves, up to 5cm (2in) long, and white flowers in spring to early summer. These are followed in autumn by yellow-green fruits. H 6–10m (20–33ft), S 8m (26ft).
Aspect Full sun or semi-shade.
Hardiness ✿✿✿ Zones 4–7.

C. laevigata
(syn. *C. oxyacantha*)
Midland hawthorn, maythorn
This rounded, deciduous tree is armed with sharp spines. It has dark green leaves, up to 5cm (2in) long, and white flowers in spring and early summer. The round, orange-red berries follow. H and S 8m (26ft).
Named varieties The widely planted cultivar 'Paul's Scarlet' (syn. 'Coccinea Plena') is one of the showiest and most striking species of hawthorn when it is in

flower, bearing red-pink, double flowers in spring. H and S 10m (33ft).
'Rosea Flore Pleno' has double pink flowers. H and S 10m (33ft).
Aspect Full sun or semi-shade.
Hardiness ✿✿✿ Zone 5.

C. x lavallei
This hybrid is grown for its bronze autumn colour and bright orange-red fruits, which ripen late in autumn. H 7m (23ft), S 10m (33ft).
Named varieties The hybrid is usually represented in cultivation by 'Carrierei', which is a strongly growing and very thorny tree. White flowers appear in clusters in early summer to midsummer. The dark green leaves turn red in autumn.
Aspect Full sun or semi-shade.
Hardiness ✿✿✿ Zones 5–7.

C. monogyna
Common hawthorn, may, quickthorn
The deciduous leaves of this rounded, small tree are dark green and glossy. The fragrant white flowers appear in late spring and are followed by red berries. H 10m (33ft), S 8m (26ft).
Named varieties The cultivar 'Stricta' is a narrowly conical small tree, with upswept, slightly twisted branches and white flowers in late spring. In autumn numerous, single-stoned, red berries are produced. H 10m (33ft), S 1.8m (6ft).
Aspect Full sun or semi-shade.
Hardiness ✿✿✿ Zones 4–7.

Cotinus 'Flame'

Crataegus laevigata 'Paul's Scarlet'

C. persimilis 'Prunifolia'
(syn. *C. prunifolia*)
This cultivar is the most widely
planted of the hawthorns. It is
grown mainly for its tidy, round-
headed habit, white flowers, autumn
colour and persistent red berries.
H 8m (26ft), S 10m (33ft).
Aspect Full sun or semi-shade.
Hardiness ❀❀❀ Zones 5–7.

CRYPTOMERIA
Japanese cedar
Although the genus contains
only a single species of evergreen
conifer, many handsome cultivars
have been selected.
Cultivation Grow in deep, fertile,
moisture-retentive but well-
drained soil in sun or semi-shade.

Pruning Formative pruning
should aim to produce a clear
trunk and a balanced crown,
while tipping the lateral branches
of young trees encourages a
denser crown.
Propagation Seed is the easiest
method of propagation and
should be collected when it is
fresh, sown into a container and
placed in an unheated glasshouse
or cold frame until germination
occurs. Semi-ripe and softwood
cuttings can be rooted during
summer and should be dipped in
a rooting hormone and placed
in a humid environment until
rooting occurs. Selected forms
are winter grafted on to seedling
raised rootstocks.

Cryptomeria japonica 'Lobbii'

Cunninghamia lanceolata

C. japonica
Japanese cedar
The species is a beautiful and
ultimately large tree. It has dark
green, slightly weeping leaves,
which are arranged in spirals
around the stems. The reddish
bark is aromatic and peels in long
strips. H 25–30m (80–100ft),
S 5–6m (16–20ft).
Named varieties Among the
best cultivars is 'Lobbii', a
beautiful form, widely grown
for its narrower and more
upright habit than the species.
The leaves are pressed more
tightly to the stem and the
branches are slightly twisted.
Aspect Full sun or semi-shade.
Hardiness ❀❀❀ Zones 5–8.

CUNNINGHAMIA
Chinese fir
This genus of evergreen conifers
is found in China and Taiwan.
They are grown for their dense,
dark green foliage.
Cultivation Grow in any deep,
moisture-retentive but well-
drained soil in sun or semi-
shade. They are not suitable
for windy sites.
Pruning Occasional pruning
is required for the removal
of dead, dying, diseased or
crossing branches.
Propagation Seed is the easiest
method of propagation and
should be collected when fresh
and sown into a container in an
unheated glasshouse or cold
frame until germination occurs.

x *Cupressocyparis leylandii*

C. lanceolata
(syn. *C. sinensis, C. unicaniculata*)
The species has soft, pointed,
slender, yew-like needles, which
have two distinct bands on the
undersides. The needles are
arranged spirally around the
stems. The bark is an attractive
shade of red-brown. H 20–25m
(65–80ft), S 6–10m (20–33ft).
Aspect Full sun.
Hardiness ❀❀❀ Zones 7–9.

x CUPRESSOCYPARIS
The evergreen conifers in this
genus are hybrids between
Chamaecyparis and *Cupressus*. They
are fast-growing and can be grown
either as specimens or for hedging.
Cultivation Grow in any moisture-
retentive but well-drained soil in
sun or semi-shade. They are not
suitable for small gardens.
Pruning Formative pruning should
aim to produce a straight trunk
with well-spaced branches and a
balanced crown. Tipping back side
shoots when young will encourage
bushy growth.
Propagation Semi-ripe cuttings
taken during late autumn or early
spring root quickly if the base of
the cutting is dipped in a rooting
hormone and the cuttings placed
in a humid environment in a frost-
free glasshouse until they root.

x C. leylandii
Leyland cypress
This hybrid between *Cupressus
macrocarpa* and *Chamaecyparis
nootkatensis* was first bred in 1870,

since when numerous hybrids have been developed. It is extremely fast-growing and in the right conditions can put on 1m (3ft) or more in a year. It is a conical tree, with dark green leaves and dark brown cones. H up to 35m (115ft), S to 5m (16ft).
Named varieties 'Castlewellan' (syn. 'Galway Gold') is a widely grown form (it is popular for hedging) with golden-yellow young foliage, which turns bronze-yellow with age. H 20–25m (65–80ft).

'Emerald Isle' is a columnar form with green foliage in flattish sprays, creating a more open habit.

'Gold Rider' is the best of the yellow-foliaged forms, with flatter foliage and semi-lax branches.

One of the first hybrids, the fast-growing, narrow 'Leighton Green' has green, flattish foliage and plenty of cones.

'Naylor's Blue' has grey-green foliage, which turns slowly blue-green in winter. The branches are loose and twisted, and the foliage is not as stiff as on other forms.
Aspect Full sun or semi-shade.
Hardiness ✤✤✤ Zones 6–10.

CUPRESSUS
Cypress
The genus contains 20–24 species of evergreen conifers, which are found throughout the northern hemisphere. They are mostly upright, columnar trees, and they can be used for hedging as long as they are not cut back to the old wood.
Cultivation Grow in any well-drained soil in sun. Do not plant in exposed sites.
Pruning Formative pruning should aim to produce a straight trunk with well-spaced branches and a balanced crown. Tipping back side shoots when young will encourage bushy growth.
Propagation Sow fresh seed into a container in an unheated glass house or cold frame until germination occurs. Semi-ripe and softwood cutting can be rooted during summer and should be dipped in a rooting hormone and placed in a humid environment until rooting occurs. Selected forms are winter grafted on to seedling raised rootstocks.

C. cashmeriana
(syn. *C. torulosa* '**Cashmeriana**')
Kashmir cypress, weeping cypress
This beautiful, slender conifer, probably from the Himalayas, is best grown in mild areas. Its blue-green, fern-like foliage is borne on long, slender, pendulous branches. H 20–30m (65–100ft), S 10m (33ft).
Aspect Full sun.
Hardiness ✤ Zone 9.

Davidia involucrata

C. macrocarpa
Monterey cypress
This is a broadly conical conifer, which develops a broader crown as it ages. It has tiny, fern-like, dark green leaves that are pressed tight to the stem. It is widely planted in coastal locations because it is tolerant of salt spray and dry, sandy soils, but young plants are susceptible to damage from late spring frosts. H 25–30m (80–100ft), S 10–12m (33–40ft).
Aspect Full sun.
Hardiness ✤✤✤ Zones 7–9.

C. sempervirens
Italian cypress
The species, which is a widely grown tree in Mediterranean areas, is distinguished by its narrow, column-like habit. A fast-growing conifer, to 50m (165ft) tall in the wild, it tends to be smaller in gardens. It has dense dark green or grey-green foliage. Although young leaves can be damaged by cold winds in spring, these trees are remarkably tolerant of salt spray. H 20m (65ft), S 3m (10ft).
Named varieties A number of forms have been selected for their narrow habit or coloured foliage, usually yellow-tinted, green or blue-green. Trees in the Stricta Group (syn. 'Pyramidalis', *C. sempervirens* var. *sempervirens*) are marginally variable forms, with a pencil-like habit and green foliage.

'Green Pencil' is another tight conical form.
Aspect Full sun.
Hardiness ✤✤✤ Zones 7–9.

DAVIDIA
Handkerchief tree, dove tree, ghost tree
The single species in the genus is a deciduous tree that is native to China. It is usually grown as a specimen tree for the showy white bracts that surround the flowerheads in spring, and which turn green as they age.
Cultivation Grow in fertile, moisture-retentive but well-drained soil in sun or semi-shade. Protect from strong winds. Young growth is susceptible to frost damage in spring.
Pruning Little pruning is required apart from the removal of dead, dying, diseased or crossing branches. Formative pruning should aim to produce a clear straight trunk and a balanced crown.
Propagation Seed should be collected in late summer once it has fallen, then the flesh should be removed and the seed can be sown into deep pots in a warm environment for three months, followed by three months in an unheated glasshouse or cold frame until germination occurs. Softwood cuttings can be taken in summer, then dipped in a rooting hormone and placed in a warm environment. Do not pot on the cuttings until the following spring.

Cupressus arizonica var. 'Glabra'

Cupressus macrocarpa

D. involucrata

This is one of the most delightful and unusual medium-sized trees when it is in flower. In late spring the small, purplish flowers are surrounded by two large, white bracts: one up to about 8cm (3in) long and the other up to about 15cm (6in) long. The leaves, up to 15cm (6in) long, are soft green and covered with silvery hairs underneath. In autumn the foliage turns yellow-brown and occasionally fiery red and orange. H 15–20m (50–65ft), S 10–15m (33–50ft).

Named varieties *D. involucrata* var. *vilmoriniana* is almost identical to the species, but there are no hairs on the underside of the leaves, which are yellow-green above and dark green below.
Aspect Full sun or semi-shade.
Hardiness ❀❀❀ Zones 6–7.

DILLENIA

There are about 60 species of evergreen shrubs and trees in the genus. They are grown for their large leaves, flowers and edible fruits. In temperate areas these potentially large trees should be grown in a frost-free conservatory and pruned to restrict their growth.
Cultivation Outdoors, grow in fertile, moisture-retentive but well-drained, neutral to acidic soil in full sun.

Pruning Formative pruning should encourage a clear trunk and balanced crown. Prune occasionally to remove dead, dying, diseased or crossing branches.
Propagation Seed is the easiest method of propagation and should be collected when fresh and sown into a container in a heated glasshouse in a frost-free and humid environment until germination occurs. Semi-ripe cuttings can also be rooted during late summer and should be dipped in rooting hormone and placed in a frost-free, humid environment until they root.

D. indica
Chulta, elephant apple
This beautiful flowering and foliage tree has large, nodding, white flowers, up to 10cm (4in) across, and large, corrugated dark green leaves, up to 30cm (12in) long. The spring flowers are followed by large green and yellow apple-like fruits. H 15–18m (50–60ft), S 10–15m (33–50ft).
Aspect Light shade or full sun.
Hardiness (Min. 15°C/59°F) Zone 11.

DIOSPYROS

This large genus, containing 475 species of slow-growing deciduous and evergreen trees and shrubs, is perhaps best known for the species *D. ebenum* (ebony), but it also includes persimmons. The

Embothrium coccineum

hardy deciduous species are native to temperate Asia and North America, while the tropical and subtropical species, which are often evergreen, are from south-western Asia to China.
Cultivation Grow in fertile soil in full sun.
Pruning Occasional pruning is required for the removal of dead, dying, diseased or crossing branches, as and when needed.
Propagation Seed is the easiest method of propagation and should be collected when fresh, removed from the fruit and sown into a container in a heated glasshouse in a frost-free and humid environment until germination occurs. Summer budding is also used and is grafted on to seedling grown rootstocks.

D. digyna
(syn. D. ebanaster)
Black sapote
This open, lax evergreen tree has glossy green leaves. Unlike many other forms of persimmon, which have brightly coloured fruits, this species has green fruits, which contain a blackish, jelly-like substance and which are widely used as flavouring for milk, fruit juice or alcoholic drinks. Outdoors it is best used as a screen or windbreak. H and S 20m (65ft).
Aspect Full sun.
Hardiness ❀ Zones 10–12.

D. ebenum
Ebony
This slow-growing, tropical evergreen tree is widely grown for its dense black wood. Although it was once native to areas of tropical India, it has been overexploited and is now rare and threatened in the wild. It is a broadly spreading tree, which bears small, velvety, rust-coloured, edible fruits. H and S 30m (100ft).
Aspect Full sun.
Hardiness ❀ Zones 10–12.

D. kaki
Japanese persimmon, Chinese persimmon, kaki
Although this deciduous species will grow in temperate climates, it requires sufficient summer heat to make the fruits that are borne on female plants palatable. The glossy, dark green leaves, up to 20cm (8in) long, turn orange-yellow in autumn. Even in temperate areas, trees will bear the tomato-sized, yellowish-orange fruits, which ripen in late autumn. It is a slow-growing tree with a broadly spreading habit. H 10–12m (33–40ft), S 7–10m (23–33ft).
Aspect Full sun to semi-shade.
Hardiness ❀❀ Zones 7–10.

D. lotus
Date plum
This deciduous species is similar to *D. kaki* but grows more quickly and the glossy, dark green leaves

Diospyros lotus

are not as colourful in autumn. On female plants the tiny, red-tinged green flowers are followed by inedible, yellow to purplish fruits. H 10–25m (33–80ft), S 6–10m (20–33ft).
Aspect Full sun to semi-shade.
Hardiness ✽✽✽ Zones 6–10.

D. virginiana
American persimmon, possumwood
This is both the hardiest and the largest species. It is grown for the durability of its timber, its long, tapering foliage and its small, orange-yellow, berry-like fruits, which are produced on female trees in autumn. Autumn colour ranges from purplish-red to orange-yellow. H 25m (80ft), S 10m (33ft).
Aspect Full sun to semi-shade.
Hardiness ✽✽✽ Zones 4–9.

EMBOTHRIUM
Chilean fire bush
The eight species of evergreen trees and shrubs in the genus, which are native to South America, are related to proteas. They are grown as ornamental trees for their vivid flowers, which are borne in late spring to early summer. They do best in climates that are moist and not too hot.
Cultivation Grow in fertile, moisture-retentive, neutral to acidic soil in sun or semi-shade.

Pruning Multi-stemmed specimens are widely grown, and pruning for these should aim to remove the lower branches and maintain a section of the trunks free of branch growth. Occasional pruning is required for the removal of dead, dying, diseased or crossing branches.
Propagation Seed is the easiest method of propagation and should be collected when fresh and sown into a container in a heated glasshouse in a frost-free and humid environment until germination occurs. Semi-ripe cuttings can also be rooted during late summer and should be dipped in a rooting hormone and placed in a frost-free, humid environment until they root.

E. coccineum
Chilean fire bush, flame flower
This upright, branched tree with an open, but columnar habit is often better grown as a multi-stemmed shrub, when it can be included in a mixed border or grown as a lawn specimen. It bears vivid orange-red, grevillea-like flowers in late spring. The long, slender leaves are evergreen, but tend to be semi-evergreen in colder areas. Plants in the Lanceolatum Group are similar to the species except that it has very long, lance-like leaves. It is hardier than the species and is the least evergreen form.

Dillenia indica

H 9–10m (30–33ft), S 4–5m (12–16ft).
Aspect Full sun to light shade.
Hardiness ✽✽ Zone 8.

ERIOBOTRYA
Loquat
The 30 or so species in the genus are evergreen shrubs and trees from eastern Asia and the Himalayas. In cold areas they can be grown under glass, although in favourable conditions they make attractive specimen trees and can be considered hardy when grown in protected locations.
Cultivation Protect plants from cold winds. Tender species grown under glass may need pruning to keep them under control. Grow in a free-draining fertile soil, in a warm and sunny location.

Although it will grow in temperate climates and take short periods of freezing temperatures, it is more at home in a subtropical climate where it will produce golden-orange fruits the size of large cherries. In cool, temperate climates it is best grown against a sunny wall.
Pruning Minimal pruning is required other than shortening back any over-vigorous shoots by one-third of their overall length, and removing any weak, crossing, diseased or dying shoots.
Propagation Sow seed in a free-draining medium in a humid environment at a temperature of 18°C (64°F). T-budding can be used to grow selected forms, using seedling loquats, quince (*Cydonia oblonga*) and hawthorns (*Crataegus*) as rootstocks.

Eriobotrya japonica

Eucalyptus dalrympleana

E. japonica
Loquat

This beautiful small tree or
spreading shrub is grown for its
handsome foliage and fruits. The
large, dark green leaves, up to
30cm (12in) long, are glossy and
strongly veined. From autumn to
winter clusters of small, fragrant,
white flowers are borne at the tips
of branches on felted brown
stems. In spring bright yellow,
edible fruits, up to 4cm (1½in)
across, appear, but these need
a hot summer to ripen fully.
H and S 8–9m (26–30ft).
Aspect Full sun.
Hardiness ❀❀ Zones 8–9.

EUCALYPTUS
Gum tree

There are more than 500 species
of evergreen trees and shrubs in
the genus. Most come from
Australia, but they are also found

throughout South-east Asia and
Melanesia. Some forms are hardy.
They are grown for their bark,
flowers and foliage, which may
be aromatic. Juvenile leaves tend
to be round and blue-green or
grey-green. Adult leaves are often
much narrower (to conserve
moisture) and less grey. Although
they often have large, straight
trunks, the trees can also be
coppiced, but require this
treatment throughout their
lives, because tall, slender
branches tend to split.
Cultivation Grow in moisture-
retentive but well-drained, neutral
to acidic soil in full sun. Protect
plants from cold winds.
Pruning Formative pruning
should aim to encourage a clear
trunk and a balanced crown,
while tipping the lateral branches
of young trees will encourage
a denser crown. Occasional

Eucalyptus cordata

pruning is required for the
removal of dead, dying, diseased
or crossing branches.
Propagation Seed is the main
method of propagation and
should be collected when fresh
and sown into a container in a
heated glasshouse in a frost-free
and humid environment until
germination occurs.

E. coccifera
Mount Wellington peppermint,
Tasmanian snow gum

This wide-spreading tree has
pendulous branches and clusters
of peppermint-scented, creamy-
white flowers in summer. The
bark shreds in long, silver-grey
plates to reveal the yellow bark
developing underneath. Juvenile
leaves are round and mid-green.
Adult leaves are narrow and grey-
green, and scented of peppermint.
H 18–20m (60–65ft), S 7m
(23ft).
Aspect Full sun.
Hardiness ❀❀❀ Zones 9–12.

E. confertifolia
Half-barked gum

The common name of this narrow
tree derives from the fact that the
upper branches and stems have
smooth, ornamental, silver-orange
bark, while the lower part of the
trunk is covered with thick,
corrugated, blackish bark, which
protects the tree against flooding
and fire. Creamy-white flowers are
borne in dense clusters in spring
together with the new leaves,
which are tinted with purple.
Adult leaves are broad and large
and grey-green with wavy margins.
H 20m (65ft), S 4m (12ft).
Aspect Full sun.
Hardiness ❀ Zones 10–12.

E. cordata
Silver gum

This dense, widely grown tree
has willow-like branches and
stunning white bark, which is
streaked with green and purple.
The silver-green leaves are flat and
angled. In late winter and early
spring clusters of white flowers
are borne. It is not a drought-
tolerant species. H 20m (65ft),
S 4m (12ft).
Aspect Full sun.
Hardiness ❀ Zones 8–11.

Eucryphia x nymansensis 'Nymansay'

E. dalrympleana
Mountain gum, broad-leaved
kindling bark

This alkaline-tolerant, fast
growing tree quickly develops a
straight trunk with smooth,
creamy-white bark, peeling in long
strands. The underbark is almost
white in spring. The emerging
foliage is bronze. Juvenile leaves
are ovate and blue-green; mature
leaves are lance-shaped and dark
green. H 20–25m (65–80ft),
S 8m (26ft).
Aspect Full sun.
Hardiness ❀❀❀ Zones 8–10.

E. ficifolia
Red-flowering gum

This beautiful, broadly spreading
tree bears large clusters of bright
red, sometimes pink or white,
flowers from summer to autumn.
The mid-green leaves have red-
tinged margins. The short trunk
is covered with rough, dark brown
bark. H 15m (50ft), S 5–15m
(16–50ft).
Aspect Full sun.
Hardiness ❀ Zones 9–12.

E. gunnii
Cider gum

This popular and highly
ornamental tree has copper-brown
bark, which shreds in long strips
in summer to reveal the pinkish-
white underbark. It is a fast-
growing tree, with silver-green
leaves and clusters of cream-
coloured flowers in summer.
H 25m (80ft), S 7m (23ft).
Aspect Full sun.
Hardiness ❀❀❀ Zones 8–10.

E. johnstonii
Tasmanian yellow gum
The bark of this attractive tree
is smooth, with orange, reddish-
yellow and green streaks. The
glossy leaves are apple-green,
and clusters of small, creamy-
white flower are borne in summer.
This is one of the best gum trees
for poorly drained, sandy soil.
H 25–30m (80–100ft), S 7–10m
(23–33ft).
Aspect Full sun.
Hardiness ❀❀ Zones 8–11.

E. nicholii
**Narrow-leaved black peppermint,
Nichol's willow-leaved
peppermint, pepper gum**
This is a slender tree when it is
young, but it develops a wider
crown as it matures. As the tree
ages it also develops flaking, dark
brown bark, and the branches
tend to weep. The apple-green
leaves smell pleasantly of
peppermint. It thrives in medium
to heavy sandy soils that remain
moist throughout the growing
season. It will survive short
periods of frost. H 15–18m
(50–60ft), S 7–12m (23–40ft).
Aspect Full sun.
Hardiness ❀❀ Zones 8–10.

E. parvula
This small tree is said to be one
of the hardiest gum trees, and it
is the most suitable variety for
a cooler climate. It has a short
trunk, often becoming multi-
stemmed, covered with dark and
light grey and green bark. The
long, narrow leaves are blue-green.

Eucryphia glutinosa

It is tolerant of a wide range of
soils, including alkaline conditions.
H 10m (33ft), S 3m (10ft).
Aspect Full sun.
Hardiness ❀❀❀ Zones 7–10.

E. pauciflora
**Snow gum, cabbage gum,
weeping gum, white sallee**
This dense, spreading, often
multi-stemmed tree develops a
weeping crown as it matures and
has grey and silver-white flaking
bark. In summer dense clusters
of creamy-white flowers are borne
in the leaf axils. The mature
leaves are long, narrow and blue-
green. H 15–20m (50–65ft),
S 15m (50ft).
Aspect Full sun.
Hardiness ❀❀❀ Zones 8–10.

EUCRYPHIA
The genus contains five species
of small, mostly evergreen garden
trees, which are native to Chile
and Australia. They bear fragrant,
mallow-like, white flowers in late
summer to early autumn.
Cultivation Grow in fertile,
moisture-retentive but well-
drained, acidic soil. E. cordifolia
and E. x nymansensis tolerate
alkaline soil. All forms require
cool growing conditions.
Pruning Formative pruning
should aim to encourage a clear
trunk and a balanced crown,
while tipping the lateral branches
of young trees will encourage
a denser crown. Occasional
pruning is required for the
removal of dead, dying, diseased
or crossing branches.
Propagation Seed is the main
method of propagation and should
be collected when fresh and sown
into a container in a heated
glasshouse in a frost-free and
humid environment until
germination occurs. Summer
softwood and semi-ripe cutting
root easily if the base of the
cutting is dipped in a rooting
hormone and the cuttings are
then placed in a frost-free, humid
environment in a glasshouse.

E. cordifolia
Ulmo, roble de Chile
In late summer this upright,
conical, evergreen tree bears
clusters of saucer-shaped, white

Eucalyptus gunnii

flowers. The oblong leaves, up to
8cm (3in) long, have wavy edges
and are dark green above and
greyish below. H 15m (50ft),
S 8m (25ft).
Aspect Full sun to light shade.
Hardiness ❀❀ Zone 9.

E. glutinosa
This popular, compact deciduous
or semi-evergreen tree has a fairly
narrowly columnar habit. The
glossy green leaves, up to 6cm
(2in) long, are narrower than
those of E. cordifolia and are heavily
toothed; they turn orange-red in
autumn. Clusters of scented
white, sometimes double,
flowers are borne in mid- to late
summer. H 10m (33ft), S 3–6m
(10–20ft).
Aspect Full sun to semi-shade.
Hardiness ❀❀❀ Zone 8.

E. x intermedia
This broadly columnar, fast-
growing, evergreen tree is a hybrid
between E. glutinosa and E. lucida.
It has pale green leaves and white
flowers. H and S 10m (33ft).
Named varieties The cultivar
'Rostrevor' bears many clusters of
beautiful, fragrant white flowers
from late summer to autumn.
Aspect Full sun to semi-shade.
Hardiness ❀❀❀ Zone 8.

E. x nymansensis 'Nymansay'
This evergreen hybrid between
E. cordifolia and E. glutinosa is grown
for its narrowly columnar habit
and mass of flowers. It is a fast-
growing tree, producing fragrant
white flowers in late summer.
H 15m (50ft), S 5m (16ft).
Aspect Full sun to semi-shade.
Hardiness ❀❀❀ Zone 7.

Fagus sylvatica 'Dawyck Purple'

FAGUS
Beech

The ten species of deciduous trees in the genus are found in temperate areas throughout the northern hemisphere. They are grown for their elegant habit and their autumn colour.

Cultivation Grow in moisture-retentive but well-drained soil in sun or semi-shade. Purple-leaved forms give best colour in full sun; yellow-leaved forms should be planted in semi-shade.

Pruning Early formative pruning should produce a clear, straight trunk and a balanced crown. Remove dead, dying, diseased or crossing branches.

Propagation Collect and sow seed in autumn. Put in an unheated glasshouse or cold frame until germination occurs. Winter grafting of ornamental European beech cultivars on to seed-raised European beech is the most effective way of propagating different forms.

F. grandifolia
American beech

A majestic, spreading tree, this specimen will require space around it as it is likely to grow as wide as it is tall. The attractive dark green leaves, up to 15cm (6in) long, are oval and toothed and turn golden-bronze in autumn. H and S 15–20m (50–65ft).
Aspect Full sun or semi-shade.
Hardiness ❀❀❀ Zones 4–9.

F. orientalis
Oriental beech

A fast-growing species native to south-east Europe as well as south-west Asia. The dark green leaves, up to 17cm (7in) long, are toothed and have wavy margins; they turn yellow-brown in autumn. A good alternative to *F. sylvatica* in poor, fast-draining soil. H 30m (100ft), S 15–20m (50–65ft).
Aspect Full sun or semi-shade.
Hardiness ❀❀❀ Zones 5–7.

F. sylvatica
Common beech, European beech

This noble, fast-growing, spreading tree is grown for its stunning orange, yellow and brown autumn colour. The leaves, up to 10cm (4in) long, have wavy margins and are pale green at first but turn glossy, dark green by midsummer. Less tolerant of dry soil conditions and high summer temperatures than *F. grandiflora* or *F. orientalis*. H 25–30m (80–100ft), S 15m (50ft).
Named varieties 'Dawyck' has a tight, conical habit and twisted, upswept branches that widen with age.
'Dawyck Gold', which is a much slower growing form, has vibrant yellow new leaves that fade to yellow-green in summer.
'Dawyck Purple' is a narrow, upright form with purple-black foliage and lovely autumn colour.
'Pendula' (syn. *F. sylvatica* f. *pendula*; weeping beech) will form a circle of new plants if the outer branches are allowed to layer themselves. H 15m (50ft), S 30m (100ft).
'Riversii' is a beautiful, wide-spreading copper beech that has dark purple leaves and good autumn colour.
Aspect Full sun or semi-shade.
Hardiness ❀❀❀ Zones 4–7.

FICUS
Fig

This large genus, which contains about 800 species of mostly evergreens, is found throughout the world in tropical and subtropical areas, where they are grown as shade trees and for their edible fruits. Many tender species are grown as houseplants

Ficus benjamina

in temperate areas, but the deciduous species *F. carica* (common fig) is hardy in sheltered temperate areas. The species below are tender and should be grown under glass in all but the warmest areas.

Cultivation Grow in fertile, moisture-retentive but well-drained soil sited in sun or semi-shade.

Pruning Prune occasionally to remove dead, dying, diseased or crossing branches.

Propagation Seed should be collected when fresh and sown into a pot in a heated glasshouse in a frost-free and humid environment until germination occurs. Semi-ripe cuttings can be rooted during late summer and placed in a frost-free, humid environment until they root. Low branches can also be layered into the soil.

F. benghalensis
Banyan, Indian fig

This evergreen species develops into a large, spreading tree with strongly horizontal branches, which are supported by prop roots growing from the branches. The prop roots layer and send up new shoots. The glossy green leaves, up to 25cm (10in) long, have distinct veins and are flushed bronze-pink in spring. H 30m (100ft), S 60m (200ft).
Aspect Light shade to full sun.
Hardiness (Min. 15°C/59°F) Zone 10–12.

F. benjamina
Weeping fig

This evergreen species has a beautiful weeping habit. The narrow leaves, up to 12cm (5in) long, are glossy and dark green. These trees develop extensive root systems and do best in deep, fertile soils and humid climates. They are widely grown in the tropics and also in protected environments, such as shopping malls. Although eventually large, trees can be easily pruned. In tropical areas they make dense hedges. H and S 30–50m (100–165ft).
Named varieties There are several cultivars, including 'Exotica', 'Golden King' (with yellow variegated leaves) and 'Starlight' (with white-edged leaves).
The widely available 'Variegata', which has glossy, dark green leaves attractively edged in white, is a popular houseplant.
Aspect Deep shade to full sun.
Hardiness (Min. 15°C/59°F) Zone 10–12.

F. elastica
India rubber tree

This is one of the most widely grown species of fig tree and found in numerous homes as a pot plant. It is now extinct in its natural habitat of India, Burma, Malaysia and Java. It is potentially a large tree with big, thick, copper-flushed leaves, which turn glossy, dark green with age. Like *F. benjamina*, it is easy to prune and shape. H and S 60m (200ft).

Ficus benghalensis

Named varieties 'Decora' has leaves with creamy-white midribs and flushed with red beneath.

The leaves of 'Doescheri' are variegated with grey-green, pale yellow and white and have pink stalks and midribs.

The large leaves of 'Robusta' are mottled with pink, cream and light green. 'Rubra' has dark copper-flushed new growth. 'Variegata' has cream-edged leaves.
Aspect Light shade to full sun.
Hardiness (Min. 15°C/59°F) Zone 10–12.

F. lyrata
Fiddle-leaf fig
This spreading evergreen tree has large, leathery, highly corrugated and twisted leaves. It is a drought-tolerant and slow-growing fig, and fruits freely. In the garden: H and S 12m (40ft); in the wild: H and S 30m (100ft).
Aspect light shade to full sun.
Hardiness (Min. 15°C/59°F) Zone 10–12.

F. macrophylla
Moreton Bay fig,
Australian banyan
This large, dense, evergreen tree has a short trunk and aerial roots, some of which are prop roots for the wide-spreading branches. The leaves, up to 25cm (10in) long, are mid-green above and rusty red below. Masses of purple-green figs are borne on mature trees. H and S 55m (180ft).
Aspect Light shade to full sun.
Hardiness (Min. 7–10°C/45–50°F) Zones 10–12.

FITZROYA
Patagonian cypress
The single species in the genus is an evergreen conifer. It is native to Chile and southern Argentina.
Cultivation Grow in fertile, moisture-retentive but well-drained soil in full sun. Shelter plants from cold winds.
Pruning Formative pruning should aim to produce a clear trunk and a balanced crown, while tipping the lateral branches of young trees will encourage a denser crown. Occasional pruning is required for the removal of dead, dying, diseased or crossing branches.
Propagation Seed is the easiest method of propagation and should be collected when fresh and sown into a container in an unheated glasshouse or cold frame until germination occurs. Semi-ripe and softwood cutting can be rooted during summer and should be dipped in a rooting hormone and placed in a humid environment until rooting occurs. Selected forms are winter grafted on to seedling raised rootstocks.

F. cupressoides (syn. F. patagonia)
Patagonian cypress, Alerce
This majestic, weeping conifer is highly prized for its timber and has been over-cropped as a result of this in Chile and Argentina. In the wild it can live up to 3,400 years, and in gardens it is grown for its dark green cypress-like foliage that hangs from long arching branches, and will develop into a broad columnar tree. Cones are small and brownish in colour

Ficus lyrata

and the bark develops with age into a rich reddish brown and shreds in long strips. Best grown in areas where annual rainfall is high, and in free-draining, humus-rich, moisture-retentive soils. H 50m (165ft), S 20m (65ft).
Aspect Light shade to full sun.
Hardiness ✹✹✹ Zone 8.

FORTUNELLA
Kumquat
The genus of five evergreen shrubs and small trees is native to woodlands from southern China to Malaysia. They are spiny plants, grown for their white flowers and edible, yellow fruits. Unlike other citrus fruits, the entire fruit of the kumquat can be eaten, including the rind and pips.
Cultivation Grow in fertile, moisture-retentive soil in full sun. Kumquats are suitable for growing in containers.
Pruning Long, whippy growth is produced during spring and summer and this should be

reduced so that a balanced, round-headed crown is produced. Occasional pruning is required for the removal of dead, dying, diseased or crossing branches.
Propagation Most citrus fruits are produced by budding and this can be done during the winter when the seedling rootstock is dormant. Kumquats will come true from seed and can be propagated this way, but require an even temperature of above 25°C (77°F) to germinate.

F. japonica
(syn. Citrus japonica, C. madurensis)
Round kumquat
This dense, bushy tree has spines in the leaf axils, glossy green leaves, up to 10cm (4in) long, and fragrant flowers. The small, slightly oval fruits are yellowish-orange, ripening to orange. H 4–5m (12–16ft), S 1.5m (5ft).
Aspect Full sun or semi-shade.
Hardiness (Min. 7°C/45°F) Zones 9–11.

Fortunella japonica

Fitzroya cupressoides

Fraxinus americana

FRAXINUS
Ash

The 65 species of usually deciduous and fast-growing trees in the genus are native to woodlands in the northern hemisphere. They are grown as specimen trees and for their attractive leaves.

Cultivation Grow in moisture-retentive but well-drained, neutral to alkaline soil in sun.

Pruning Little pruning is required apart from the removal of dead, dying, diseased or crossing branches. Early formative pruning should produce a clear straight trunk and a balanced crown.

Propagation Seed should be collected fresh and have three months warm treatment followed by three months in an unheated glasshouse or cold frame until germination occurs. Summer budding on to seedling-grown ash is used for propagation.

F. americana
White ash

The species, which is native to eastern North America, is a fast-growing tree with dark green, pinnate leaves, up to 35cm (14in) long and with 5–9 leaflets. In autumn the leaves turn yellow or purple. H 25–30m (80–100ft), S 15m (50ft).

Named varieties The cultivar 'Autumn Purple' is a smaller, conical tree with dark green leaves that turn red-purple in autumn. H 18m (60ft), S 12m (40ft).

Aspect Full sun or semi-shade.
Hardiness ✿✿✿ Zones 4–9.

F. angustifolia
Narrow-leaved ash

This spreading tree, from northern Africa and south-west Europe, has glossy, dark green leaves, up to 25cm (10in) long, with 13 leaflets. These turn yellow-gold in autumn. H 25m (80ft), S 12m (40ft).

Named varieties The species is not often grown in gardens but is usually represented by the form 'Raywood' (claret ash), which is an upright, fast-growing tree with glossy, dark green leaves that turn dark red-purple in autumn. H 20m (65ft).

Aspect Full sun or semi-shade.
Hardiness ✿✿✿ Zone 5.

F. excelsior
Common ash, European ash

This is a very large, broadly columnar tree, which may be identified by its black winter buds. The dark green leaves, up to 30cm (12in) long, have 9 to 13 leaflets and turn yellow in autumn. Winged fruits (keys) hang in clusters from the stems in winter and fall in spring. H 30–40m (100–130ft), S 20m (70ft).

Named varieties There are several fine cultivars. 'Jaspidea' has stunning yellow new shoots, yellow-green stems in winter and good yellow autumn colour. 'Pendula' (weeping ash) is a weeping form, often grafted on a straight trunk and producing an umbrella-like shape. It is one of the most widely planted weeping trees. 'Westhof's Glorie' has a narrow conical habit, which broadens with age, and is often used as a street tree in Europe.

Aspect Full sun or semi-shade.
Hardiness ✿✿✿ Zones 5–7.

F. ornus
Manna ash, flowering ash

One of the most attractive ashes for general planting, this beautiful, medium-sized, round-headed tree from southern Europe and south-western Asia bears showy clusters of small, scented, creamy-white flowers in early summer. The dark green leaves, which are up to 20cm (8in) long, have 5–9 leaflets and turn purple-red in autumn. H 20m (65ft), S 15m (50ft).

Aspect Full sun or semi-shade.
Hardiness ✿✿✿ Zones 5–6.

GINKGO
Maidenhair tree

This extraordinary tree is sadly now extinct in the wild. It is an ancient tree, and 200 million years ago the species was widespread across the world. The only species in the genus, it is a deciduous conifer. Male and female trees exist, and it is the female that produces the fruit that is harvested for its nut. Female fruits also have a strong, pungent aroma, so the male form is more widely grown as a garden or street tree, and it is widely planted in towns, streets and gardens because it is tolerant of pollution. It is also relatively disease-free.

Cultivation Grow in well-drained soil in full sun.

Pruning Occasional pruning only is required for the removal of dead, dying, diseased or crossing branches.

Propagation Seed is the easiest method of propagation and should be collected when fresh and sown into a container in an unheated glasshouse or cold frame until germination occurs. Semi-ripe and softwood cutting can be rooted during summer and should be dipped in a rooting hormone and placed in a humid environment until rooting occurs. Selected forms are winter grafted on to seedling-raised rootstocks.

Ginkgo biloba

G. biloba

It is an upright, conical tree with upswept branches. The unusual two-lobed leaves are green with linear veins, and they turn golden-yellow in autumn. H 30–40m (100–130ft), S 8–15m (26–50ft).
Named varieties Numerous cultivars have been developed for their habit or for their autumn colour. 'Autumn Gold', one of the most widely distributed male forms, has a semi-upright but broadly conical shape and fantastic autumn colour. The male 'Fastigiata' is a tight, upright column with twisted branches and good autumn colour. 'Princeton Sentry', a male form, is widely grown in the USA as a street tree; the autumn colour is excellent. The fast-growing male 'Saratoga' is a more compact but still conical tree with good autumn colour. 'Tremonia' is a widely planted European form that originated in Germany. It has beautiful autumn colour, twisted branches and a narrow habit.
Aspect Full sun or semi-shade.
Hardiness ✲✲✲ Zones 6–10.

GLEDITSIA

The genus contains 12–14 species of deciduous, rather spiny trees, which are native to North and South America and Asia. They are grown for their attractive pinnate leaves and for the large seedpods that follow the insignificant flowers.
Cultivation Grow in fertile, well-drained soil in full sun.
Pruning Early formative pruning should aim to produce a clear straight trunk and a balanced crown; little pruning is required apart from the removal of dead, dying, diseased or crossing branches as and when needed.
Propagation Seed is widely used. It should be collected fresh and have three months warm treatment followed by three months in an unheated glasshouse or cold frame until germination occurs. Summer budding on to seedling-grown trees and winter grafting is used to propagate the different forms. Trees can also be propagated by softwood cuttings taken during summer, dipped into a rooting

Gleditsia triacanthos

hormone, and placed in a humid environment until rooted, and then hardened off and potted on.

G. sinensis
Chinese honey locust

A graceful, medium-sized tree, this is armed with numerous thorns on the stems and branches, but it has delicate, light green foliage. When it is grown in free-draining, fertile soil it will bear whitish, pea-like flowers in summer, followed by bean-like pods in autumn. H 20m (65ft), S 15m (50ft).
Aspect Full sun.
Hardiness ✲✲✲ Zone 5.

G. triacanthos
Honey locust

This widely grown tree from North America has a spreading habit and spiny branches and trunk. The glossy, dark green leaves, up to 25cm (10in) long, turn yellow in autumn, when the seedpods, which can be up to 45cm (18in) long, are borne. H 30m (100ft), S 20m (65ft).
Named varieties 'Rubylace' is an unusual, beautiful tree, with an almost weeping habit. The foliage is purple-red as it emerges and remains purple-green through the summer. It never produces seedpods. H and S 8–10m (26–33ft).
The fast-growing 'Shademaster' is a stunning, semi-weeping tree with green foliage, persisting long

into autumn before turning pale yellow. It is almost thornless, and therefore is one of the most widely planted of this group. H and S 10m (33ft).
The broadly conical and thornless 'Sunburst' has golden-yellow young leaves that fade to pale yellow-lemon in summer. H 12m (40ft), S 10m (33ft).
Aspect Full sun.
Hardiness ✲✲✲ Zones 4–9.

GREVILLEA
Spider flower

The 250 species of evergreen trees and shrubs in the genus are mostly native to Australia, with a few coming from South-east Asia.
Cultivation Outdoors, grow in fertile, neutral to acidic soil in full sun.
Pruning Occasional pruning only is required for the removal of dead, dying, diseased or crossing branches.
Propagation Seed is the easiest method of propagation and should be collected when fresh and sown into a container in a heated glasshouse in a frost-free and humid environment until germination occurs. Softwood

cuttings can also be rooted during early summer and should be dipped in a rooting hormone and placed in a frost-free, humid environment until they root.

G. banksii

This is a widely branching large shrub or small tree with deeply cut, fern-like leaves, up to 25cm (10in) long. In late winter and spring dense clusters of pale pink or dark red flowerheads are produced at the tips of the stems. With regular pruning to maintain its shape, this is a beautiful small flowering tree for moist, acidic soil. H 10m (33ft), S 5m (16ft).
Aspect Full sun.
Hardiness ✲ Zones 8–11.

G. robusta
Silky oak

A large, fast-growing, flowering and foliage tree, this has deeply cut, fern-like leaves, up to 30cm (12in) long, and one-sided, radially arranged clusters of spidery, bright yellow flowerheads in spring. H 30m (100ft), S 20m (65ft).
Aspect Full sun.
Hardiness (Min. 5°C/41°F) Zones 8–11.

Gleditsia sinensis

HALESIA
Snowdrop tree, silver bell

The five species of attractive deciduous shrubs or small trees in the genus are native to south-eastern USA and eastern China. They have attractive bell-shaped flowers, which are followed by winged fruits.

Cultivation Grow in fertile, moisture-retentive but well-drained, neutral to acidic soil in sun or semi-shade.

Pruning Early formative pruning should aim to produce a clear straight trunk and a balanced crown; little pruning is required apart from the removal of dead, dying, diseased, or crossing branches as and when needed.

Propagation Trees can be propagated by softwood cuttings taken during summer, which are dipped into a rooting hormone, and placed in a humid environment until rooted, and then hardened off and potted on. Cuttings are best potted on the following spring, as they establish more quickly.

H. carolina
(syn. H. tetraptera)

In spring, before the leaves emerge, masses of pendent, bell-shaped, pink-tinged, white flowers are borne along the branches. They are followed by green fruits with four wings. The mid-green leaves, up to 15cm (6in) long, turn yellow in autumn. H and S 10–20m (33–65ft).

Aspect Semi-shade to full sun.
Hardiness ✿✿✿ Zones 4–9.

H. monticola
Mountain snowdrop tree

The mid-green leaves, up to 20cm (8in) long, of this fast-growing, conical tree turn yellow in autumn. Bell-shaped white flowers are borne in spring, before the leaves, and are followed by four-winged, green fruits, which are sometimes up to 5cm (2in) long. H 12m (40ft), S 8m (26ft).

Named varieties *H. monticola* var. *vestita* has even larger flowers, which are sometimes tinged with pink. *H. monticola* var. *vestita* f. *rosea* has large, pale pink flowers.

Aspect Semi-shade to full sun.
Hardiness ✿✿✿ Zones 5–8.

ILEX
Holly

The genus contains about 400 species of both evergreen and deciduous trees and shrubs. They are found in temperate, tropical and subtropical areas and can vary immensely in their height and spread, habit, shape, leaf shape and colour and even the colour of the berries. Female trees bear fruit, and most hollies require that both male and female trees are present to produce berries. Although there are some self-fertile forms, these are not common.

Halesia monticola

Cultivation Grow in fertile, moisture-retentive but well-drained soil in sun or semi-shade.

Pruning Early formative pruning should aim to produce a dense conical habit and will involve tipping back side shoots and branches to create a dense crown. A single leader should be produced along with a clear straight trunk and a balanced crown; little pruning is required apart from the removal of dead, dying, diseased or crossing branches as and when needed.

Propagation Trees can be propagated by softwood or semi-ripe cuttings taken from early to late summer, dipped into a rooting hormone, and placed in a humid environment until rooted, and then hardened off and potted on. Seed can also be used, and should be collected when fresh, soaked to remove the pulp, and then grown in an unheated glasshouse or cold frame until it germinates.

I. x altaclerensis
Highclere holly

This hybrid between *I. aquifolium* and *I. perado* forms a large evergreen shrub or small tree. These plants are more heat-tolerant than *I. aquifolium* and have a greater resistance to pollution. The glossy, dark green leaves, up to 12cm (5in) long, are larger than, but not as spiky as, those of *I. aquifolium*. Female forms produce berries, but require a male holly nearby to pollinate the flowers. H to 20m (65ft), S 12–15m (40–50ft).

Named varieties There are many cultivars. The popular, strongly growing female form 'Belgica' has narrow, pale green leaves and an abundance of orange-red fruits in autumn. Its conical habit makes it a popular choice as a focal point.

'Belgica Aurea' (syn. 'Silver Sentinel') is one of the best variegated hollies. It is a female fruiting form, with the attributes of 'Belgica', but it has narrow, yellow-margined leaves. H 12m (40ft), S 5m (16ft).

The pyramidal female form 'Camelliifolia' is widely grown for its glossy, camellia-like, dark green leaves, red berries and purple stems. H 14m (46ft).

'Golden King' is another female form with red berries, but it has a much wider and flatter leaf than 'Belgica Aurea', and mature trees are slightly more open in habit. H 6m (20ft).

The male form 'Hodginsii' does not bear berries, but it is widely planted as a pollinator for this group and for *I. aquifolium*. H 14m (46ft), S 10m (33ft).

'Lawsoniana' is a delightful, open-growing, female form. The broad leaves have a distinct yellow blotch in the centre of the leaf, and the foliage colour contrasts well with the red-brown fruits. H 6m (20ft).

Aspect Full sun to semi-shade.
Hardiness ✿✿ Zone 7.

I. aquifolium
English holly, common holly

This species is widely planted in cool temperate climates where it develops into a broadly columnar

Ilex aquifolium 'Amber'

Ilex aquifolium 'Golden Queen'

tree with dark green stems and a dense crown of spiny, evergreen foliage. The glossy, dark green leaves, up to 10cm (4in) long, are spiny. It is not tolerant of high summer temperatures, and specimens grown in poor, free-draining soils are prone to leaf fall during late summer. H 20–25m (65–80ft), S 8–10m (26–33ft).

Named varieties The female form 'Amber' has spiny green leaves. Bright orange-yellow berries are borne in dense clusters at the tips of the stems. H to 6m (20ft), S 2.4m (8ft).

'Argentea Marginata' (syn. 'Argentea Variegata') is a beautiful female form with pinkish new leaves, which develop a crisp creamy-white variegation and sharp spines. These leaves are a wonderful foil for the bright red berries. H 15m (50ft), S 4m (12ft).

The female 'Bacciflava' (syn. 'Fructu Luteo') is the best of the yellow-berried hollies. H 15m (50ft), S 4m (12ft).

'Golden Milkmaid' is one of the most beautiful variegated hollies. The spiny leaves have a striking golden blotch in the centre.

Despite the name, 'Golden Queen' (syn. 'Aurea Regina') is a male form with spiny, grey-green leaves that are edged with yellow. H 10m (33ft), S 6m (20ft).

The widely planted female form 'Madame Briot' has attractive purple shoots and spiny, dark green leaves that are mottled and edged with golden-yellow. H 10m (33ft), S 5m (16ft).

'Pyramidalis Fructu Luteo' is a wonderful conical holly, which makes a fine specimen tree when fully grown. It is widely planted for its habit, glossy green leaves with distinct yellow margins and plentiful bright red berries. H 6m (20ft), S 4m (12ft).
Aspect Full sun to semi-shade.
Hardiness ❋❋ Zone 7.

I. x *koehneana*
This hybrid between *I. aquifolium* and *I. latifolia* is a narrow evergreen shrub. It has large, spiny, glossy green leaves and red berries. H 7m (23ft), S 5m (16ft).
Aspect Full sun.
Hardiness ❋❋❋ Zone 7.

I. latifolia
This pyramidal evergreen species is sometimes known as the magnolia leaf holly as it bears very long, tapering, glossy green, almost spineless leaves, nearly 30cm (12in) long. Female trees produce berries in autumn and these ripen in winter, starting greenish-red and ripening to salmon-pink. This species enjoys high summer temperatures, when the wood can ripen fully before winter, and in more maritime climates it may suffer occasional frost damage. H 7–20m (23–65ft), S 5–10m (16–33ft).
Aspect Full sun.
Hardiness ❋❋ Zone 7.

I. opaca
American holly
This columnar evergreen species is a useful understorey tree, which does much better in a continental climate where the summers are hot and the winters are cold. The spiny leaves are dull green and can grow up to 12cm (5in) long. They are a good contrast with the bright red berries, borne in clusters on female plants. This species needs acidic soil. H 10–15m (33–65ft), S 7–8m (23–26ft).
Aspect Full sun or semi-shade.
Hardiness ❋❋❋ Zone 5.

JACARANDA
There are about 45 species of evergreen and deciduous trees in the genus, and they are found in tropical and subtropical

Jacaranda mimosifolia

America. They have attractive foliage, and mature plants bear bell-shaped flowers. In temperate areas they make good foliage plants for conservatories, although they can get tall and leggy.
Cultivation Outdoors, grow in fertile, moisture-retentive but well-drained soil in full sun.
Pruning Formative pruning should aim to encourage a clear trunk and a balanced crown, while tipping the lateral branches of young trees will encourage a denser crown.
Propagation Seed is the easiest method of propagation and should be collected when fresh and be sown into a container in a heated glasshouse in a frost-free and humid environment until germination occurs. Softwood cuttings can be rooted during early summer and should be dipped in a rooting hormone and placed in a frost-free, humid environment such as a greenhouse until they root. Low branches can also be layered into the soil.

J. mimosifolia
(syn. *J. acutifolia*, *J. ovalifolia*)
This deciduous Argentinian species is widely planted wherever it will grow. As the light green, fern-like leaves emerge in spring, many large panicles of bluish-purple flowers are produced. It will not thrive in climates with high winter rainfall. H 15m (50ft), S 10–15m (33–50ft).
Aspect Full sun.
Hardiness (Min. 5–7°C/41–45°F) Zones 9–11.

Ilex x *koehneana* 'Chestnut Leaf'

Juglans ailanthifolia

Juniperus chinensis

JUGLANS
Walnut

The 15 or so species of deciduous trees in the genus are native to North and South America and an area stretching from south-eastern Europe to South-east Asia. They are grown for their decorative habit, attractive foliage, spring catkins, autumn fruits and distinctively patterned timber.
Cultivation Grow in deep, fertile, well-drained soil in full sun. Plant in a sheltered position.
Pruning Early formative pruning should aim to produce a clear straight trunk and a balanced crown. Subsequently, little pruning is required apart from the removal of dead, dying, diseased or crossing branches.
Propagation Collect seed when fresh, remove the fleshy pulp, crack the hard nut case, and then grow in an unheated glasshouse or cold frame until it germinates. Winter grafting is used to produce the coloured leaved form, which is grafted on to the common walnut.

J. ailanthifolia
Japanese walnut

This deciduous tree is native to Japan and Sakhalin, and due to its bold foliage it makes a good ornamental specimen for large gardens. It has yellow-green pinnate leaves, up to 16cm (6¼in) long, and produces yellow-green catkins in spring. The nuts have a pleasant flavour and an oily texture. H and S 10m (50ft).
Aspect Full sun.
Hardiness ❋❋❋ Zones 4–9.

J. nigra
Black walnut

This large, slow-growing, often straight-trunked tree is valued for the quality of the timber. A noble parkland tree, it has dark green, pinnate, aromatic leaves, up to 60cm (24in) long, which turn yellow in autumn, and large, edible, oily nuts. H 30m (100ft), S 20 (65ft).
Aspect Full sun.
Hardiness ❋❋❋ Zones 4–7.

J. regia
Common walnut

A widely grown tree in Europe for both its wood and edible nuts, this spreading species has glossy green, pinnate leaves, up to 30cm (12in) long, which are flushed with bronze when they first emerge, fading to green in early summer. H 30m (100ft), S 15–20m (50–65ft).
Named varieties Among the various cultivars the slow-growing 'Purpurea' has dark purple leaves, which fade to a purple-green colour in summer.
Aspect Full sun.
Hardiness ❋❋❋ Zones 4–9.

JUNIPERUS
Juniper

The 60 species of evergreen, coniferous shrubs and trees in this genus are found throughout the northern hemisphere. They exhibit an enormous range of shape, size and colour, and numerous cultivars have been developed, providing plants for ground cover as well as tall specimen trees.

Cultivation Grow in fertile, well-drained soil in sun or semi-shade.
Pruning Formative pruning should aim to produce a balanced crown, while tipping the tips of lateral branches of young trees will encourage a denser crown. Occasional pruning only is required for the removal of dead, dying, diseased, or crossing branches.
Propagation Seed is the easiest method of propagation and should be collected when fresh and sown into a container in an unheated glasshouse or cold frame until germination occurs. Semi-ripe and softwood cutting can be rooted during summer and should be dipped in a rooting hormone and placed in a humid environment until rooting occurs.

J. chinensis
Chinese juniper

This narrowly conical tree is similar in habit and appearance to *Cupressus sempervirens*. The dark brown bark peels in long strips. Trees often have spiky juvenile foliage and soft, scale-like, greenish-blue foliage at the same time. H 20–25m (65–80ft), S 5–6m (16–20ft).
Named varieties 'Aurea' is a slow-growing, narrow conifer with both adult and juvenile foliage. The golden-yellow foliage is susceptible to sun scorch. H 10m (33ft), S up to 5m (16ft).
'Obelisk' is a tightly conical tree with blue-green foliage. H 2.4m (8ft), S 60cm (2ft).
Aspect Full sun or semi-shade.
Hardiness ❋❋❋ Zones 6–10.

J. recurva
Himalayan weeping juniper, drooping juniper

This broadly conical tree has slender, scale-like, blue-green leaves borne on pendulous branches. The reddish bark peels in long flakes. It will flourish in sheltered locations with moist, free-draining but fertile soil. H 10–15m (33–50ft), S 5m (16ft).
Named varieties *J. recurva* var. *coxii* (coffin juniper) has more open foliage than the species and long, weeping stems of blue-green foliage.
Aspect Full sun.
Hardiness ❋❋❋ Zone 7.

Juniperus chinensis 'Aurea'

Koelreuteria paniculata

KOELREUTERIA

The three species in the genus are deciduous trees from China and Taiwan. They are grown for their lovely flowers, borne in large panicles in late summer, and seedpods. Trees flower best in hot summers, and although they are hardy they are still susceptible to damage from late spring frosts and do best in a sheltered position.

Cultivation Grow in fertile, moisture-retentive but well-drained soil in full sun.

Pruning Early formative pruning should aim to produce a clear trunk and a balanced crown.

Subsequently, little pruning is required apart from the removal of dead, dying, diseased or crossing branches. Branch damage is common and any such damaged material should be removed as soon as possible.

Propagation Seed is the most common form of propagation. It should be collected when fresh, and be given three months warm treatment followed by three months cold treatment and grown on in an unheated glasshouse or cold frame until it germinates. Root cuttings can be taken in early winter. Upright forms are winter grafted on to seedling rootstocks.

K. paniculata
Golden rain tree, pride of India
This is a spreading tree, with pinnate leaves, up to 45cm (18in) long, which are tinged with pink when they first emerge and which turn yellow in autumn. From mid- to late summer panicles of yellow flowers are borne, and these are followed by papery, translucent, yellow seedheads, which turn brown as they age. H and S 10–12m (33–40ft).
Named varieties The slow-growing 'Fastigiata' has a tight, conical habit.

'Rose Lantern' has rosy-pink fruit cases, which persist long into autumn.

'September' is later flowering than other species. The flowers are followed by yellowish-green seedheads that turn brown.
Aspect Full sun or semi-shade.
Hardiness ❀❀❀ Zones 6–8.

Laburnum anagyroides

LABURNUM
Golden rain
The two species of deciduous tree in the genus, which are native to south-eastern Europe and western Asia, are grown for their racemes of yellow flowers. They are easy-to-grow plants, but all parts are very poisonous.

Cultivation Grow in well-drained soil in full sun.

Pruning Early formative pruning should aim to produce a clear trunk and a balanced crown, followed by minimal pruning in order to remove any dead, dying, diseased or crossing branches. Canker is common in many laburnums so quickly cut back and discard diseased shoots to healthy growth.

Propagation Seed and softwood cuttings are the most common form of propagation. Seed should be collected when it is fresh, then sown in to a humid environment such as a heated greenhouse or conservatory until germination occurs. Softwood cuttings can

be taken in summer, dipped in a rooting hormone and then placed in a humid environment until rooting occurs.

L. alpinum
Scotch laburnum
This delightful tree produces racemes, up to 40cm (16in) long, of yellow flowers in late spring to early summer. These are followed by narrow seedpods. The glossy, dark green leaves have three leaflets, up to 8cm (3in) long. H and S 6–8m (20–26ft).
Aspect Full sun or semi-shade.
Hardiness ❀❀❀ Zones 4–7.

L. anagyroides (syn. L. vulgare)
Common laburnum
In late spring to early summer racemes, up to 30cm (12in) long, of bright yellow, wisteria-like flowers are produced. The grey-green leaves, each with 3 leaflets, have hairy undersides. H 7–8m (23–26ft), S 3–4m (10–12ft).
Aspect Full sun or semi-shade.
Hardiness ❀❀❀ Zones 5–7.

Juniperus x media pfitzeriana

L. × watereri 'Vossii'
This cultivar, developed from a hybrid between *L. alpinum* and *L. anagyroides*, is the most widely planted of the laburnums. It bears racemes, 50–60cm (20–24in) long, of golden-yellow flowers in late spring to early summer. The leaves are dark green. H and S 7–8m (23–26ft).
Aspect Full sun or semi-shade.
Hardiness ❀❀❀ Zones 5–7.

LAGERSTROEMIA

The genus contains more than 50 species of evergreen and deciduous trees and shrubs. Native to tropical and subtropical regions from Asia to Australasia, they are often grown for their beautiful, colourful flowers and do best where summer temperatures are high. In temperate areas with mild winters they require the heat of a south-facing wall to ripen the wood before the first frosts.
Cultivation Outdoors, grow in well-drained soil in full sun.
Pruning Early pruning should aim to produce a clear trunk and a balanced crown. Apart from that little pruning is required apart from the removal of dead, dying, diseased or crossing branches. They are grown as multi- or single-stemmed trees, with the canopy lifted away from their stems.
Propagation Seed and softwood cutting is the most common form of propagation. Seed should be collected when fresh, and be sown into a container at 10–13°C (50–55°F). Softwood cuttings should be taken during early summer, dipped in a rooting hormone and placed in a humid environment until rooting occurs.

L. fauriei
This beautiful small, often multi-stemmed, deciduous tree is grown for its stunning reddish-brown bark and panicles of fragrant white flowers, which appear in midsummer. In autumn the dark green leaves, up to 10cm (4in) long, turn yellow. The trees have an arching, vase-shaped habit. H and S 8–10m (26–33ft).
Named varieties The vigorous 'Fantasy' bears masses of off-white flowers in summer on strongly arching branches. The light copper-brown bark is very attractive. H 12m (40ft).
'Sarah's Favorite' has large clusters of dense white flowers and orange-yellow autumn colour.
Aspect Full sun.
Hardiness ❀❀ Zones 7–9.

L. indica
There are numerous selections of this spectacular small to medium-sized autumn-flowering tree, which are grown for their 30cm (12in) long clusters of white, pink, lavender, red or purple coloured flowers. H 4.5–7.5m (15–25ft). S 4.5m (15ft).

Named varieties 'Byers Wonderful White' is an upright growing form with dense clusters of white flowers. H 6m (20ft)
'Carolina Beauty' is the most commonly grown red flowering variety, but it is susceptible to mildew. H 6m (20ft).
'Catawba' has good mildew resistance, stunning autumn colour and rich purple flowers. H 4.5m (15ft).
'Pink velour' is crimson-coloured when in bud but the flowers are lavender. H 4m (12ft).
Aspect Full sun.
Hardiness ❀ Zones 6–9.

L. indica × *L. fauriei*
A number of hybrids between *L. fauriei* and *L. indica* have been developed with the aim of increasing disease resistance, improving bark colour and intensifying flower colours. H and S 5–6m (16–20ft).
Named varieties 'Acoma' is a broadly spreading small tree, with beautiful white flowers and light silver-grey, brown bark.
The upright 'Miami' bears pink flowers and has chestnut-brown bark. H 5m (16ft), S 2.4m (8ft).
'Muskogee' is popular for its pretty lavender-pink flowers. The bark is silver-grey and brown, and in autumn the leaves turn vibrent shades of yellow, red and purple.
'Tuskegee' has pale brown and silver-grey bark and vivid coral-pink flowers. H and S 5m (16ft).
Aspect Full sun.
Hardiness ❀❀ Zones 7–9.

LARIX
Larch

The 12–14 species in the genus are unusual in being deciduous conifers. They are found throughout the northern hemisphere and are generally fast-growing trees, grown for their graceful habit, autumn colour and timber. The attractive lime-green foliage may be tinted blue-green in early spring. The needles turn bright golden or butter yellow in autumn. In spring bright red female catkin-like flowers are borne along the stems, and the male cones are small, golden-brown and persist for a long time.

Larix kaempferi

Cultivation Grow in deep, well-drained soil in full sun.
Pruning Early formative pruning should aim to produce a clear trunk and a balanced crown. Otherwise little pruning is required apart from the removal of dead, dying, diseased or crossing branches.
Propagation Seed should be collected when fresh, and be sown into a container outside or in an unheated glasshouse or cold frame until germination occurs. Cultivars are produced in winter by being grafted on to seedling-raised larch rootstocks. Hardwood cuttings can also be taken in winter.

L. decidua
European larch
In Europe this species is grown for its timber, and it is also often used as a pioneer species in reforestation projects because it is tolerant of a wide range of soil conditions. They are fast-growing, strongly conical trees, with long, pendulous branches and good yellow autumn colour. H 30–40m (100–130ft), S 6–10m (20–33ft).
Named varieties 'Fastigiata' has a strongly upright habit and short, twisted branches. It is an excellent choice for a focal point or lawn specimen. H 20m (65ft), S 5m (16ft).
'Pendula' is usually grown as a graft on a clean stem of the species so that the foliage will arch and weep. Although this

Lagerstroemia 'Acoma'

Larix decidua

gives an attractive shape when the tree is young, with age the crown becomes somewhat dense and overcrowded. H and S 10m (33ft).
Aspect Full sun.
Hardiness ❁❁❁ Zones 3–6.

L. griffithii
Himalayan larch, Sikkim larch
This larch has a pendulous habit, reddish-brown bark, golden autumn colour and soft, green needles in spring and summer. It also has the largest cones of any of the genus – they may reach 10cm (4in) across – and they persist on the branches. This requires a more sheltered site than *L. decidua*. H 20m (65ft), S 10m (33ft).
Aspect Full sun to light shade.
Hardiness ❁❁❁ Zones 6–7.

L. kaempferi
(**syn.** *L. leptolepis*)
Japanese larch
This large, spreading tree has blue-green foliage that turns an attractive golden-yellow in autumn. It is planted for its quick growth and good-quality timber. H 30m (100ft), S 6–10m (20–33ft).
Aspect Full sun.
Hardiness ❁❁❁ Zones 3–6.

L. laricina
Tamarack, American larch
The species has a conical habit with short branches clothed in blue-green foliage, which turns

Laurus nobilis

Licuala grandis

yellow in autumn. It is widely grown in North America for the quality of its timber and its ability (unusual among larches) to tolerate waterlogged soil. Among the hardiest of the larches, it is intolerant of high summer temperatures and is best grown in areas of high annual rainfall in acidic soil. H 25m (80ft), S 10m (33ft).
Aspect Full sun.
Hardiness ❁❁❁ Zones 1–5.

LAURUS
Laurel, bay
The two species of evergreen trees and shrubs in the genus are native to southern Europe, the Azores and the Canary Islands. They are grown for their small flowers and their aromatic leaves.
Cultivation Grow in moisture-retentive but well-drained soil in full sun.
Pruning Early formative pruning should aim to produce a clear trunk and a balanced crown. Bay trees can be grown as multi- or single-stemmed trees, so training should encourage either type.
Propagation Softwood and semi-ripe cuttings can be taken during early and late summer, then be dipped in a rooting hormone and placed in a humid environment such as a greenhouse until rooting occurs. Low branches can be layered during the autumn or spring, then removed and potted on a year later.

L. nobilis
Bay, sweet bay
This is the species that is grown for culinary purposes. The dark green leaves, up to 10cm (4in) long, are highly aromatic. In spring small yellow-green flowers are borne in dense clusters, and these are followed in autumn on female plants by greenish-black berries. This is a useful evergreen for hedging in maritime areas, and it is tolerant of regular clipping. H and S 15m (50ft).
Named varieties 'Aurea' is a slower growing form. In spring the foliage is yellow, fading to greenish-yellow in summer. H 10m (33ft).
Aspect Full sun to semi-shade.
Hardiness ❁❁ Zone 8.

LICUALA
Palas
There are more than 100 species of stemless or shrubby, sometimes suckering, palms in the genus, mostly found in swamps or rainforests of Australasia and South-east Asia.

Cultivation Outdoors, grow in fertile, moisture-retentive but well-drained soil in full sun.
Pruning Little pruning is required apart from the removal of dead leaves and spent flower clusters.
Propagation Sow fresh seed into a container in a humid environment at 29°C (84°F) until germination occurs.

L. grandis
(syn. *Pritchardia grandis*)
Ruffled fan palm
The stem of this tropical palm is initially covered with a mat of brown fibres, which falls away as the palm ages, revealing the whitish-green trunk beneath. The large, glossy, semicircular leaves are sometimes divided into three sections, each up to 1m (3ft) across and deeply corrugated with serrated edges. Long spikes of pale green flowers are borne in summer. H and S 3m (10ft).
Aspect Semi-shade when young, full sun when mature.
Hardiness (Min. 15–16°C/59–61°F) Zone 11.

Laurus nobilis 'Aurea'

Liquidambar styraciflua 'Variegata'

L. ramsayi
(syn. *L. muelleri*)

This single-stemmed palm is native to Australia. It has large, corrugated, semicircular, green leaves, up to 1m or more across, which are divided into several sections, some joined together at the tips. Cream-coloured flowers, borne in large spikes in summer, are followed by round red fruits. H 12m (40ft), S to 5m (16ft).
Aspect Semi-shade when young, full sun when mature.
Hardiness ✽ Zone 11.

LIGUSTRUM
Privet

The genus of about 50 evergreen, semi-evergreen and deciduous trees and shrubs is best known for hedging plants, but a number of the species can be grown as focal points or specimen trees, when they display an attractive round-headed shape, bold foliage, attractive flowers and bark.
Cultivation Grow in well-drained soil in sun or semi-shade.

Pruning Early formative pruning should aim to produce a clear trunk and a balanced crown. Tipping the branches of young trees will encourage a denser crown. Occasional pruning only is required for the removal of dead, dying, diseased or crossing branches.
Propagation Seed should be collected when fresh, and be sown into a container in an unheated glasshouse or cold frame until germination occurs. Semi-ripe cuttings are taken during late summer, and are dipped in a rooting hormone, then placed in a humid environment until rooting occurs. The variegated forms are often winter grafted on to seedling privet as they are difficult to root from cuttings.

L. lucidum
Chinese privet

This evergreen is a stunning large shrub or small garden tree, especially if given sufficient space to develop, when it will assume an almost symmetrical shape. The glossy, dark green leaves, up to 8cm (3in) long, taper to a point and are an excellent foil for the masses of fragrant creamy-white flowers that appear in summer. In late summer small blue-black berries follow the flowers. Eventually, it will develop smooth, silver-grey, fluted bark. It can be planted as a lawn specimen in a small garden or grown as a multi-stemmed tree, and it is widely planted as a small street tree in warmer climates. A good choice for urban locations as it seems to be tolerant of atmospheric pollution. H and S 12m (40ft).
Named varieties 'Excelsum Superbum' is a slower growing form, which is one of the most beautiful of all variegated evergreen trees. The leaves have bold yellow margins and silver-white variegation. New foliage is tinged with pink.
Aspect Full sun or semi-shade.
Hardiness ✽✽✽ Zone 7.

LIQUIDAMBAR

The four species of deciduous tree in the genus have maple-like leaves, which colour well in autumn. Trees bear insignificant flowers in spring, and after long, hot summers these are followed by clusters of round fruit. They are grown to their conical habit, which makes them excellent specimen trees.
Cultivation Grow in moisture-retentive but well-drained, neutral to acidic soil in full sun (for best autumn colour) or semi-shade. Protect young plants from cold winter winds.

Pruning Sweet gums are prone to wind damage. Ensure that an even balanced crown is developed by formative pruning and any narrow angled, weakly attached codominant stems are removed.
Propagation Collect seed when fresh and sow in a pot in an unheated glasshouse or a cold frame until germination occurs. Take softwood cuttings in early summer and keep in a humid environment until rooting occurs. Selected forms are grafted on to seed-grown sweet gums and are either indoor grafted in winter or budded in summer.

L. styraciflua
Sweet gum

This widely grown, broadly conical, ornamental tree has large, maple-like leaves and good autumn colour. The three- to seven-lobed leaves, up to 15cm (6in) across, are green in summer, turning shades of red, purple and orange in autumn. Older stems have a corky appearance. H 25m (80ft), S 10–12m (33 40ft).
Named varieties 'Burgundy' is a strongly growing form with purple-tinted foliage which turns dark purple in autumn and persists into winter.

The clone 'Lane Roberts' has foliage that turns purple in late summer before becoming crimson-purple-black in autumn.

'Moonbeam' has pinkish-yellow mottled leaves, which turn green in summer and red, yellow and purple in autumn. H 10m (33ft), S 6m (20ft).

'Palo Alto' has one of the neatest habits of growth, and has scarlet and orange autumn colour.

Ligustrum lucidium

Liriodendron tulipifera

'Slender Silhouette' is an upright form with red and purple autumn colour; it only occasionally produces fruit.

'Stared' is a graceful form with deeply lobed leaves that turn red-orange in autumn.

The beautiful 'Variegata' has new leaves that are edged with cream and are flushed pink in summer before turning yellow and orange in autumn. H 15m (50ft), S 8m (26ft).

The leaves of the popular form 'Worplesdon' turn purple and then orange-yellow in autumn; it occasionally bears fruit.
Aspect Full sun or semi-shade.
Hardiness ❀❀❀ Zones 5–9.

LIRIODENDRON
The two large, fast-growing deciduous trees are often grown as specimen trees, when the leaves take on good autumn colour.
Cultivation Grow in fertile, moisture-retentive but well-drained, slightly acidic soil in full sun or semi-shade.
Pruning The branches are brittle so care should be taken to ensure that an even balanced crown is developed by formative pruning. Remove narrow angled, weakly attached codominant stems.
Propagation Seed, softwood cuttings, grafting and budding are the most common forms of propagation. Collect seeds when fresh, and sow into a container in an unheated glasshouse or cold frame until germination occurs. Take softwood cuttings during early summer, then dip them in a rooting hormone and place in a humid environment until rooting occurs. The selected forms are grafted on seed-grown tulip trees and are either winter indoor grafted or budded during summer.

L. chinense
Chinese tulip tree
Initially upright in habit, this tree becomes more spreading with age. The three-lobed leaves are dark green, turning yellow in autumn. Greenish-yellow, tulip-like flowers, up to 4cm (1½in) long, are produced in summer. H 20–22m (65–72ft), S 10–12m (33–40ft).
Aspect Full sun.
Hardiness ❀❀❀ Zones 6–9.

L. tulipifera
Tulip tree
This ultimately large tree often sheds its lower branches as it ages. The dark green leaves, up to 15cm (6in) long, are shallowly lobed and turn yellow in autumn. In spring numerous, yellow-green tulip-like flowers, up to 6cm (2½in) long, are borne. H 35m (115ft), S 15–20m (50–65ft).
Named varieties
'Aureomarginatum' is a slower growing form. The leaves are broadly edged with bright yellow, which turns yellow-green in summer to leave a lighter shadow around the edge of the leaves, which turn yellow in autumn. H 20m (65ft), S 10m (33ft).

'Fastigiatum' is an erect, columnar form with twisted, upswept branches. H 15–20m (50–65ft), S 4–8m (12–26ft).

The leaves of 'Mediopictum' have a yellow blotch in the centre, and this does not fade in summer.
Aspect Full sun.
Hardiness ❀❀❀ Zones 4–9.

LITHOCARPUS
This is a large genus of about 300 species of evergreen trees and shrubs. They are found mostly in eastern and southern Asia, but one species is native to North America.
Cultivation Grow in fertile, moisture-retentive but well-drained, neutral to acidic soil in sun or semi-shade.
Pruning Early formative pruning should produce a clear trunk and a balanced crown. Tipping the branches of young trees will encourage a denser crown. Occasional pruning is required for the removal of dead, dying, diseased or crossing branches.
Propagation Seed should be collected when fresh, and sown into a container in an unheated glasshouse or cold frame until germination occurs.

L. edulis
This species is a spreading, small tree, with long, tapering leaves, which are glossy, pale green above and dull green beneath. It produces erect clusters of creamy-white flowers in spring, followed in autumn by masses of acorns with an edible nut inside. H and S 10m (33ft).
Aspect Full sun.
Hardiness ❀❀ Zone 7.

L. henryi
This slow-growing, ornamental tree has pale green, lance-shaped leaves, up to 25cm (10in) long, and a rounded habit. Small white flowers are borne in spikes in late summer, followed by clusters of acorns. H and S 10m (33ft).
Aspect Full sun.
Hardiness ❀❀ Zone 7.

LIVISTONA
Fountain palm
The 28 species of palm in the genus are native to Asia and Australasia. They have single, erect, grey stems. As they age they become ringed and marked with the scars from old leaf cases.
Cultivation Outdoors, grow in fertile, moisture-retentive but well-drained soil in sun or semi-shade. These palms will not tolerate winter wet.
Pruning Little pruning is required apart from the removal of dead leaves and spent flower clusters during early summer.
Propagation Seed is the easiest method of propagation. Sow fresh seed into a pot in a heated glasshouse in a humid environment at 29°C (84°F) until germination occurs.

L. australis
Australian fan palm, cabbage palm
The upright trunk becomes silver-grey as it ages. The semicircular leaves, which can be 1.8m (6ft) or more across and which are borne on long stems, have up to 70 linear lobes, each about half the length of the leaves. These droop gracefully. Flower spikes, to 1.8m (6ft) long, are borne in summer and are followed by brownish, red or black fruits. H 25m (80ft), S 5m (16ft).
Aspect Full sun to light shade.
Hardiness (Min. 3–5°C/37–41°F) Zones 9–11.

L. chinensis
Chinese fan palm, Chinese fountain palm
The glossy green leaves of this palm, to 1.8m (6ft) wide, are nearly circular but have longer drooping tips than *L. australis*, and these give an elegant appearance. H 12m (40ft), S 5m (16ft).
Aspect Full sun to light shade.
Hardiness (Min. 3–5°C/37–41°F) Zones 9–11.

Lithocarpus edulis

Maackia amurensis

MAACKIA

There are about eight species of slow-growing, deciduous trees in the genus, and they are native to eastern Asia. They have attractive foliage and flowers and are grown as small specimen trees.

Cultivation Grow in moisture-retentive but well-drained, neutral to acidic soil in full sun.

Pruning Early formative pruning should aim to produce a clear trunk and a balanced crown. Occasional pruning is required for the removal of dead, dying, diseased or crossing branches.

Propagation Seed is the main method of propagation and should be collected when fresh, then be soaked in hot water for 24 hours and sown into a container in an unheated glasshouse or cold frame until germination occurs.

M. amurensis

This attractive tree has dark green, walnut-like foliage and small, erect clusters of bluish-white flowers in late summer. The flowers are followed in autumn by seedpods up to 5cm (2in) long, and the leaves turn pale yellow. H and S 15m (50ft).
Aspect Full sun.
Hardiness ❀❀❀ Zones 4–7.

MAGNOLIA

The 125 species of deciduous and evergreen trees and shrubs in the genus include some of the most beautiful of all flowering trees. They have been widely hybridized to produce numerous named forms, developed not only for their flower size and colour, including yellow, but also in an attempt to create later flowering forms so that the delicate blooms are not damaged by late spring frosts.

Cultivation Grow in fertile, moisture-retentive but well-drained, acidic soil in sun or semi-shade. *M. delavayi* and *M. grandiflora* will grow in dry alkaline soil. *M. kobus*, *M.* x *loebneri*, *M. sieboldii*, *M. stellata* and *M. wilsonii* will grow in moisture-retentive, alkaline soil. Protect plants from strong winds.

Pruning Magnolias need a lot of formative pruning when young so that a clear stem and even branch work can be developed. Long, whippy branches are often produced and these should be reduced in overall length during summer. Grafted and budded plants sometimes produce root suckers, which should be removed during summer.

Propagation Seed, softwood cuttings, grafting and budding are the most common forms of propagation. Seed should be collected when fresh, the brightly coloured seed coat should be removed and then sown into a container out-of-doors in an unheated glasshouse or cold frame until germination occurs. Softwood cuttings are taken during early summer, dipped in a rooting hormone and then placed in a humid environment until rooting occurs. Selected forms are grafted on to seed-grown magnolias and are either winter indoor grafted or budded during summer. Evergreen magnolias can be propagated by semi-ripe cuttings during summer, dipped in a rooting hormone and then placed in a humid environment until rooting occurs.

M. 'Albatross'

This fast-growing hybrid of *M. cylindrica* and *M.* x *veitchii* has large white flowers, flushed pink toward the base, borne in mid-spring. It makes a small, upright, deciduous tree. H and S 6m (20ft).
Aspect Full sun to semi-shade.
Hardiness ❀❀ Zone 7.

M. 'Apollo'

This free-flowering, medium-sized, deciduous tree bears dark purple-pink flowers. H and S 6m (20ft).
Aspect Full sun to semi-shade.
Hardiness ❀❀ Zone 7.

M. 'Athene'

This deciduous tree has an upright habit and bears large, white, scented flowers that are tinged with pink at the base. H and S 6m (20ft).
Aspect Full sun to semi-shade.
Hardiness ❀❀ Zone 7.

M. 'Atlas'

This quick-growing deciduous tree produces lilac-pink flowers soon after planting. H and S 6m (20ft).
Aspect Full sun to semi-shade.
Hardiness ❀❀ Zone 7.

Magnolia campbellii subsp. *mollicomata* 'Lanarth'

Magnolia grandiflora 'Goliath'

M. 'Butterflies'
This upright tree produces beautiful, canary yellow flowers. H and S 6m (20ft).
Aspect Full sun to semi-shade.
Hardiness ❀❀❀ Zones 4–9.

M. campbellii
Campbell's magnolia
This vigorous deciduous magnolia, sometimes called the Queen of Magnolias, is native to the Himalayas, from eastern Nepal, Sikkim and Bhutan to Assam. It is a variable tree, with elliptic mid-green leaves, up to 25cm (10in) long, and white, red or pale pink flowers with 12–16 tepals, which are borne before the leaves in late winter to early spring.

The flowers are known as cup-and-saucer type because the inner tepals remain upright, while the outer ones flop outwards. The flowers are particularly susceptible to frosts in late winter and early spring. H 15–20m (50–65ft), S 10m (33ft).
Named varieties The Alba Group includes a number of seed-raised forms with pretty white flowers, which are more common in the wild than the pink-flowering form that was first introduced .

M. campbellii subsp. *mollicomata* 'Lanarth' is a hardier and more compact form that produces masses of lilac-purple flowers in late winter and early spring.

M. campbellii (Raffilli Group) 'Charles Raffill' is a fast-growing, tree like magnolia with dark pink flowers that open purple-pink.
Aspect Full sun to semi-shade.
Hardiness ❀❀❀ Zones 7–9.

M. 'Elizabeth'
This stunning deciduous form produces bright yellow, scented flowers, up to 15cm (6in) across, on bare branches in spring. The dark green leaves, up to 20cm (8in) long, are tinged with bronze when they emerge. H 10m (33ft), S 6m (20ft).
Aspect Full sun to semi-shade.
Hardiness ❀❀❀ Zones 5–9.

M. 'Galaxy'
This small, fast-growing deciduous tree bears large, fragrant, purple-pink flowers, up to 20cm (8in) across, just before the leaves appear in spring. H 12m (40ft), S 8m (26ft).
Aspect Full sun to semi-shade.
Hardiness ❀❀❀ Zone 7.

M. 'Gold Star'
Attractive, star-shaped, ivory-white to pale yellow flowers are produced on this pyramidal deciduous tree, which is a hybrid of *M. acuminata* var. *subcordata* 'Miss Honeybee' and *M. stellata* 'Rubra'. It has red-tinged young growth. H and S 10m (33ft).
Aspect Full sun to semi-shade.
Hardiness ❀❀❀ Zones 5–9.

M. grandiflora
Bull bay
This exceptional tree, which exhibits great heat tolerance, is one of the most imposing of the evergreen magnolias – indeed, of all flowering trees. It is native to the southern USA, from North Carolina to central Florida and into Texas and Arkansas. It has glossy, dark green leaves, up to 20cm (8in) long, and from late summer to early autumn it bears creamy-white, cup-shaped flowers, which may be up to 25cm (10in) across. In cooler areas it is often grown against walls so that it can benefit from the warmth in winter and the shelter from cold, drying winds. H 25m (80ft), S 10m (33ft).
Named varieties 'Alta' is a strongly growing, upright form. The dark green leaves have brown undersides. Glossy, creamy-white flowers are produced in summer and then occasionally in autumn. H 10m (33ft).

The widely grown 'Bracken's Brown Beauty' is a dense tree. It has glossy, dark green leaves with russet brown undersides and produces masses of flowers.

The fast-growing 'Claudia Wannamaker' is a fine form with dark green leaves with rusty-brown undersides, and it flowers from an early age.

'Goliath', a rather bushy form, is grown for its scented, creamy-white flowers, up to 30cm (12in) across, and large pale green leaves. 'Hasse' is a small-leaved form, with masses of flowers and a strongly pright habit. H 14m (46ft), S 4m (12ft).
Aspect Full sun to semi-shade.
Hardiness ❀❀ Zones 7–9.

Magnolia stellata

M. 'Ivory Chalice'

This hybrid produces masses of pale yellow flowers throughout spring, with the main flush appearing just before the leaves. H and S 6m (20ft).
Aspect Full sun to semi-shade.
Hardiness ❁❁❁ Zones 5–9.

M. kobus

This small, generally round-headed but rather variable, deciduous tree is found in forests throughout Japan. The mid-green leaves, up to 20cm (8in) long, smell of aniseed if crushed. It has creamy-white flowers, sometimes tinged purple at the base, in mid-spring. H 12m (40ft), S 10m (33ft).
Aspect Full sun to semi-shade.
Hardiness ❁❁❁ Zones 4–8.

M. x loebneri
Loebner's magnolia

This hybrid between *M. kobus* and *M. stellata* is a fast-growing, broadly spreading deciduous tree. The mid-green leaves are about 12cm (5in) long, and star-shaped white flowers, flushed pink-purple inside and out, are borne in mid-spring. H 10m (33ft), S 7m (23ft).
Named varieties The popular cultivar 'Leonard Messel' is widely planted for its frost-resistant, pink-tinged white flowers. H 8m (26ft), S 6m (20ft).

'Neil McEacharn' is an early-flowering form with pink-tinged buds that open creamy-white.

'Raspberry Fun', a form with darker pink flowers, originated in Korea from seed collected from 'Leonard Messel'.

'White Stardust' is a vigorous form, flowering early in spring with masses of white flowers and good dark green foliage.
Aspect Full sun to semi-shade.
Hardiness ❁❁❁ Zones 3–7.

M. 'Lois'

This is one of the best and most reliable of the yellow-flowered magnolias for cooler climates where it reliably produces primrose yellow flowers, which are borne just before the leaves emerge. H and S 6m (20ft).
Aspect Full sun to semi-shade.
Hardiness ❁❁❁ Zones 5–9.

M. obovata
(syn. M. hypoleuca)
Japanese big-leaf magnolia

This strongly growing, deciduous species, which is native to Japan, has large, mid-green leaves, up to 40cm (16in) long, and creamy-white, highly scented flowers in late spring to early summer. It is a hardy species but must have acidic soil. H 15m (50ft), S 10m (33ft).
Aspect Full sun to semi-shade.
Hardiness ❁❁❁ Zones 5–7.

M. x soulangeana
Chinese magnolia, saucer magnolia

This variable, deciduous hybrid between *M. denudata* and *M. liliiflora* is one of the most widely planted of the hybrid magnolias thanks to its tolerance of a wide range of soils and atmospheric pollution. It is a spreading small tree or multi-stemmed large shrub, with dark green leaves and goblet-shaped flowers, which may be white, deep pink or purple-pink and are borne in mid- to late spring. H and S 6m (10ft).
Named varieties Several lovely cultivars have been developed. 'Alba' (syn. 'Alba Superba') is a dense, erect small tree with scented white flowers.

The upright 'Alexandrina', one of the most widely planted forms, has masses of large saucer-shaped,

white flowers, which are flushed purple at the base and have a lovely scent.

The larger and later flowering 'Brozzonii' has large white flowers, up to 25cm (10in) across and flushed with purple at the base. H 8m (26ft).
Aspect Full sun to semi-shade.
Hardiness ❁❁❁ Zones 4–9.

M. stellata
Star magnolia

This is perhaps the best-known and possibly the most widely planted species, with its compact habit and lovely, star-shaped flowers. It is a slow-growing, deciduous plant, eventually making a dense shrub or, sometimes, a small tree. The dark green leaves are up to 20cm (8in) long, and the flowers, which range in colour from white to rose pink and purple, are borne in mid- to late spring, just as the leaves are emerging. It does best in moisture-retentive soil in a sunny position. Protect the flower buds from cold, drying winds. H 3m (10ft), S 4m (12ft).
Named varieties Among the many cultivars 'Centennial' is an upright, conical form with numerous, 28- to 32-tepalled white flowers up to 14cm (5½in) across.

'Rosea' is a vigorous form, occasionally suckering, but quickly forming a small tree that

Malus 'John Downie'

produces masses of white flowers, delicately tinged with pink and striped with pink on the outside.
Aspect Full sun to semi-shade.
Hardiness ❁❁❁ Zones 4–9.

M. x veitchii

This deciduous hybrid between *M. campbellii* and *M. denudata* is a large, upright magnolia. It has obovate leaves, up to 30cm (12in) long, which are tinged with purple when they first emerge. The pink to white flowers are borne in mid-spring, before the leaves. H 30m (100ft), S 10m (33ft).
Named varieties In late spring, before the leaves appear, the

Magnolia x *loebneri* 'Merrill'

Malus 'Butterball'

Malus 'Evereste'

hardier cultivar 'Peter Veitch' has goblet-shaped, white flowers, faintly flushed with purple pink.
Aspect Full sun to semi-shade.
Hardiness ❀❀ Zone 7.

MALUS
Apple, crab apple
This genus of about 35 deciduous trees and shrubs includes the orchard apple, *Malus sylvestris* var. *domestica*. It also includes a group of ornamental hybrid crab apples, which are grown for their spring flowers and autumn fruits and also the good autumn colour that many display. They have been hybridized to tolerate a range of soil conditions and to have good disease resistance.
Cultivation Grow in moisture-retentive but well-drained soil in sun. Purple-leaved forms produce their best colour in sun.
Pruning Early formative pruning should aim to produce a clear trunk and a balanced crown. Tipping the branches of young trees will encourage a denser crown. Crab apples are prone to fireblight, canker and occasionally silver leaf and this should be removed as soon as symptoms occur. Occasional pruning is required to remove dead, dying, diseased or crossing branches.
Propagation Seed is used to propagate the species while cultivars are budded on to seed-grown rootstocks. Seed should be collected when fresh, and be sown into a container in an

unheated glasshouse or cold frame until germination occurs. Budding is undertaken during summer.

M. 'American Beauty'
This vigorous US form has exceptionally large, double, red flowers, up to 4cm (1½in) across, and bronze-red foliage that turns bronze-green. It does not produce fruit. H and S 8m (26ft).
Aspect Full sun.
Hardiness ❀❀❀ Zones 4–7.

M. 'Butterball'
In spring this small, spreading tree produces pink-tinged buds, which open to white flowers. The orange-yellow fruits, to 2.5cm (1in) across, persist long into winter. H and S 8m (26ft).
Aspect Full sun.
Hardiness ❀❀❀ Zones 4–7.

M. 'Callaway'
Popular in the USA because of its disease resistance, this small tree bears single, scented, white flowers in spring, which open from pink buds, and large reddish-maroon fruits on pendulous branches. H and S 8m (26ft).
Aspect Full sun.
Hardiness ❀❀❀ Zones 4–7.

M. 'Evereste'
This small, conical tree has dark green leaves, which are sometimes lobed. In late spring, white flowers open from red buds, followed by large, orange-yellow,

Malus 'Striped Beauty'

red-flushed fruits. Unlike some other crab apples, it retains a good shape as it matures. H and S 7m (23ft).
Aspect Full sun.
Hardiness ❀❀❀ Zones 4–7.

M. floribunda
Japanese crab apple
This graceful, broadly spreading tree has lobed, dark green leaves. In mid-spring the tree is covered with crimson buds, from which open white or pale pink flowers. In autumn small yellow fruits hang from the branches in clusters. It is usually the first crab apple to flower in spring.

H and S 5m (16ft).
Aspect Full sun.
Hardiness ❀❀❀ Zones 4–7.

M. hupehensis
Rather larger than the average crab apple, this vigorous species develops into a spreading tree. In early summer the dark green leaves are almost completely hidden by the white flowers, and these are followed in autumn by small, cherry-like, dark red fruits. H and S 12m (40ft).
Aspect Full sun.
Hardiness ❀❀❀ Zones 4–7.

M. 'John Downie'
Initially erect but developing into a broadly conical tree, this has attractive bright green leaves. In spring small, starry, white flowers open from pink buds. These are followed by orange and red fruits, which are borne in long-stalked clusters. H 10m (33ft), S 6m (20ft).
Aspect Full sun.
Hardiness ❀❀❀ Zones 4–7.

M. 'Red Sentinel'
This self-fertile tree is best known for its clusters of attractive red crab apples which persist well into the winter. The blossom is white with pink tinges, and is scented. It makes an attractive specimen tree for a small to medium-sized garden.

Malus pumila

Malus 'Red Sentinel'

It is also attractive to wildlife.
H and S 8m (26ft).
Aspect Full sun or partial shade.
Hardiness ❀❀❀ Zones 4–7.

M. transitoria

This wide-spreading, semi-weeping tree has small, bright green leaves, which turn yellow in autumn. In spring white flowers open from pink buds, and in autumn there are masses of small, cherry-like, golden-yellow fruits, which are hidden among the stunning orange-yellow autumn colour but are revealed again once the leaves fall. H 8m (26ft), S 10m (33ft).
Aspect Full sun.
Hardiness ❀❀❀ Zones 5–7.

MALUS SYLVESTRIS VAR. DOMESTICA
Common apple

This is a huge range of trees that produce edible apples. They are usually upright, spreading and covered in white, cup-shaped flowers in mid- and late spring, followed by apples in autumn.
Cultivation Apples fruit best if they are grown in full sun, with some shelter from wind to allow pollination by bees. Soil conditions can vary, but a free-draining, fertile soil is best.
Pruning Remove any dead, diseased or damaged branches during winter. Thin out spurs that are over-congested along the stems leaving the strongest to encourage large healthy fruit.
Propagation Propagate either by chip- or T-budding in summer or whip-and-tongue grafting on to certified rootstock in early spring to control the ultimate size.

M. s. var. d. 'American Golden Russet' (syn. 'Sheep Snout')

This is a widely grown Irish dessert and culinary apple that was exported to America, and became known as the 'American Golden Russet'. It is not self-fertile and so requires a pollinator. It produces large, yellow-russet fruits that are sharp and crisp to taste and shaped like a sheep's nose. Widely grown on MM.106. rootstock where it will grow to 5m tall and wide (18ft x 18ft).
Aspect Full sun.
Hardiness ❀❀❀ Zones 5–8.

M. s. var. d. 'Braeburn'

Bred in New Zealand, this is now widely grown for its medium to large apples that have a sweet and crisp flavour and a yellow-green skin with reddish stripes. Often grafted onto a M.26. rootstock where it will grow 4m wide and tall (12ft x 12ft).
Aspect Full sun.
Hardiness ❀❀❀ Zones 5–9.

M. s. var. d. 'Bramley Seedling'

This classic and widely grown cooking apple needs to be pollinated by two different types of apples as it is a triploid variety. Large green, blushed red apples are produced in mid-autumn and can be stored all winter. Ultimately 10m tall and wide (33ft x 33ft), although if grafted on to a dwarfing rootstock such as M.26. it may only reach 4m tall and wide (12ft x 12ft).
Aspect Full sun.
Hardiness ❀❀❀ Zones 5–9.

M. s. var. d. 'Cox's Orange Pippin'

Enduringly popular since its introduction in the early 19th century, this reddish, orange and green apple has a distinct, sharp and sweet taste and holds its shape well when baked. If it is grafted on to a vigorous rootstock it can become quite a large and unruly tree, so it is best grafted on to a less vigorous rootstock. On M.7. it will grow to 5m tall and wide (18ft x 18ft).
Aspect Full sun.
Hardiness ❀❀❀ Zones 5–9.

M. s. var. d. 'Discovery'

One of the most widely planted eating apples, this is especially suitable for garden use since the fruit is best picked straight from the tree as soon as it is ripe. It is also partially self-fertile so can be pollinated easily by a crab apple or another fruiting apple. Often grafted on to an M.26. rootstock where it will grow 4m wide and tall (12ft x 12ft).
Aspect Full sun.
Hardiness ❀❀❀ Zones 5–9.

M. s. var. d. 'Egremont Russet'

This is the best of the russets and is grown for its strong but sweet taste, crisp and firm flesh, and because it stores relatively well. It is most often grafted on to an M.26. rootstock where it will grow 4m wide and tall (12ft x 12ft).
Aspect Full sun.
Hardiness ❀❀❀ Zones 5–9.

M. s. var. d. 'Golden Delicious'

This popular dessert apple is grown in warmer climates, where it is quick-growing and yields large crops of pale-yellow-skinned, light-flavoured apples. Requires additional pollinators and is often

Malus x schiedeckeri 'Hillieri'

Malus sylvestris var. *domestica*

M. s. var. d. 'Laxton's Superb'
This is a late cropping 'Cox's Orange Pippin' hybrid that was bred at Laxton's Nursery, England, in 1904, and was an immediate success due to its late ripening, good flavour and reddish orange-yellow colour. Often grown on M.26. rootstock where it will grow to 4m tall and wide (12ft x 12ft).
Aspect Full sun.
Hardiness ❀❀❀ Zones 5–9.

M. s. var. d. 'Liberty'
A widely grown American selection, this is bred for its disease resistance, its well-balanced sweet and sharp flavour and attractive red skin. Requires additional pollinators and is often grown on MM.106. rootstock where it will grow to 5m tall and wide (18ft x 18ft).
Aspect Full sun.
Hardiness ❀❀❀ Zones 5–8.

M. s. var. d. 'Spartan'
This Canadian introduction has extreme cold hardiness. The tree produces apples that have a soft and sweet flesh and a crimson red skin. It makes an excellent cropping tree and one of the best cold climate apples. Best grown on M.26., where it will reach 4m tall and wide (12ft x 12ft).
Aspect Full sun.
Hardiness ❀❀❀ Zones 3–9.

grown on MM.106. rootstock where it will grow to 5m tall and wide (18ft x 18ft).
Aspect Full sun.
Hardiness ❀❀❀ Zones 5–8.

M. s. var. d. 'Golden Pippin'
An old-fashioned variety with small fruits, this has a distinct lemon aftertaste and can be used for eating, cooking and cider or juice making. Holds it shape and colour well when cooked. It is best picked in autumn and can be stored all winter. Requires another apple to pollinate it as it is not self-fertile. Widely grown on MM.106. rootstock where it will grow to 5m tall and wide (18ft x 18ft).
Aspect Full sun.
Hardiness ❀❀❀ Zones 5–8.

M. s. var. d. 'Granny Smith'
This is one of the most famous and widely grown eating apples. Originally introduced from Australia in the 1900s, it is known for its lime green colour, tart, crisp flesh and late cropping. Requires another pollinator, and is often grown on MM.106.,

where it can grow to 4m tall and wide (12ft x12ft).
Aspect Full sun.
Hardiness ❀❀❀ Zones 5–8.

M. s. var. d. 'Howgate Wonder'
This apple is mainly grown for exhibition purposes since it can grow to an enormous size – up to 1.7kg (3lb 14oz).
Aspect Full sun.
Hardiness ❀❀❀ Zones 3–9.

M. s. var. d. 'Idared'
This apple is grown for both culinary and dessert use and has a sharp but sweet taste and long storability. It is an excellent garden variety, especially if it is grafted on to a dwarfing rootstock such as M.26., where it will reach 4m tall and wide (12ft x 12ft).
Aspect Full sun.
Hardiness ❀❀❀ Zones 4–9.

M. s. var. d. 'James Grieve'
This very sweet and juicy green apple is suitable for both dessert use and cooking. It ripens during early autumn and is best used before the end of the season. Reasonable fruit set is always

guaranteed as it is self-fertile, although fertilization by another apple will dramatically increase the yield. Grown on M.26. rootstock, it will reach 4m tall and wide (12ft x 12ft).
Aspect Full sun.
Hardiness ❀❀❀ Zones 5–8.

Malus sylvestris var. *domestica* 'Laxton's Epicure'

MAYTENUS

The genus contains about 225 species of evergreen trees and shrubs, which are native to tropical Africa and North and South America.

Cultivation Grow in moisture-retentive but well-drained soil in full sun. Protect plants from cold, drying winds.

Pruning Early formative pruning should aim to produce a clear trunk and a balanced crown.

Propagation Seed is the main method of propagation and should be collected when fresh and sown into a container in an unheated glasshouse or cold frame until germination occurs.

M. boaria
(syn. *M. chilensis*)
Mayten

This fast-growing but variable tree has a beautiful weeping habit, although some plants weep more strongly than others. In addition, some forms produce a thicket of root suckers, whereas other forms do not produce any suckers at all. It has glossy, dark green leaves, up to 5cm (2in) long. In sunny areas small clusters of pale green flowers are borne in mid- to late spring, and these are followed by red-orange seedpods. Hardiness can depend on where exactly the seeds or cuttings were collected, because the species has a wide

Maytenus boaria

natural range in Chile. H 20m (65ft), S 10m (33ft).
Aspect Full sun.
Hardiness ❀❀❀ Zone 8.

MELIA

There are three to five species of deciduous or semi-evergreen trees and shrubs in the genus. They are native to India, China, South-east Asia and northern Australia and are grown as specimen trees in warm areas.

Cultivation Outdoors, grow in well-drained soil in full sun.

Pruning Formative pruning should aim to encourage a clear trunk and a balanced crown. Occasional pruning is required for the removal of dead, dying, diseased or crossing branches.

Propagation Seed should be collected when fresh and sown into a container in a heated glasshouse in a frost-free and humid environment until germination occurs.

M. azedarach
Bead tree, pride of India, Persian lilac

A fast-growing but fairly short-lived deciduous tree, it is grown for its fragrant, star-shaped, lilac-coloured flowers, which are borne from spring to early summer, and for the attractive yellow fruits that follow and that persist into winter, when they are readily distributed by birds. H 10–15m (33–50ft), S 8–10m (26–33ft). Named varieties 'Jade Snowflake' is a pretty and more compact form with creamy-white speckled leaves. H and S 8m (26ft).
Aspect Full sun.
Hardiness (Min. 7°C/45°F) Zones 7–12.

METASEQUOIA
Dawn redwood

The single species of deciduous coniferous tree in the genus is native to central China. It was originally known only from fossil records until it was discovered growing in a valley in China in 1941. Since then it has been widely grown throughout the world because of its extreme beauty and year-round interest.

Cultivation Grow in fertile, moisture-retentive but well-

Metasequoia glyptostroboides 'Gold Rush'

drained soil in full sun. Trees seem to do better in areas with warm summers.

Pruning Formative pruning should aim to produce a clear trunk and a balanced crown. Tipping the lateral branches of young trees will encourage a denser crown.

Propagation Seed is the easiest method of propagation and should be collected when fresh and sown into a container in an unheated glasshouse or cold frame until germination occurs. Semi-ripe and softwood cuttings can be rooted during summer and should be dipped in a rooting hormone and placed in a humid environment until rooting occurs. Hardwood cuttings will also root during the winter if a rooting hormone is applied to the cutting.

M. glyptostroboides

This beautiful and fast-growing tree has fern-like, bright green foliage, which turns yellow-brown or pinkish-brown in autumn. Mature trees have corrugated fluted trunks, clothed in cinnamon-brown bark. H 40m (130ft), S 10–20m wide (33–65ft).
Named varieties The fast-growing 'Emerald Feathers' has an

attractive habit, with weeping new shoots. The lime-green leaves colour well in autumn.

'Gold Rush' (syn. 'Ogon') has stunning yellow foliage in spring, and this fades to yellow-green in summer. It is slower growing than the green-leaved forms.

'National' (syn. 'Fastigiata') is a fast-growing, narrow cultivar.
Aspect Full sun.
Hardiness ❀❀❀ Zones 3–7.

METROSIDEROS
Rata, pohutakawa

There are about 50 species of evergreen trees and shrubs in the genus. They are native to South Africa, Malaysia and Australasia.

Cultivation Outdoors, grow in fertile, moisture-retentive but well-drained, neutral to acidic soil in sun. Protect plants from cold, drying winds.

Pruning Formative pruning should aim to encourage a clear trunk and a balanced crown, while tipping the lateral branches of young trees will encourage a denser crown. Occasional pruning is required for the removal of dead, dying, diseased or crossing branches.

Propagation Seed is the easiest method of propagation and should be collected when fresh and sown into a container in a heated glasshouse in a frost-free and humid environment until germination occurs. Low branches can also be layered into the soil.

M. excelsus
(syn. *M. tomentosa*)
Common pohutakawa, New Zealand Christmas tree
This tree is native to New Zealand, and in summer masses of stunning, bright scarlet, spider-like inflorescences cover the foliage as the tree explodes into bloom. (The flowers themselves are small, but the stamens are long and feathery.) The attractive leaves, up to 10cm (4in) long, are glossy, dark green above and covered with silver-white hairs beneath. H 20m (65ft), S 15m (50ft).
Aspect Full sun.
Hardiness ❋ Zone 9–11.

M. robusta
Northern rata
This tall but slender tree from New Zealand has dark green leaves, which are covered with silver-white hairs on the undersides. The inflorescences, up to 3cm (1½in) long, are matt crimson and are displayed in dense terminal clusters. H 30m (100ft), S 10–12m (33–40ft).
Aspect Full sun.
Hardiness ❋ Zones 9–11.

Metrosideros excelsus

MICHELIA
Banana shrub, port wine magnolia
There are about 45 species of evergreen or deciduous trees and shrubs in the genus, which is closely related to *Magnolia*. Like magnolias, these plants produce lovely flowers, which are often fragrant, in spring or early summer, but the flowers are borne in the leaf axils, not terminally, as on magnolias.
Cultivation Outdoors, grow in fertile, moisture-retentive but well-drained, neutral to acidic soil in semi-shade.
Pruning For a formal appearance, trim annually after flowering.
Propagation Grow from softwood cuttings or from seed. Collect ripe seeds from fruit cones as they open. Otherwise, store the fruit cones until they open naturally, but do not allow the seeds to dry out too much. Sow in a peat-based compost, cover with 6mm (¼in) grit and place in a frost-free greenhouse until they germinate.

M. doltsopa
This small, rather shrubby, evergreen tree has glossy, dark green leaves, which are covered with grey hairs beneath. In spring to early summer fragrant, creamy-white flowers, up to 10cm (4in) across, are borne. H 15m (50ft), S 5–10m (16–33ft).
Named varieties 'Silver Cloud' is a large-flowering selection, originally raised in New Zealand. Semi-evergreen in cooler climates, it is totally evergreen in milder areas. In spring it bears masses of fragrant, large, white, magnolia-like flowers.
Aspect Full sun to semi-shade.
Hardiness (Min. 5°C/41°F) Zones 8–9.

MORUS
Mulberry
The genus contains 10–12 species of deciduous trees and shrubs. They are native to South and North America, Africa and Asia and are grown as specimen trees for their attractive toothed and lobed leaves and for their edible autumn fruits.
Cultivation Grow in fertile, moisture-retentive but well-drained soil in full sun. Protect

Michelia doltsopa

from cold, drying winds. Mulberries have brittle roots and should be planted and transplanted with care.
Pruning This must be done when the tree is completely dormant as if it is left until spring any wounds will bleed profusely. Pruning should aim to create an open, balanced canopy, and to remove any dying, damaged, dead or diseased branches.
Propagation Seed, grafting, or hardwood cuttings are the main methods of propagation. Sow fresh seed into a container in an unheated glasshouse or cold frame until germination occurs. Winter grafting on to seed-grown mulberries is commonly practised. Hardwood cuttings taken during the winter root easily and produce trees quickly.

M. alba
White mulberry
This spreading tree from eastern and central China is quite tolerant of drought, pollution and poor soil. It develops twisted branches as it matures. It has attractive heart-shaped, glossy, light green leaves, up to 20cm (8in) long, which turn yellow in autumn. In late spring and summer greenish-yellow catkins appear, followed in late summer by white fruits, up to 2.5cm (1in) long, which turn pink and red when they are ripe. H and S 10–15m (33–50ft).
Aspect Full sun.
Hardiness ❋❋❋ Zones 5–7.
Named varieties 'Pendula' is a low-growing weeping form.
  'Russian' is very hardy and drought-resistant form, which produces good-quality fruit.

Morus alba 'Pendula'

Nothofagus dombeyi

M. nigra
Black mulberry

More compact than *M. alba*, this species, which is believed to come from south-western Asia, has coarser, mid-green leaves, up to 15cm (6in) long, which turn golden-yellow in late autumn. The oval fruits are green when they first appear but ripen to red and dark purple. H and S 10m (33ft). Aspect Full sun.
Hardiness ❈❈❈ Zones 5–7.

M. rubra
Red mulberry

The species, which is native to North America, is larger than *M. alba* and *M. nigra*. It has dark green leaves, up to 12cm (5in) long, which turn yellow in autumn. The fruits are green at first, ripening to red and then purple. H 12m (40ft), S 15m (50ft). Aspect Full sun.
Hardiness ❈❈❈ Zones 5–7.

MYRTUS
Myrtle

The genus contains two species of evergreen trees, which are native to Mediterranean countries, including northern Africa. They are grown for their aromatic leaves and fragrant flowers.
Cultivation Grow in moisture-retentive but well-drained soil. Protect from cold, drying winds.
Pruning Responds well to pruning in autumn or winter.
Propagation Sow seed in pots in a cold frame, or take semi-ripe cuttings in late summer.

M. communis

The glossy, dark green leaves, up to 5cm (2in) long, form a dense canopy. In mid- to late summer saucer-shaped, creamy-white flowers almost hide the foliage, followed in autumn by small black berries. H and S 3m (10ft). Aspect Full sun.
Hardiness ❈❈ Zones 9–10.

NOTHOFAGUS
Southern beech

Native to the southern hemisphere, where they grow in forests in South America and Australasia, there are about 20 species of evergreen and deciduous trees in the genus. They can be grown as specimen trees or included in a woodland.
Cultivation Grow in fertile, moisture-retentive but well-drained, acidic soil in full sun. They are susceptible to damage from late spring frosts.
Pruning Early formative pruning should aim to produce a clear trunk and a balanced crown.

Myrtus communis

Occasional pruning is required for the removal of dead, dying, diseased or crossing branches as and when required.
Propagation Seed is the main method of propagation and should be collected when fresh and be sown into a container in an unheated glasshouse or cold frame until germination occurs.

N. betuloides

This is an exceptionally beautiful, broadly columnar evergreen, which is an excellent shade tree for the garden, where its toothed, glossy green leaves, to 2.5m (1in) long, produce light, dappled shade. It is quick-growing when young and can be used in screens and windbreaks as well as for upper-canopy shade. H 15–20m (50–65ft), S 6–10m (20–33ft). Aspect Full sun or semi-shade.
Hardiness ❈❈ Zone 7.

N. dombeyi
Coigue, Dombey's southern beech

This columnar to conical evergreen tree is faster growing than *N. betuloides*. The finely toothed leaves, up to 4cm (1½in) long, are glossy, dark green. This may be semi-evergreen in areas with very cold winters. H 20m (65ft), S 10m (33ft). Aspect Full sun or semi-shade.
Hardiness ❈❈ Zone 8.

N. obliqua
Roblé

This broadly conical deciduous species is often used in forestry because it is extremely fast-growing. The dark green leaves, up to 8cm (3in) long, are blue-green beneath and irregularly toothed. They turn yellow, orange and red in autumn. H 20m (65ft), S 15m (50ft). Aspect Full sun.
Hardiness ❈❈❈ Zone 8.

NYSSA

There are approximately four or five species of deciduous trees in the genus, which are found in woodland in eastern Asia and North America. They are grown as specimen trees for their foliage and excellent autumn colour.

Cultivation Grow in fertile, moisture-retentive but well-drained, neutral to acidic soil. Protect from cold, drying winds.
Pruning Early formative pruning should aim to produce a clear trunk and a balanced crown. Occasional pruning is required for the removal of dead, dying, diseased or crossing branches as and when required.
Propagation Seed and budding are the main methods of propagation and seed should be collected when fresh and sown into a container in an unheated glasshouse or cold frame until germination occurs. Summer budding on to seed-grown sweet gums is also commonly practised.

N. sylvatica
Tupelo, black gum, sour gum

This medium-sized broadly conical to columnar tree is native to North America. It has glossy, dark green leaves, up to 15cm (6in) long, which glow yellow, orange and red in autumn. H 25m (80ft), S 10m (33ft).
Named varieties Numerous selections have been made for their autumn colour. 'Autumn Cascades', an excellent tree for a small garden, has a strongly weeping habit, and it is probably best trained with a straight stem and then allowed to weep. The leaves turn a beautiful red-orange in autumn.
'Jermyns' is a strongly growing form, pyramidal when young but spreading with age, with leaves that are yellow-orange in autumn.
'Red Rage' has glossy, dark green leaves that are vibrant red in autumn.
'Sheffield Park' has a broad habit; its glossy, dark green foliage turns orange-red in autumn.
'Wisley Bonfire' has slightly weeping tips and a lovely red autumn colour.
Aspect Full sun or semi-shade.
Hardiness ❈❈❈ Zone 4–9.

OLEA
Olive

The 20 or so species of evergreen trees and shrubs in the genus are found in Mediterranean countries, including northern Africa, Central Asia and Australasia. They are grown for their fruits, from which oil is extracted. In warm areas they may be grown as specimen trees.

Cultivation Olives require a fertile but free-draining soil, in a warm sunny location.

Pruning Should be undertaken when the tree is young to encourage a dome-shaped tree and an evenly balanced canopy. The only other regular pruning should be done to remove dead, dying, diseased and crossing branches.

Propagation Olives are usually propagated by semi-ripe stem cuttings taken during late autumn. T-budding is also used when faster growing specimens are required and these are grafted on to seedling-grown rootstocks.

O. europaea
European olive
This slow-growing tree from Mediterranean Europe has twisted, gnarled branches and a short trunk, eventually developing into a broad-headed tree. The small, leathery leaves, up to 8cm (3in) long, which are slightly toothed, are grey-green above and lighter, silver-green beneath. In summer clusters of small white flowers appear, and these are followed by green fruits, which ripen to black. H and S 10m (33ft).
Aspect Full sun.
Hardiness ❋❋ Zones 8–10.

Olea europaea

Oxydendron arboreum

OXYDENDRON
Sorrel tree, sourwood
There is a single species of deciduous tree in the genus, and it is native to North America. This is a good woodland tree, and it is grown for its autumn colour.
Cultivation Grow in fertile, moisture-retentive but well-drained, acidic soil. Protect from cold, drying winds.
Pruning Occasional pruning only is required for the removal of any dead, dying, diseased or crossing branches.
Propagation Seed should be collected when fresh and sown into a container in an unheated glasshouse or cold frame until germination occurs.

O. arboreum
This small tree or large shrub will develop into a conical or columnar plant. The dark green leaves, up to 20cm (8in) long, are glossy and toothed and turn red, yellow and purple in autumn. Clusters of creamy-white, heather-like flowers are borne in late summer to early autumn at the tips of the branches. H 15m (50ft), S 8–10m (26–33ft).
Aspect Full sun or semi-shade.
Hardiness ❋❋❋ Zones 5–9.

PARROTIA
Persian ironwood
This genus of deciduous trees is found in the Caucasus and northern Iran. Parrotia is grown as a specimen tree for its autumn colour and early spring flowers.

Cultivation Grow in deep, fertile, moisture-retentive but well-drained, acidic soil in full sun or semi-shade. Trees are susceptible to damage from late spring frosts.
Pruning Formative pruning should aim to produce a clear trunk and a balanced crown. Occasional pruning only is required for the removal of any dead, dying, diseased or crossing branches.
Propagation Seed should be collected when fresh and sown into a container in an unheated glasshouse or cold frame until germination occurs. Winter grafting on to seedlings is also a good method.

P. persica
This spreading tree is tolerant of both drought and heat. It has a short trunk, and in winter the bark is a mixture of grey-brown and green flaking patterns, which reveal attractive pink, yellow and cinnamon patches underneath. The glossy green leaves, up to 12cm (5in) long, turn vivd shades of orange, red-purple and yellow in autumn. In late winter to early spring small red flowers emerge from hairy brown buds, before spring growth appears. H 8–10m (26–33ft), S 10m (33ft).
Aspect Full sun or semi-shade.
Hardiness ❋❋❋ Zones 4–8.

Nyssa sylvatica 'Sheffield Park'

Parrotia persica

PAULOWNIA

The six species of deciduous trees in the genus are found throughout eastern Asia. They are handsome specimen trees, grown for their pretty flowers, which do best in hot summers.

Cultivation Grow in fertile, well-drained soil in full sun. Protect from cold winds. Young shoots are susceptible to late spring frosts.

Pruning Formative pruning should aim to produce a clear trunk and a balanced crown.

Propagation Seed should be collected when fresh and sown into a container in a protected frost-free environment until germination occurs. Hardwood cuttings can be taken in winter and planted in the ground, left for a year and then transplanted the following spring.

P. tomentosa
(syn. *P. imperialis*)
Empress tree, foxglove tree, princess tree

This stunning and fast-growing tree from China is grown for its highly prized timber, large panicles of flowers and velvety leaves. The light green leaves, 30–40cm (12–16in) long, are covered in hairs, densely beneath. In late spring fragrant, pale pink-purple flowers, up to 5cm (2in) long, are produced in upright clusters. This species is often grown as a coppiced tree, when it produces astonishingly large leaves. It is tolerant of pollution. H 15m (50ft), S 10m (33ft).

Paulownia tomentosa

Named varieties 'Lilacina' (syn. *P. fargesii*), which may be slightly hardier than the species, has paler, lilac-coloured flowers.
Aspect Full sun or semi-shade.
Hardiness ❋❋❋ Zones 6–9.

PHELLODENDRON

The genus contains ten species of deciduous trees, which are found in eastern Asia. Male and female flowers are borne on separate plants, both of which must be present to produce the round, blue-black fruits. They have aromatic, attractive foliage and make large specimen trees.

Cultivation Grow in deep, fertile, well-drained soil in full sun.

Pruning Formative pruning should aim to produce a clear trunk and a balanced crown. Occasional pruning is required to remove dead, dying, diseased or crossing branches.

Propagation Seed should be collected when fresh and sown into a container in an unheated glasshouse or cold frame until germination occurs.

P. amurense
Amur cork tree

A broadly spreading, fast-growing, medium-sized tree from north-eastern Asia, with bark that grows corky as the tree ages. The glossy, dark green leaves, up to 35cm (14in) long, are pinnate and turn yellow in autumn. H and S 12m (40ft).
Aspect Full sun or semi-shade.
Hardiness ❋❋❋ Zones 3–7.

PHOENIX
Date palm

The 17 species of palms in the genus are found in tropical and subtropical areas in the Canary Islands, Africa, Greece and western and southern Asia. They are tender plants, which are often grown in conservatories and as houseplants in areas that are too cold for them outdoors.

Cultivation Best grown in a fertile, free-draining loam-based potting compost that retains some moisture and light shade protection in tropical climates.

Pruning Date palms require little annual pruning with the exception of the cosmetic removal of the dead fronds and fruit spikes.

Phoenix canariensis

Propagation: Seed should be collected fresh and sown in a humus-rich compost in a humid environment above 24°C (66°F).

P. canariensis
Canary Island date palm

This species is one of the most widely planted palms for tropical and Mediterranean planting. The trunk is straight with a slight taper at the base, and the arching, narrowly V-shaped, bright to mid-green fronds, which have many leaflets, may get to 6m (20ft) long. In summer bright yellow or creamy-yellow flowers are produced in clusters, up to 1.8m (6ft) long, and these ripen to edible, orange fruits. H 15m (50ft), S 12m (40ft).
Aspect Full sun.
Hardiness (Min. 10–16°C/ 50–61°F) Zones 8–11.

P. dactylifera
Date palm

This species is a tall, fast-growing and occasionally suckering plant. It has arching, grey-green leaves, up to 6m (20ft) long, consisting of many leaflets. The large, straw-coloured flower spikes are followed by the sweet fruits, which ripen to orange on the tree in dry conditions. H 20–30m (65–100ft), S 6–12m (20–40ft).
Aspect Full sun.
Hardiness (Min. 10–16°C/ 50–61°F) Zones 9–11.

PICEA
Spruce

The genus contains about 35 species of coniferous evergreen trees, which are found throughout the northern hemisphere (except Africa). They make handsome specimen trees and can also be planted to create windbreaks. Numerous cultivars have been developed, displaying a wide range of habit, size and foliage colour.

Cultivation Grow in deep, moisture-retentive but well-drained, neutral to acidic soil in full sun.

Pruning Formative pruning should aim to produce a clear trunk and a balanced crown, while tipping the lateral branches of young trees will encourage a denser crown. Occasional pruning is required to remove dead, dying, diseased or crossing branches.

Propagation Seed is the easiest method of propagation and should be collected when fresh and sown into a container in an unheated glasshouse or cold frame until germination occurs. Semi-ripe and softwood cuttings can be rooted during summer and should be dipped in a rooting hormone and placed in a humid environment until rooting occurs. Selected forms are winter grafted on to seedling-raised rootstocks.

P. abies
Norway spruce, common spruce
This highly adaptable, conical conifer, which will grow in a range of soil types, is widely grown in Europe for its timber; it is also farmed to supply Christmas trees. It has long branches, densely clothed with dark green, needle-like foliage. The needles are attached by short, woody pegs, which remain once the needles fall and give the branches a spiky appearance. Pendulous cones ripen to light brown. There are many dwarf forms, which are more suitable for gardens than the species. H 40m (130ft), S 6m (20ft).
Aspect Full sun.
Hardiness ✿✿✿ Zones 3–7.

P. breweriana
Brewer's spruce
This large, slow-growing, broadly conical tree has graceful, slightly weeping branches. The dark green, needle-like foliage, white-green beneath, is arranged on pendent side shoots. The cones are green

at first but turn purple as they mature. H 25m (80ft), S 10m (33ft).
Aspect Full sun.
Hardiness ✿✿✿ Zone 5.

P. orientalis
Caucasian spruce, oriental spruce
One of the most beautiful of the spruces, this ultimately large tree from the Caucasus and north-eastern Turkey has glossy, dark green needles that lie almost flat along the shoots. The long, brown cones hang from the foliage in winter and are highly distinctive. The stunning silhouette and slender, slightly weeping branches combine with the plant's tolerance of a range of conditions to make this a desirable addition to a large garden. H 50m (165ft), S 20m (65ft).
Named varieties 'Aurea' has an open, but graceful habit. In spring, for about six weeks, the new leaves are light creamy-gold before turning yellow-green. H 10m (33ft).
'Skylands' is similar to 'Aurea' in habit but the needles are golden-yellow throughout the year. This slender but vigorous small tree is one of the most stunning garden conifers.
Aspect Full sun.
Hardiness ✿✿✿ Zone 5.

P. pungens
Colorado spruce
This large, strongly conical tree from the north-western USA has green-grey or blue-grey

Pinus ayacahuite

needles arranged around the stem. The slender horizontal branches sweep upwards, while lower limbs may weep, often growing right down to the ground. H 35m (115ft), S 4.5m (15ft).
Named varieties The beautiful and slow-growing 'Hoopsii' has silver-blue needles and a dense conical habit. H 15m (50ft).
'Koster', a smaller but equally slow-growing form, is sometimes called the Colorado blue spruce because of its stunning silver-blue foliage. H 10m (33ft).
Aspect Full sun.
Hardiness ✿✿✿ Zones 3–7.

PINUS
Pine
This is a large genus, containing about 120 species of coniferous evergreen trees and shrubs, which are found throughout the northern hemisphere. Pines are grown as specimen trees and as windbreaks, and a vast number of cultivars have been developed, offering a range of size, habit and foliage colour.
Cultivation Grow in well-drained soil in full sun.

Pruning Early formative pruning should aim to produce a clear trunk and a balanced crown, while tipping the lateral branches of young trees encourages a denser crown.
Propagation Seed is the easiest method of propagation and should be collected when fresh and sown into a container in an unheated glasshouse or cold frame until germination occurs. Selected forms are winter grafted on to seedling-raised rootstocks.

P. ayacahuite
Mexican white pine
This broadly conical, spreading conifer is native to Mexico, Honduras and Guatemala. A five-needle pine, it has long, slender, blue-green leaves, which are borne in clusters along the stems. The light brown cones, up to 10cm (4in) long, drip a lot of white resin. Although the foliage is tolerant of heat, this pine is not drought tolerant and prefers fertile, moisture-retentive soil. H 35m (115ft), S 10m (33ft).
Aspect Full sun.
Hardiness ✿✿✿ Zone 7.

Picea breweriana

P. bungeana
Lacebark pine

Native to northern and central China, this beautiful, often multi-stemmed, three-needle pine spreads as it ages. The short, pale green needles are borne in dense clusters, giving a tufted effect to the branches. The ornamental bark flakes in patches to reveal the creamy-white, darkening to grey-green and purplish-green, bark beneath. The cones, up to 8cm (3in) long, change from yellow-brown to warm red as they mature. It prefers a warm position. H 10–15m (33–50ft), S 6m (20ft).
Aspect Full sun.
Hardiness ✿✿✿ Zones 3–7.

P. coulteri
Big-cone pine, Coulter pine

This large, three-needled pine from the south-western USA develops into a broadly spreading tree. The long grey-green or blue-green needles are borne in clusters at the tips of branches, giving a tufted appearance. The large cones, which may get up to 35cm (14in) long, are spiny and remain attached to the branches for many years, opening only in high temperatures. Mature bark is deeply furrowed with scaly ridges and is dark grey to black. They are tolerant of drought. H 25m (80ft), S 10m (33ft).
Aspect Full sun.
Hardiness ✿✿✿ Zone 7.

P. densiflora
Japanese red pine

This two-needled pine from north-eastern Asia and Japan is similar in many respects to *P. sylvestris*. It has sandy-red bark, which flakes near the top of the trunk but is grey near the base. The bright green needles are up to 12cm (5in) long, and yellow cones, up to 6cm (2½in) long, open during their second summer. This pine needs acidic soil. H 35m (115ft), S 20m (65ft).
Aspect Full sun.
Hardiness ✿✿✿ Zones 3–7.

P. palustris
Pitch pine, longleaf pine, southern yellow pine

This fast-growing, three-needled pine is native to the south-eastern USA. It has dark green needles, up to 45cm (18in) long, and reddish-brown, flaking bark. With age the lower branches die, and the crown becomes a sparse dome of tufted foliage above a clear, straight trunk. It will endure extreme summer heat. H 40m (130ft), S 15m (50ft).
Aspect Full sun.
Hardiness ✿✿ Zones 7–10.

P. patula
Mexican weeping pine, jelecote pine

A highly ornamental landscape tree for mild climates, this pine from central Mexico develops into a spreading tree. It has reddish-brown bark, and the light green needles, which are usually in threes but are occasionally in fours or even fives, are up to 30cm (12in) long. It needs acidic soil. H 20m (65ft), S 10m (33ft).
Aspect Full sun.
Hardiness ✿✿ Zone 8.

P. strobus
Eastern white pine, Weymouth pine

The species, which is native to North America, is a fast-growing, five-needled and highly resinous pine. It is grown for its attractive, slender-branched crown and blue-green foliage. The grey-green needles are up to 14m (56ft) long, and green cones, up to 15cm (6in) long, ripen to brown. H 35m (115ft), S 10m (33ft).

Pinus sylvestris

Named varieties 'Fastigiata' has upright branches clothed in dense clusters of blue-green foliage. H 20m (65ft), S 3m (10ft).
'Pendula' has a strongly weeping habit and is often trained as a straight-trunked standard before being allowed to weep, when it produces blue-green foliage.
Aspect Full sun.
Hardiness ✿✿✿ Zones 3–7.

P. sylvestris
Scots pine

Native to Europe and temperate Asia, this two-needled species is widely grown for its timber. It is also an ornamental tree with short blue-green, twisted needles, up to 8cm (3in) long, and orange-brown bark. The green cones, up to 8cm (3in) long, mature to grey or reddish-brown. It is a broadly spreading, often flat-topped tree with a clear trunk and light 'clouds' of foliage. It does best in neutral to acidic soil. H 30m (100ft), S 9m (30ft).
Named varieties The trees in Aurea Group (syn. 'Aurea') are slower growing with golden-yellow needles in spring, turning green-yellow later in the year. H 10–15m (33–50ft).
Trees in Fastigiata Group have twisted, upright branches clothed with blue-green foliage. They are among the most beautiful of all upright garden trees. H 8m (26ft), S 1.8m (6ft).
Aspect Full sun or semi-shade.
Hardiness ✿✿✿ Zones 3–7.

Pinus bungeana

P. wallichiana
Bhutan pine, blue pine, Himalayan pine
A beautiful, fast-growing, five-needled pine, native to the Himalayas, this develops a broadly conical habit. The smooth, grey bark ages to dark brown. The grey-green leaves, up to 20cm (8in) long, are borne in dense clusters at the ends of the branches. The resinous green cones, up to 30cm (12in) long, mature to brown. H 35m (115ft), S 10–12m (33–40ft). Aspect Full sun.
Hardiness ❋❋❋ Zones 5–7.

PISTACIA
Pistachio
The genus, which contains nine to eleven species of evergreen and deciduous shrubs and small trees, is known for the nuts from *P. vera*, which is grown commercially. The species are found in warm but temperate areas of the northern hemisphere, and they are grown for their flowers, foliage and fruit. Most species are tender, but *P. chinensis* will survive in sheltered temperate gardens.
Cultivation Grow in fertile, well-drained soil. Protect from cold, drying winds.
Pruning The trees should be trained to a modified central leader with four or five main scaffold limbs branching about 1.2m (4ft) from the ground. Little subsequent pruning is needed except to remove interfering branches.

Propagation By chip-budding or grafting selected scions on to one-year rootstocks of *P. atlantica*, *P. terebinthus* and *P. integerrima*.

P. chinensis
Chinese mastic
This deciduous tree has glossy, dark green pinnate leaves, up to 25cm (10in) long, which turn golden-yellow in autumn. In mid- to late spring clusters of aromatic red flowers are borne with the new leaves, and these are followed by small, round, red fruits that mature to blue. H 15m (50ft), S 10m (33ft). Aspect Full sun.
Hardiness ❋❋ Zones 6–10.

PITTOSPORUM
There are about 200 species of evergreen trees and shrubs in the genus, many of them from Australasia, but some from south and east Asia, southern Africa and the Pacific islands. They are grown mainly for their attractive foliage, although some pittosporums have interesting and sweetly scented flowers. Most are frost hardy to frost tender, but some varieties can be grown outdoors in mild, sheltered areas.
Cultivation Outdoors, grow in fertile, moisture-retentive but well-drained soil. Plants with purple and variegated leaves give the best colour when grown in full sun.
Pruning Only light pruning is required to maintain shape and avoid crossing branches.

Pistacia vera

Propagation By semi-hardwood cuttings. Seeds are difficult to obtain and viability is poor.

P. adaphniphylloides
This unusual species will develop into a small, round-headed tree with long, narrow, deep green leaves and delicate, cream-coloured, deliciously scented flowers, which are borne in early summer. H and S 10m (33ft). Aspect Full sun or semi-shade.
Hardiness ❋ Zones 9–10.

P. dallii
This New Zealand tree is one of the hardiest of this group. It is a highly ornamental form, with purple shoots and long, dark green, serrated leaves up to 10cm (4in) long. Fragrant, creamy-white flowers are borne in summer. H 6m (20ft), S 4m (12ft).
Aspect Full sun or semi-shade.
Hardiness ❋❋ Zones 8–10.

P. eugenioides
Lemonwood, tarata
Also native to New Zealand, this pretty, ultimately densely crowned tree has crinkled, glossy green leaves, up to 10cm (4in) long, and honey-scented, pale yellow flowers in summer. The foliage smells pleasantly of lemons when it is crushed, and stems are widely used in the cut-flower trade. H 7–10m (23–33ft), S 3m (10ft). Aspect Full sun or semi-shade.
Hardiness ❋ Zones 9–10.

P. tenuifolium
Kohuhu
This widely grown pittosporum is native to New Zealand, and it has been extensively hybridized to produce a range of different forms and foliage colours, including variegated, purple and mottled. The foliage is widely used in the cut-flower trade. The species, which is fast-growing, is a large shrub or small tree. The distinctive, glossy green leaves, up to 6cm (2½in) long, have wavy edges, and young shoots are black. In late spring to early summer small, fragrant, bell-shaped, black-red flowers are borne amid the leaves. H 10m (33ft), S 5m (16ft).
Aspect Full sun or semi-shade.
Hardiness ❋❋ Zones 8–10.

Pinus strobus 'Pendula'

Pittosporum tenuifolium 'Purpurea'

P. undulatum
**Australian mock orange,
cheesewood, Victorian box**
This Australian species is a dense,
rounded tree with glossy, dark
green leaves, up to 15cm (6in)
long, with wavy edges. In late
spring to midsummer fragrant,
creamy-white flowers are borne
in clusters. H 14m (46ft), S 7m
(23ft).
Aspect Full sun or semi-shade.
Hardiness ❁ Zones 9–10.

PLATANUS
Plane
The genus contains six species
of mostly deciduous trees, which
have attractive, maple-like foliage
and flaking bark. They are native
to North and Central America,
South-east Asia and south-eastern
Europe and are highly ornamental
trees suitable for planting as
specimen trees in large gardens.
They are also tolerant of poor soil
and pollution.
Cultivation Grow in fertile, well-
drained soil in full sun.
Pruning Formative pruning should
aim to produce a clear trunk and
a balanced crown.
Propagation Collect fresh seed
and sow into a pot outdoors, or
in an unheated glasshouse or cold
frame until germination occurs.

P. x hispanica
(syn. *P. x acerifolia*)
London plane
This hybrid between *P. occidentalis*
and *P. orientalis* is widely planted in
London as a street tree, hence its
common name. It is a vigorous,
broadly spreading, deciduous tree,
with flaking bark and palmate,
bright green leaves, up to 35cm
(14in) long. Clusters of green
fruit, ageing to brown, are borne
in autumn and last into winter.
Pollard in restricted spaces.
H 30m (100ft), S 20m (65ft).
Aspect Full sun or semi-shade.
Hardiness ❁❁❁ Zones 4–9.

P. orientalis
Oriental plane
This popular and attractive
spreading deciduous species
originates from south-eastern
Europe, but is widely planted in
Asia. It has attractive flaking bark
and large, deeply lobed, glossy
green leaves, up to 25cm (10in)
long. Clusters of up to six green
fruits, which age to brown, are
borne in autumn, and last into
winter. It grows better in
temperate areas than in the
continental climate of the USA.
H and S 30m (100ft).
Aspect Full sun or semi-shade.
Hardiness ❁❁❁ Zones 4–9.

Platanus orientalis

Platanus x hispanica

PLUMERIA
**Frangipani, temple tree,
pagoda tree**
There are seven to eight species
of deciduous shrubs and trees
in this genus, which is native to
tropical and subtropical America.
Grown for their lovely, fragrant
flowers, they are popular in the
tropics as they are salt-spray-
and drought tolerant. Although
tender, frangipani can be grown
as houseplants or in a warm
greenhouse or conservatory.
Cultivation Outdoors, grow in
fertile, well-drained soil in sun.
Pruning Formative pruning should
aim to encourage a number of
clear trunks and a balanced crown,
while tipping the lateral branches
of young trees will encourage a
denser crown.
Propagation Take softwood
cuttings in early summer and
place in a frost-free, humid
environment until they root.
Low branches can be layered.

P. rubra
Common frangipani
This rather variable large shrub
or small tree develops an upright
habit as it matures. The leaves are
mid- to dark green, up to 40cm
(16in) long, and have pale red-
green midribs. In the wild the
highly scented flowers, which are
borne in clusters above the foliage
in summer to autumn, range from
white, to pink, yellow and deep
pink-red. In dry regions during
periods of drought the foliage will
fall, but the tree will still flower.
H 7m (23ft), S 5m (15ft).

Named varieties An array of
vividly coloured forms have been
developed, including 'Bridal
White', which is a slow-growing
cultivar with white flowers with
reflexed petals and green foliage.
 'June Bride' bears large clusters
of white flowers, tinted pink at the
edges, with orange-yellow centres.
 'Royal Flush' has clusters of
magenta flowers without the
coloured centre.
 'Sunbathed' has yellow flowers
that are white around the edge.
Aspect Full sun.
Hardiness (Min. 10–13°C/
50–5°F) Zones 10–12.

PODOCARPUS
Podocarp, yellow-wood
There are 90–100 species of
evergreen coniferous trees and
shrubs in the genus. The leaves
are usually arranged in spirals
around the stems, and they have
fleshy, berry-like fruits. They
make excellent specimen plants
and mixed border trees.
Cultivation Grow in fertile,
moisture-retentive but well-
drained soil. Protect plants from
cold, drying winds.
Pruning Young plants often grow
straight up, with no side branching.
To rectify, cut them back hard,
which will result in re-growth along
the stem. Pinch back new growth as
necessary to promote bushiness.
Propagation Plants can be started
from seeds or cuttings. Seeds
often sprout while still attached
to the fleshy stalk on the plant.
Tip cuttings take 10 to 12 weeks
to root.

Plumeria rubra

P. lawrencei

This species from New Zealand is a spreading shrub or small tree with narrow green leaves, flushed with bronze, and red berries. H 10m (33ft), S 6m (20ft).
Aspect Full sun.
Hardiness ✺✺ Zone 7.

P. macrophyllus
Kusamaki, big-leaf podocarp, Japanese yew

This slow-growing conical tree, which is native to eastern China, has red-brown bark. The feathery leaves are dark green above and lighter green beneath. Red-purple fruits are borne on female plants in autumn. It requires a moist, temperate climate to thrive and long, hot, humid summers to develop into a tree. It will not survive prolonged periods of frost. H 10–15m (33–50ft), S 8–10m (26–33ft).
Aspect Full sun.
Hardiness ✺✺ Zones 9–10.

P. salignus
(syn. *P. chilinus*)
Willow-leaf podocarp

This slow-growing, graceful, small garden tree has drooping branches covered with curtains of foliage. The narrow leaves, up to 15cm (6in) long, are glossy, dark blue-green above and yellow-green beneath. Female plants produce green or purple fruits in autumn. H 15m (50ft), S 10m (33ft).
Aspect Full sun.
Hardiness ✺✺✺ Zones 9–10.

P. totara
Totara

In its native New Zealand this is a fast-growing tree, but in less favourable climates it is slower growing. It has a broadly conical habit with large, yew-like leaves, up to 2.5cm (1in) long. The brown to grey bark peels in strips. H 20m (65ft), S 10m (33ft).
Aspect Full sun.
Hardiness ✺ Zone 10.

POPULUS
Poplar, aspen, cottonwood

This genus of about 35 species of large, fast-growing deciduous trees are grown for their foliage and catkins. They make good specimens in large gardens. They are unsuitable for small gardens because their questing roots can damage foundations and drains.
Cultivation Grow in moisture-retentive but well-drained soil in sun. Poplars will not tolerate waterlogged soil.
Pruning Formative pruning should aim to produce a clear trunk and a balanced crown. Many poplars are prone to canker, so any diseased wood should be removed as it appears. Occasional pruning is required to remove dead, dying, diseased or crossing branches.
Propagation Collect fresh seed and sow in a pot in an unheated glasshouse or cold frame until germination occurs. Softwood cuttings are taken during summer and placed in a humid environment until rooting occurs. Hardwood cuttings are taken in winter.

P. x canadensis
Canadian poplar

This hybrid between *P. deltoides* and *P. nigra* is a fast-growing tree with a conical to columnar habit. The broadly triangular leaves, up to 10cm (4in) long, are glossy green, flushed bronze in summer and turn yellow in autumn. Red male catkins and yellow female catkins, both up to 10cm (4in) long, are borne in spring. H 30m (100ft), S 20m (65ft).
Named varieties 'Aurea' (syn. 'Serotina Aurea') is a columnar, male form with young leaves that are flushed with bronze, turning butter yellow in autumn. H 25m (80ft), S 10m (33ft).
Aspect Full sun.
Hardiness ✺✺✺ Zones 5–7.

P. x jackii
(syn. *P. x candicans*, *P. gileadensis*)

This columnar hybrid between *P. balsamifera* (balsam poplar) and *P. deltoides* (eastern cottonwood) has dark green, heart-shaped leaves, up to 15cm (6in) long, which are white-green beneath. Green female catkins, up to 15cm (6in) long, appear in early spring. H 25m (80ft), S 15m (50ft).
Named varieties 'Aurora' has ovate leaves that are variegated and mottled yellow along the margins and green and pink-purple in the centres. The most vivid colours are produced on the strongest growing shoots. It is often treated as a short-stemmed pollard to retain the coloured leaves. H 15m (50ft), S 6m (20ft).
Aspect Full sun.
Hardiness ✺✺✺ Zones 5–7.

Plumeria alba

Populus maximowiczii

P. lasiocarpa
Chinese necklace poplar
A graceful, medium-sized, conical tree, this has large, heart-shaped, dark green leaves, up to 30cm (12in) long. Yellow-green catkins, up to 10cm (4in) long, appear in mid-spring. H 20m (65ft), S 10m (33ft).
Aspect Full sun.
Hardiness ❋❋❋ Zones 5–7.

P. nigra
Black poplar
This fast-growing tree has very dark, deeply fissured bark. The triangular to ovate leaves, up to 10cm (4in) long, are dark green, initially bronze and turning yellow in autumn. Green female and red male catkins are borne in early to mid-spring. H 35m (115ft), S 20m (65ft).
Named varieties The well-known form 'Italica' (syn. *P. nigra* var. *italica*; Lombardy poplar) has been cultivated in Europe for a long time and is widely used as a windbreak tree on agricultural land. It is a beautiful, fast-growing tree with a narrow, conical shape. The close branches are erect and covered with glossy green leaves that turn yellow in autumn. H 30m (100ft), S 3m (10ft).
Aspect Full sun.
Hardiness ❋❋❋ Zones 3–9.

P. tremuloides
American aspen, quaking aspen
This adaptable, medium-sized tree, found from Canada to Mexico, has distinctive, shallowly toothed, glossy green leaves, up to 6cm (2½in) long, which are bronze when they emerge, turning yellow in autumn. The ovate leaves flutter and quiver in the lightest of winds. Green female and red-grey male catkins, both up to 6cm (2½in) long, are borne in early spring. Planted in sufficient numbers, these trees can be used to block out unwanted vehicle noise. H 15–20m (50–65ft), S 10m (33ft).
Aspect Full sun.
Hardiness ❋❋❋ Zones 3–9.

PORTLANDIA
There are over 20 species in the genus of evergreen shrubs and small trees. They are native to Central America and the Caribbean and are grown for their fragrant flowers.
Cultivation Outdoors, grow in fertile, well-drained, alkaline soil in sun or light shade.
Pruning Formative pruning should aim to encourage a clear trunk, or multiple trunks, and a balanced crown. Occasional pruning is required for the removal of any dead, dying, diseased or crossing branches.

Propagation Seed is the easiest method and should be collected when fresh and sown into a container in a heated glasshouse in a frost-free and humid environment until germination occurs. Low branches can also be layered into the soil; when rooted they should be detached from the parent tree and potted up.

P. grandiflora
Tree lily
This small tree has glossy green, magnolia-like leaves, up to 15cm (6in) or more long. The funnel-shaped flowers, up to 15cm (6in) long, are borne in summer. They are white with a reddish throat and smell of vanilla. H 6m (20ft), S 1.8m (6ft).
Aspect Full sun to light shade.
Hardiness (Min. 10°C/50°F) Zones 10–12.

PROTEA
The genus contains about 115 species of evergreen shrubs and just a few trees. They are found in Africa and are prized for their large flowerheads.
Cultivation Outdoors, grow in well-drained, neutral to acidic soil in sun. These plants will not tolerate wet winters.
Pruning Formative pruning should aim to encourage a clear trunk and a balanced crown, while tipping the lateral branches of young trees will encourage a denser crown. Occasional

pruning is required for the removal of dead, dying, diseased or crossing branches.
Propagation Seed is the easiest method of propagation and should be collected when fresh and sown into a container in a heated glasshouse in a frost-free and humid environment until germination occurs.

P. eximia
This small, upright tree from South Africa has ovate leaves, up to 10cm (4in) long. The leaves, silver-green to glaucous green, are flushed and sometimes edged with red-purple. In spring and summer, cone-shaped scarlet flowers are surrounded by large bracts, creating showy flowerheads, up to 15cm (6in) across, that resemble those of *Banksia*. H 5m (16ft), S 3m (10ft).
Aspect Full sun.
Hardiness ❋ Zones 9–11.

PRUMNOPITYS
The ten species of coniferous evergreen trees in the genus are found in Central and South America, Malaysia and New Zealand. They are similar in many respects to podocarps and have yew-like foliage. They can be grown as specimen trees or used as hedging.
Cultivation Grow in fertile, moisture-retentive but well-drained soil in sun. Protect plants from cold, drying winds.

Protea eximia

Pruning Formative pruning should aim to produce a clear trunk and a balanced crown, while tipping the lateral branches of young trees will help to encourage a denser crown. Occasional pruning is required for the removal of any dead, dying, diseased or crossing branches.

Propagation Seed is the easiest method of propagation and should be collected when fresh and sown into a container in an unheated glasshouse or cold frame until germination occurs. Semi-ripe cuttings can be taken in late summer and early autumn. The base of the cutting should be dipped in a rooting hormone before planting it and placing in a humid environment in a glasshouse until it roots.

P. andina
(**syn.** *P. elegans, Podocarpus andinus*)
Plum-fruited yew, plum yew
This species from Chile and Argentina will eventually develop into a broadly conical tree. The narrow blue-green leaves, up to 3cm (1½in) long and with two pale bands on the undersides, are arranged in whorls. The cones, up to 2.5cm (1in) long, are pale yellow, and female plants produce plum-like, yellowish fruits, up to 2cm (½in) long, which ripen to purple. H 15–20m (50–65ft), S 8–10m (26–33ft).
Aspect Full sun to semi-shade.
Hardiness ✻✻✻ Zones 8–10.

Prumnopitys andina

Prunus 'Accolade'

PRUNUS
Ornamental cherry
This enormous genus contains some 430 species of deciduous and evergreen trees and shrubs, which provide almonds, apricots, cherries, peaches and nectarines, plums and damsons and sloes. There are also many ornamental trees, grown for their delightful white, pink or red spring flowers, colourful fruits and attractive autumn colour. They are often small trees, useful for their long period of interest in gardens where space is limited. The Japanese cherries, the Sato-zakura Group, have been especially developed for their beautiful blossom, which is borne from early spring.

Cultivation Grow in fertile, moisture-retentive but well-drained soil in sun. Deciduous forms prefer full sun.

Pruning Formative pruning should aim to produce a clear trunk and a balanced crown. Many cherries are prone to canker and silver leaf, so any diseased wood should be removed as soon as it appears. Pruning should be done during summer to reduce the risk of infection from silver leaf.

Propagation Seed is used for the species while summer budding and winter grafting are the main means of propagation. Collect fresh seed and sow in a pot in an unheated glasshouse or cold frame until germination occurs. Summer budding and winter grafting are both quite popular and should be done on to disease-resistant rootstocks or on to seed-raised bird cherry stock.

P. 'Accolade'
This is an outstanding small deciduous tree, which has been developed from *P. sargentii* and *P. subhirtella*. It has dark green leaves, up to 10cm (4in) long, which turn vivid orange-red in autumn. In early spring clusters of semi-double, pale pink flowers open from dark pink buds. Like most Japanese cherries, they are best grown in moisture-retentive soils. H and S 8–10m (26–33ft).
Aspect Full sun or semi-shade.
Hardiness ✻✻✻ Zones 5–6.

Prunus sargentii

P. 'Amanogawa'
(syn. P. serrulata 'Erecta')

A small, upright, deciduous Japanese cherry, with erect branches that open with age, this has ovate leaves, up to 12cm (5in) long, which are slightly bronzed in spring. In autumn the foliage is red, yellow and green. The fragrant, semi-double, pale pink flowers, up to 4cm (1½in) across, are borne in dense clusters in mid- to late spring. H 8–10m (26–33ft), S 4m (12ft).
Aspect Full sun or semi-shade.
Hardiness ✿✿✿ Zones 5–6.

P. cerasifera
Cherry plum, myrobalan

A small deciduous tree, this is often grown as a hedge, when it will be covered with single, white flowers, up to 2.5cm (1in) across, in spring. Mature plants sometimes produce red or yellow, plum-like fruits. H and S 10m (33ft).
Named varieties The species is most often represented in gardens by the highly decorative 'Pissardii' (syn. *P. pissardii*; purple-leaved plum). This has reddish-purple leaves, which darken to purple as they mature. In mid-spring masses of white flowers open from pink buds. It is an adaptable, ultimately broadly spreading tree, often used as a hedge. H and S 8m (26ft).
Aspect Full sun or semi-shade.
Hardiness ✿✿✿ Zones 5–8.

P. 'Ichiyo'

This spreading deciduous tree has dark green leaves, up to 10cm (4in) long, which are tinged with bronze in spring. Double, frilly, pale pink flowers, up to 5cm (2in) across, are borne in clusters in mid- to late spring. H and S 8m (26ft).
Aspect Full sun or semi-shade.
Hardiness ✿✿✿ Zones 5–6.

P. sargentii
Sargent cherry

This spreading deciduous tree has dark green leaves, up to 12cm (5in) long, which are initially reddish then turn shades of orange, yellow and red in autumn. Pale pink flowers, up to 4cm (1½in) across, are borne in mid-spring, followed by red, cherry-like fruits. H 20m (65ft), S 15m (50ft).
Aspect Full sun or semi-shade.
Hardiness ✿✿✿ Zones 4–7.

P. serrula
(syn. P. tibetica)

This medium-sized, fast-growing deciduous tree is grown for its glossy, mahogany-red or orange-brown bark. The dark green leaves, up to 10cm (4in) long, turn yellow in autumn. White flowers, up to 2cm (3/4in) across, are borne in late spring, followed by small, bright red fruits. H and S 10–15m (33–50ft).
Aspect Full sun or semi-shade.
Hardiness ✿✿✿ Zones 5–7.

P. 'Shirofugen'

This attractive, deciduous Japanese cherry develops a spreading habit. The dark green leaves, up to 12cm (5in) long, are coppery-red in spring, turning reddish-orange in autumn. The long-lasting, fragrant flowers are white, up to 5cm (2in) across, and open from pink buds in late spring, turning purple-pink before they fall. H 8m (26ft), S 10m (33ft).
Aspect Full sun or semi-shade.
Hardiness ✿✿✿ Zones 5–6.

P. 'Shirotae'
(syn. P. 'Mount Fuji')

This is a spreading, deciduous tree, which develops a slightly weeping habit. The dark green leaves, up to 12cm (5in) long, are light green when they first emerge in spring and turn vibrant red and orange in autumn. The fragrant, double, white flowers, which are up to 5cm (2in) across, are borne in pendent clusters in mid-spring. H 6m (20ft), S 8m (26ft).
Aspect Full sun or semi-shade.
Hardiness ✿✿✿ Zones 5–6.

P. 'Taihaku'
Great white cherry

This broadly spreading, vigorous, deciduous Japanese cherry has long, arching branches. The dark green, rather leathery leaves, up to 20cm (8in) long, are red-bronze when they emerge in spring and sometimes turn red-orange in autumn. The single white flowers, up to 7cm (2³/4in) across, are borne in clusters in mid-spring. H 8m (26ft), S 10m (33ft).
Aspect Full sun or semi-shade.
Hardiness ✿✿✿ Zones 5–6.

PRUNUS ARMENIACA
Apricot

These are one of the most difficult of the stone fruits to grow. This is because they flower very early in the year and the delicate flowers are very easily damaged by frost. They can also be affected by peach leaf curl, especially in areas where winters are cool and wet. They are best sited in free-draining but fertile soils and in areas where summer temperatures are high.

Prunus armeniaca

Cultivation Depending on the selection, chilling requirements can vary, but these difficult trees generally require about 350 hours below 7°C (45°F). Flowers are prone to frost damage and germination can be improved by hand pollination. The best fruit is produced after hot summers, but drought conditions can cause premature fruit drop.

Pruning Fruits are borne on one-year-old shoots and on spur shoots, so regular yearly pruning is required to remove any unproductive or old shoots during winter and pruning to encourage an open-bowl-shaped tree.

Propagation Apricots are normally propagated by chip- or T-budding during summer on to a good dwarfing rootstock.

P. a. 'Goldbar'

This warm climate selection produces very large, light yellow-orange fruit with a reddish blush to the skin. The flesh is light orange, very firm, meaty and moderately juicy. It is a vigorous tree that flowers heavily and requires pollinating, but sets a light crop.
Aspect Full sun, in a moisture-retentive soil.
Hardiness ❋❋ Zones 4–8.

P. a. 'Goldstrike'

This is a free-fruiting variety that produces large and firm fruit. The skin is a light orange colour and slightly glossy. The flesh is light orange, firm, meaty and moderately juicy. 'Goldstrike' blooms heavily but fruit set is often moderate to light under natural pollination, although it will cross-pollinate very well with 'Goldbar'.
Aspect Full sun, in a moisture-retentive soil.
Hardiness ❋❋ Zones 4–8.

P. a. 'Tilton'

This popular variety is widely grown in the USA. It is very good for freezing, drying and eating fresh, and is one of the tastiest of all varieties of apricot. It has a distinct appearance, with a slightly flatter shape than most varieties and a concave line that goes halfway around the fruit.

It has a light orange skin, and the flesh is firm, tender and juicy with a sweet and sour taste. It has a golden colour with a red blush. It is a vigorous tree, bearing heavy crops that are resistant to late frosts, and its fruits ripen earlier than those of many other varieties. However, since the delicate flowers are produced very early in spring they may be prone to frosts.
Aspect Full sun, in a moisture-retentive soil.
Hardiness ❋❋ Zones 4–8.

P. a. 'Tom Catt'

This variety produces very juicy, very large, orange fruits if the crop is thinned properly, and they are often the first apricots to ripen each season. One of the best cool climate varieties, it is widely grown in the UK. The firm orange flesh is delicious eaten fresh. It requires either a pollinator or hand pollination, but is one of the best of the garden varieties as it has good disease resistance.
Aspect Full sun, in a moisture-retentive soil.
Hardiness ❋❋ Zones 4–8.

P. a. 'Pedigree Bush'

This variety is normally grafted on to an extreme dwarfing rootstock, which makes it suitable for growing in containers as a patio plant. Medium-sized succulent, orange-red fruits are produced late in summer on trees that are pollinated. Plants seldom exceed 2m (6ft) tall.
Aspect Full sun, in a moisture-retentive soil.
Hardiness ❋❋ Zones 4–8.

P. a. 'Wenatachee'

Synonymous with 'Moorpark', this variety bears large fruit, and is grown for its distinct light yellow fruits. The fruit is widely used in jams. Its main attraction is its self-pollination, which produces fruit annually. However, it flowers early in the spring and is prone to frost damage. It is also the least tolerant of heavy soils.
Aspect Full sun, in a moisture-retentive soil.
Hardiness ❋❋ Zones 4–8.

Prunus avium

PRUNUS AVIUM
Sweet cherry

These are generally more vigorous and adaptable to a wider range of soils than *P. cerasus*. Plant in an open location as a specimen garden tree or as part of an orchard. When selecting, it is important to note that only a few cultivars are self-fertile. Netting or bird scarers may be necessary to protect the cherry crop. H and S 7–8m (23–26ft).
Aspect Full sun, in a moisture-retentive soil.
Hardiness ❋❋❋ Zones 3–9.
Cultivation Grow in fertile, well-drained, moisture-retentive soil. Avoid soils that flood or become waterlogged in winter and spring. They do best in a sunny, warm position with some protection to maximize pollination.
Pruning Sweet cherries fruit on spurs of wood that is two years or older. Mature trees are best pruned in summer. Slow down the vegetative growth by pruning every tip back to 5–6 nodes, which encourages the tree to produce spurs.
Propagation Use chip- or T-budding in summer on an appropriate rootstock. Malling F12/1 is a vigorous rootstock that can encourage the growth of slower growing forms, and it is used on poorer, shallower soils. More vigorous rootstocks are becoming available, including

Inmil, Camil, Edabriz and the Gisela series, and these will reduce the overall size of the tree and enhance disease resistance. Trees can be raised from seed, but are often inferior and take many years to produce fruit.
Named varieties The following sweet cherries will achieve a height and spread of 5m (16ft) if they are grown on Colt rootstock.

The prolific 'Bigarreau Napoléon' bears unusual red-flushed, yellow fruits, which are quite large and very sweet. They are often referred to as 'Naps' cherries. It is not self-fertile.

'Merchant' is a well-flavoured cherry with large, dark red fruits, which are produced quite early in summer. It has reasonably good resistance to cherry canker but is not self-fertile.

The widely grown 'Merton Favourite' bears delicious fruit and is also a beautiful spring-flowering garden tree. It is not self-fertile.

'Stella' is a reliable, self-fertile, late-fruiting cultivar, which bears large, dark red fruit.

PRUNUS CERASUS
Sour cherry

Acid or sour cherries tend to be hardier than sweet cherries and can even be grown against shady walls. H and S 7–8m (23–26ft).

Prunus cerasus

Prunus insititia

Cultivation As for *Prunus avium*.
Pruning Sour cherries fruit on one-year-old wood, so pruning is undertaken in spring and summer to remove about one-third of the older shoots and to encourage new growth.
Propagation As for *Prunus avium*.
Named varieties 'Morello' is one of the most reliable and widely grown of all cherries, but it is best to buy plants from a professional grower because the stock used can vary considerably. Trees bear masses of bright red cherries, which are widely used for pies, jams and even wine. It is self-fertile. H and S 5m (16ft) if grown on Colt rootstock.
Aspect Full sun or light shade, in a moisture-retentive soil.
Hardiness ❀❀❀ Zones 3–9.

PRUNUS DOMESTICA
Plum, gage

These attractive garden trees have been grown for many centuries for their edible fruits as well as their lovely, pure-white early spring flowers. The sweet and juicy purple fruits can be eaten fresh, or can be dried, in which case they are called prunes. They are represented in gardens by various fruiting selections.
Cultivation Grow in fertile, well-drained soil in a sheltered position in full sun. The trees will do best if the soil is not too wet in winter and early spring. Plums and gages are usually grown on rootstocks in order to limit their growth. Pixy is the

smallest of the dwarfing rootstocks and is one of the best for small, confined spaces, although it is not tolerant of difficult soil conditions; it will produce trees with a height and spread of 3m (10ft). St Julien A is a widely used rootstock as it will tolerate a wider range of soils. Brompton and Myrobalan are vigorous rootstocks that will produce trees with a height and spread greater than 4m (12ft).
Pruning Fruits are produced at the base of one-year-old shoots as well as on two-year-old wood and on small spurs. The aim is to prune back tip growth in summer by cutting back about one-third of the lateral shoots to develop and encourage the growth of fruiting wood. At the same time remove dead and dying, diseased and crossing branches.
Propagation Chip- or T-bud in summer on to suitable rootstocks.
Named varieties The following cultivars will achieve a height and spread of 5m (16ft) if grown on St Julien A rootstock.
'Cambridge Gage' is a widely grown, partially self-fertile greengage that produces greenish-golden fruits.
'Czar' is an old-fashioned plum that is still widely cultivated today for its abundant crop of small, round, purplish-blue, sweet fruits.
'Golden Transparent' is a wonderful, self-fertile gage, grown for its large crops of sweet yellow fruits, which are produced late in autumn.

The widely grown 'Jefferson' is a heavy-cropping form with sweet, bright yellow plums. It requires an additional pollinator.
'Oullin's Gage', which will crop regularly without a pollinator, and bears green-skinned greengages that ripen to golden-yellow. Larger crops can be achieved with a pollinator.
'Reine Claude Verte' (syn. 'Purple Gage') bears firm but juicy green-fleshed greengages with a sweet taste. It is partially self-fertile but performs better with another pollinator.
The widely grown 'Stanley' is a heavy-cropping, self-fertile plum with sweet bluish-purple fruits.
The self-fertile and reliable 'Victoria' bears one of the largest fruits of any plum – they can be the size of duck eggs. They are a distinctive yellow-tinted red and very sweet.
Aspect Semi-shade or full sun.
Hardiness ❀❀❀ Zones 4–9.

PRUNUS DULCIS
Almond

The common almond is grown for its edible seed, which is contained within a hard nut, and requires high summer temperatures to ripen properly. The trees are widely grown in Mediterranean regions on a commercial basis, and in this climate the small, fleshy, peach-like fruits split in early autumn to reveal the hard seed capsule.
Cultivation Grow in fertile, free-draining soil in full sun in a frost-free position. Most fruiting forms

are grown on St Julien rootstock to dwarf their growth to 5m (16ft). They are self-fertile.
Pruning The nuts are produced on one-year-old wood. In summer remove about one-third of the previous year's fruiting wood to encourage new growth.
Propagation Trees are propagated by chip-budding on to field-grown dwarfing rootstocks in summer.
Named varieties 'Robin' is an attractive tree for a small garden. Vivid pink flowers appear in spring, and it produces good autumn colour. H and S 8m (26ft).
Aspect Full sun.
Hardiness ❀❀❀ Zone 7.

PRUNUS INSITITIA
(syn. *Prunus domestica* var. *insititia*)
Damson

Cultivated since Roman times, damsons are believed to originate from Damascus, and they are still known as the Damask plum. In gardens, this small tree is easily identified by its sprawling habit, small white spring flowers and its distinctive yellow or purple fruits that ripen in September.
Cultivation As *Prunus domestica*.
Pruning As *Prunus domestica*.
Propagation As *Prunus domestica*.
Named varieties The following damsons will achieve a height and spread of 5m (16ft) if grown on St Julien A rootstock.
'Farleigh Pacific' is a reliable, heavy-cropping damson that is partially self-fertile, but to get bumper crops an additional pollinator is required.

Prunus dulcis

Psidium guajava

'Merryweather' is a reliable, old-fashioned damson that produces sweet and juicy black fruits. It is self-fertile.

'Prune Damson' (syn. 'Shropshire Damson') produces masses of black, sweet fruits in late autumn. It is self-fertile.
Aspect Semi-shade or full sun.
Hardiness ❀❀❀ Zones 4–9.

PSEUDOLARIX
Golden larch
The genus contains a single species of deciduous coniferous tree, which is native to China. The trees are grown in gardens for their foliage, cones and elegant habit.
Cultivation Grow in deep, fertile, moisture-retentive but well-drained, neutral to acidic soil in sun. These trees need a sheltered position and do best in areas that regularly have long, hot summers.

Pruning Formative pruning should aim to produce a clear trunk and a balanced crown, while tipping the lateral branches of young trees will encourage a denser crown.
Propagation Seed is the easiest method of propagation and should be collected when fresh and sown into a container in an unheated glasshouse or cold frame until germination occurs.

P. amabilis
(syn. P. kaempferi)
This beautiful but slow-growing, broadly conical tree has wide-spreading branches and larch-like, lime-green leaves, which turn intense yellow in autumn before they fall. Yellow-green cones ripen to brown. H 15–20m (50–65ft), S 12–15m (40–50ft).
Aspect Full sun or semi-shade.
Hardiness ❀❀❀ Zones 4–7.

PSEUDOTSUGA
There are about eight species of evergreen coniferous trees in the genus, and they are found in North America, China, Taiwan and Japan. They are broadly conical trees with whorled branches and are grown as specimen trees. H 60m (200ft), S10m (33ft).
Cultivation Grow in moisture-retentive but well-drained, neutral to acidic soil in sun.
Pruning Formative pruning should aim to produce a clear trunk and a balanced crown, while tipping the lateral branches of young trees will encourage a denser crown.
Propagation Seed is the easiest method of propagation and should be collected when fresh and sown into a container in an unheated glasshouse or cold frame until germination occurs.

P. menziesii
Douglas fir, green Douglas fir, Oregon Douglas fir
This fast-growing tree from western North America is often grown for its timber; it is also often planted as a nurse species to protect slower growing trees and to create windbreaks and screens in gardens. In addition, its elegant conical shape makes it a handsome specimen tree. The grey, corky bark becomes deeply furrowed with age. The linear leaves, to 3cm (1½in) long, are dark green, with two white bands beneath, and are aromatic when crushed. H 50m (165ft), S 10m (33ft).
Aspect Full sun.
Hardiness ❀❀❀ Zones 4–7.

PSIDIUM
Guava
The genus of 100 species of evergreen trees and shrubs comes from the Americas. These are tender plants, grown mostly for their large fruits, some of which are edible.
Cultivation: Guavas prefer a sheltered site that is protected from strong winds. Although they will tolerate a wide range of soils, a fertile, well-drained neutral soil is preferred.
Pruning Formative pruning, done after fruiting, is required to encourage a rounded shape and at the same time crossing, diseased and dead branches and shoots should be removed.
Propagation Cultivars can be propagated by softwood cuttings in summer. Keep them in a humid environment, such as a heated propagator or mist unit. Chip-budding, which produces plants more quickly, is done in summer. Plants are also grafted on to seedling-raised trees. Seed propagation produces variable offspring, so only the strongest seedlings should be grown on.

P. guajava
Common guava, yellow guava, apple guava
This shrub or small tree, which is sometimes semi-evergreen, originated in tropical America but is now widely grown and naturalized throughout tropical and subtropical areas. It is grown mainly for the yellow, pear-shaped

Pseudolarix amabilis

Psidium guajava

Pterocarya stenoptera

fruits, up to 8cm (3in) across, with pinkish flesh, which are eaten fresh and also canned and used for making jellies and juice. The white flowers are borne throughout the year. H and S 10m (33ft).
Aspect Free-draining but moisture-retentive soil in a sunny location.
Hardiness ❀ Zones 10–12.

P. littorale
Strawberry guava
This smaller plant from Brazil has bronze-red bark and pink fruits with whitish flesh. H and S 8m (26ft).
Aspect Free-draining but moisture-retentive soil in a sunny location.
Hardiness ❀ Zone 10.

PTEROCARYA
Wing nut
The genus contains about ten species of deciduous trees, which are native to Asia. They are related to the walnut and are grown for their attractive foliage and catkin-like inflorescences and for the long spikes of winged fruits that appear in summer. They make handsome specimen trees in gardens that are large enough to accommodate them.
Cultivation Grow in fertile, deep, moisture-retentive but well-drained soil in sun. Unwanted suckers, which are an especial problem with trees growing near water, should be removed as soon as they are noticed, otherwise they will quickly develop into an almost impenetrable thicket.
Pruning Formative pruning should aim to produce a clear trunk and a balanced crown. Wing nuts are prone to both root and stem suckers and these are best removed, as and when they appear. Occasional pruning is required for the removal of dead, dying, diseased or crossing branches.
Propagation Seed, softwood and hardwood cuttings are the main methods of propagation. Seed should be collected when fresh and sown into a container in an unheated glasshouse or cold frame until germination occurs.

Softwood cuttings are taken during summer, dipped in a rooting hormone and placed in a humid environment until rooting occurs. Hardwood cuttings are taken in winter and can be rooted in the garden bed or in containers, after which they can be lifted and transplanted the following spring.

P. fraxinifolia
Caucasian wing nut
This vigorous and broadly spreading tree has glossy, dark green, pinnate leaves, consisting of about 21 leaflets and 40–60cm (16–24in) long. In autumn they turn yellow. In spring catkins appear; the small, yellowish male catkins soon fall, but the pinkish female ones, initially up to 15cm (6in) long, persist and grow to 50cm (20in) long, becoming covered with winged green fruits. H 25–30m (80–100ft), S 20–25m (65–80ft).
Aspect Full sun or semi-shade.
Hardiness ❀❀❀ Zones 5–9.

P. stenoptera 'Fern Leaf'
This beautiful cultivar of the Chinese wing nut has deeply cut, fern-like leaves, tinted purple at first and turning green in summer. It is a fast-growing tree but suckers less than other wing nuts; however, if roots are damaged by lawnmowers they may throw up suckers some way from the main trunk. H and S 25m (80ft).
Aspect Full sun or semi-shade.
Hardiness ❀❀❀ Zones 5–8.

PUNICA
Pomegranate
Of the two species of deciduous shrubs or small trees in the genus, only *P. granatum* is widely cultivated. The trees are grown for their attractive flowers and large, edible fruits. They are not hardy plants but are small enough to be grown in conservatories, and in warmer areas they can be grown as specimen trees or included in a mixed border.
Cultivation Grow in fertile, well-drained soil in sun.
Pruning Formative pruning should aim to encourage a short trunk and a balanced crown, while tipping

the lateral branches of young trees will encourage a denser crown. Occasional pruning is required for the removal of dead, dying, diseased or crossing branches.
Propagation Seed is the easiest method of propagation and should be collected when fresh and be sown into a container in a heated glasshouse in a frost-free and humid environment until germination occurs. Softwood cuttings can also be rooted during early summer and should be dipped in a rooting hormone and placed in a frost-free, humid environment until they root. Root suckers can also be carefully separated from the parent plant and potted on.

P. granatum
In tropical areas this small tree bears fruits and flowers almost all year round. The glossy green leaves, which have red veins at first, are up to 8cm (3in) long. Funnel-shaped, orange-red flowers are borne over a long period in summer to autumn and are followed by round, yellow-brown fruit. H and S 6m (20ft).
Aspect Full sun.
Hardiness ❀❀ Zones 8–10.

PYRUS
Pear
Among the 30 or so species of deciduous trees and shrubs in the genus is *P. communis*, which is

Punica granatum

Pyrus communis 'Williams Bon Chrétien'

Pyrus communis 'Conference'

the parent of the many forms of culinary and dessert pear. However, the ornamental forms, with attractive foliage, spring flowers and good autumn colour, make excellent specimen trees, especially in small gardens.
Cultivation Grow in fertile, free-draining but moisture-retentive soil in a warm, sunny and sheltered position. If the soil does not retain enough moisture the tree will produce inferior fruit unless extra water is given as the fruits begin to develop. Quince A rootstock will grow on poor soil but does best in deep, fertile, nutrient-rich soil. Quince C is a more widely available rootstock that produces slightly smaller trees. It is less tolerant of poor soil, although it does produce earlier, if slightly smaller, fruits.
Pruning The aim is to encourage the production of fruiting spurs and to remove older, less productive wood. This should only be done during the summer or winter.
Propagation Pears are usually grafted on to rootstocks of the species, *Pyrus communis*, or on to *Cydonia* (quince) rootstock, which provide some semi-dwarfing effects. Pears can also be propagated from seed, which should be collected when fresh and be sown into a container in an unheated glasshouse or cold frame until germination occurs. Winter grafting is popular, and is done on to seedlings of species closely related to the top stock or scion material.

Pyrus calleryiana
This ornamental pear has white spring flowers and good autumn colour. The two most popular forms are 'Bradford' and 'Chanticleer', both of which have a conical habit. H and S 15m (45ft).
Aspect Full sun.
Hardiness ✸✸✸ Zones 4–9.

P. communis 'Blake's Pride'
This is a widely grown and hardy American pear tree. Apart from producing very reliable, heavy crops of juicy, golden russet-like fruit in early autumn, it is also very resistant to fireblight (a disease that affects members of the rose family, Rosaceae). Grafted on to the common domestic pear, *Pyrus communis*, it can be maintained at 4m tall and wide (12ft x 12ft).
Aspect Full sun
Hardiness ✸✸✸ Zones 4–9.

P. c. 'Charneaux'
If planted in an orchard setting with other pears nearby, this will produce a profusion of extremely juicy sweet fruit. Grown on Quince A it can be maintained at 4m tall and wide (12ft x 12ft).
Aspect Full sun.
Hardiness ✸✸✸ Zones 4–9.

P. c. 'Clapp's Favourite'
This early fruiting variety requires an additional pollinator. Fruits are large, very tasty and juicy with a distinct flavour. Grown on Quince A it can be maintained at 4m tall and wide (12ft x 12ft).
Aspect Full sun.
Hardiness ✸✸✸ Zones 4–9.

P. c. 'Concorde'
This variety is an excellent garden pear that fruits regularly if a pollinator is nearby. Large, juicy fruits are produced in mid-autumn. Grown on Quince A it can be maintained at 4m tall and wide (12ft x 12ft).
Aspect Full sun.
Hardiness ✸✸✸ Zones 4–9.

P. c. 'Conference'
This widely grown variety is one of the best pears for cooler climates. A good pollinator for other pears, it is partially self-fertile. It is a very heavy cropping form if a suitable pollinator is nearby. The firm, yellowish fruits can be cooked or eaten fresh. Grown on Quince A it can be maintained at 4m tall and wide (12ft x 12ft).
Aspect Full sun.
Hardiness ✸✸✸ Zones 4–9.

P. c. 'Jeanne De Arc'
A traditional French variety, this has been cultivated for many years. It is a very heavy cropping form if a suitable pollinator is nearby. Although fruits are slightly smaller than those of some other varieties, they are very juicy and sweet. Grown on Quince A it can be maintained at 4m tall and wide (12ft x 12ft).
Aspect Full sun.
Hardiness ✸✸✸ Zones 4–9.

P. c. 'Packham's Triumph'
This smaller pear fruits late in the year. Small fruits are produced in large quantities if a suitable pollinator is grown nearby. Grown on Quince A it can be maintained at 4m tall and wide (12ft x 12ft).
Aspect Full sun.
Hardiness ✸✸✸ Zones 4–9.

P. c. 'Hosui'
This is a specially selected variety of the Asian pears that are grown for their round, sweet fruits and disease resistance. 'Hosui' produces masses of round, copper-coloured fruits which are very juicy and sweet. It can be pollinated by another Asian or common pear. Grown on Quince A it can be maintained at 4m tall and wide (12ft x 12ft).
Aspect Full sun.
Hardiness ✸✸✸ Zones 4–9.

QUERCUS
Oak
The genus contains about 600 species of evergreen and deciduous trees and shrubs. They vary widely in size and habit and are found in North and South

Pyrus calleryana 'Chanticleer'

Quercus alnifolia

America, northern Africa, Europe and Asia in tropical forests, arid areas, temperate mountainous regions and even swamps. They produce acorns (nuts) in scaly cups. They are best grown as specimen trees in large gardens.

Cultivation Grow in deep, fertile, well-drained soil in sun or semi-shade. Evergreen forms do best in full sun. Species that require acidic soil are noted below.

Pruning Formative pruning should produce a clear trunk and a balanced crown. Prune occasionally to remove dead, dying, diseased or crossing branches.

Propagation Seed and winter grafting are the main means of propagation. Many species of oaks are highly promiscuous so seed collected from gardens will have variable results, but seed collected from pure native stands will often come true. Sow fresh seed into a container in an unheated glasshouse or cold frame until germination occurs. Tender species and evergreen seed should be sown in a frost-free environment. Winter grafting can be done using seedlings of species closely related to the top stock or scion material.

Q. acutissima
Sawtooth oak

This fast-growing deciduous tree from China and Japan has an open crown. The glossy, green leaves, up to 20cm (8in) long, are edged with bristly teeth and turn yellow and golden-brown in autumn. H and S 15–20m (50–65ft). Aspect Full sun or semi-shade. Hardiness ❀❀❀ Zones 5–9.

Q. alba
White oak, American white oak

This beautiful deciduous tree, which is native to the eastern USA, has roughly flaking, dark grey bark. The lobed leaves, up to 23cm (9in) long, are bright green, tinged with pink in spring and becoming purple-red in autumn. Sadly, it is too large for most gardens. H and S 30–35m (100–115ft). Aspect Full sun or semi-shade. Hardiness ❀❀❀ Zones 3–9.

Q. alnifolia
Golden oak

This evergreen shrub or small, spreading tree from Cyprus is slow-growing but spectacular. The leaves, up to 6cm (2½in) long, are dark green above with golden-yellow felted undersides. It is tolerant of heat and of dry soils. H and S 8m (26ft). Aspect Full sun or semi-shade. Hardiness ❀❀ (borderline) Zones 6–9.

Q. bicolor
Swamp white oak

A spreading, deciduous tree from the south-eastern USA, this has pale grey-brown bark, which becomes deeply fissured as the tree ages. The glossy, dark green leaves, up to 15cm (6in) long, are obovate, and the undersides of young leaves are covered with white hairs. The leaves turn orange and coppery-red in autumn. It is more tolerant of wet soils than some other species and it is often found growing in flood plains. H and S 20m (65ft). Aspect Full sun or semi-shade. Hardiness ❀❀❀ Zones 4–8.

Q. castaneifolia
Chestnut-leaved oak

This spreading deciduous tree from the Caucasus and Iran has corky brown bark. The leaves are glossy, dark green, 15cm (6in) or more long, with triangularly toothed edges and greyish undersides. They turn brown-yellow in autumn. H and S 30m (100ft). Aspect Full sun or semi-shade. Hardiness ❀❀❀ Zones 6–9.

Q. cerris
Turkey oak

An adaptable deciduous species, this fast-growing oak from southern and central Europe has pale grey bark and a wide trunk. The flowers appear as red buds on the catkins in spring. The lance-shaped, dark green leaves, up to 12cm (5in) long, are pale blue-green beneath, turning yellow-brown in autumn. H and S 35m (115ft). Aspect Full sun or semi-shade. Hardiness ❀❀❀ Zones 5–7.

Q. coccinea
Scarlet oak

This fast-growing deciduous species is native to the eastern USA. It has a straight trunk and smooth, silver-grey bark. The glossy, dark green leaves, up to 15cm (6in) long, have deep C-shaped lobes and bristle-tipped teeth and turn scarlet-brown in autumn, persisting on the tree over a long period. H 20–25m (65–80ft), S 15–20m (50–65ft). Aspect Full sun or semi-shade. Hardiness ❀❀❀ Zones 4–9.

Q. dentata
Daimio oak, Japanese emperor oak

A spreading deciduous oak from eastern Asia, this has brown bark that becomes deeply fissured as the tree ages. The dark green leaves, 30cm (12in) or more long, are shallowly lobed and turn brown in autumn. It is a slow-growing species that needs acidic soil and warm summers. H 15m (50ft), S 20m (65ft).

Q. falcata
Spanish oak, southern red oak

This spreading deciduous tree, native to the southern USA, has grey-brown bark in scaly plates. The dark green, elliptical leaves, up to 23cm (9in) long, are covered with white-grey hairs on the undersides. The rounded lobes are smooth or have a few bristles. The leaves turn brown in autumn and hang on the tree for a long period. The almost spherical acorns are red-brown. This species needs acidic soil. H 15–20m (50–65ft), S 12–15m (40–50ft). Aspect Full sun or semi-shade. Hardiness ❀❀❀ Zones 6–7.

Q. frainetto
(syn. *Q. conferta*)
Hungarian oak

This fast-growing, deciduous tree, which is native to south-eastern Europe, develops a spreading habit. The bark is pale grey, eventually becoming fissured. The obovate, dark green leaves, 20cm (8in) or more long, are initially tipped with red and have grey hairs on the undersides, which soon fall off. The leaves have many rounded lobes and turn yellow-brown in autumn. It is tolerant of a range of soil conditions, including chalk. H 30m (100ft), S 25m (80ft). Aspect Full sun or semi-shade. Hardiness ❀❀❀ Zones 6–7.

Quercus coccinea 'Splendens'

Q. georgiana
Georgia oak, Stone Mountain oak
This deciduous species from the eastern USA is a large shrub or small tree, which develops a dense head. The shallowly lobed leaves, with a bristle at the end of each lobe, turn reddish-purple, occasionally orange, in autumn. H and S 10m (33ft).
Aspect Full sun or semi-shade.
Hardiness ❀❀ Zones 5–8.

Q. glauca
Japanese blue oak
This evergreen species, which develops into a broadly spreading, small tree, is native to China and Japan. The narrow, toothed leaves, up to 10cm (4in) long, are bronze-coloured when they emerge but by summer fade to mid-green above and blue-green beneath. Although fairly hardy, new growth is susceptible to damage from late spring frosts. It tolerates most soil conditions, including heavy clay soil. H and S 10–18m (33–60ft).
Aspect Full sun or semi-shade.
Hardiness ❀❀ Zones 8–9.

Q. x hispanica
Lucombe oak
In mild areas this hybrid between Q. cerris and Q. suber is almost evergreen, although it is usually semi-evergreen. It develops into a large, fairly upright tree. It has grey-brown, rather corky bark, which becomes deeply fissured. The dark green leaves, up to 5cm (2in) long, are blue-white beneath and each leaf lobe has a small spine at its tip. H 20m (65ft), S 15m (50ft).
Aspect Full sun or semi-shade.
Hardiness ❀❀❀ Zones 8–9.

Q. ilex
Holm oak, holly-leaved oak
This round-headed evergreen tree from south-western Europe has dark grey bark and ovate to lance-shaped dark green leaves, up to 8cm (3in) long, with white-grey hairs on the undersides. It is tolerant of a range of conditions and can even be grown as a hedge or pollarded. H 25m (80ft), S 20m (65ft).
Aspect Full sun or semi-shade.
Hardiness ❀❀ Zones 7–9.

Quercus ilex

Quercus robur

Q. imbricaria
Shingle oak
This deciduous species, native to the eastern USA, is a spreading, round-headed tree with smooth, brownish-grey bark. The narrow, willow-like leaves, up to 18cm (7in) long, are tinged red when they emerge in spring, turning green in summer and red-orange in autumn. It is tolerant of high temperatures. Although it will tolerate a range of conditions, it does best on well-drained, acidic soil. H 20m (65ft), S 25m (80ft).
Aspect Full sun or semi-shade.
Hardiness ❀❀❀ Zones 6–9.

Q. marilandica
Black jack oak
A deciduous species, native to the south-eastern USA, this is a slow-growing, spreading, fairly small tree with dark brown bark. The glossy, dark green leaves, up to 18cm (7in) long, taper towards the base and have three lobes at the broad end. They turn yellow-brown in autumn. The timber is hard and dense. H 12m (40ft), S 12–15m (40–50ft).
Aspect Full sun.
Hardiness ❀❀❀ Zones 6–9.

Q. myrsinifolia
Chinese evergreen oak, bamboo oak
This spreading, densely branched, evergreen tree from China, Japan and Laos has smooth, dark grey bark. The lance-shaped and slightly toothed leaves are glossy, dark green, up to 12cm (5in) long and tinged with bronze-red or bronze-purple when they first emerge. This species needs acidic soil. H 12m (40ft), S 10m (33ft).
Aspect Full sun or semi-shade.
Hardiness ❀❀ Zones 7–9.

Q. palustris
Pin oak
This popular, fast-growing deciduous species from the eastern USA develops into a broad-headed tree with smooth grey bark that darkens and develops thin ridges with age. The deeply lobed leaves are glossy mid-green, up to 15cm (6in) long, turning red-brown or scarlet in autumn. The acorns are almost spherical. Although it will tolerate a range of conditions, it does best on acidic soil. H 20–30m (65–100ft), S 12–20m (40–65ft).
Aspect Full sun or semi-shade.
Hardiness ❀❀❀ Zones 4–8.

Q. petraea
(syn. Q. sessiflora)
Sessile oak, Durmast oak
This spreading, deciduous tree from Europe develops an upright trunk with grey bark. The glossy, dark green leaves, up to 17cm (7in) long, are quite rounded and toothed. H 30–40m (100–130ft), S 25–30m (80–100ft).
Aspect Full sun.
Hardiness ❀❀❀ Zones 4–8.

Q. phellos
(syn. Q. pumila)
Willow oak
A deciduous species from the eastern USA, this has a spreading crown and grey bark. It has slender, dark green leaves, up to 12cm (5in) long, which turn yellow, then brown, in autumn. It needs acidic soil. H 20m (70ft), S 15m (50ft).
Aspect Full sun or semi-shade.
Hardiness ❀❀❀ Zones 5–9.

Quercus rubra

Quercus suber

Q. rhysophylla
Loquat oak

This evergreen species from Mexico is fast-growing, with a pyramidal habit at first but broadening with age, and dark brown bark. The glossy, heavily corrugated, dark green leaves, up to 25cm (10in) long, are shallowly lobed and tinged with bronze-red in spring. H 20–25m (65–80ft), S 15m (50ft). Aspect Full sun or semi-shade. Hardiness ❁ Zones 8–9.

Q. robur
(syn. *Q. pedunculata*)
Common oak, English oak, pedunculate oak

This spreading, fast-growing and long-lived tree from Europe has smooth brown-grey bark, which becomes fissured with age. The almost stalkless leaves are dark green, up to 15cm (6in) long, and shallowly lobed. The acorns have long stalks. The species thrives in drier conditions than *Q. petraea*. H 25m (80ft), S 20m (65ft). Aspect Full sun. Hardiness ❁❁❁ Zones 4–7.

Q. rubra
(syn. *Q. borealis*)
Red oak, northern red oak

A fast-growing deciduous species from North America, this develops a smooth, grey-brown bark. The dark green leaves, up to 20cm (8in) long, are oval and have lobes tipped with bristles. In autumn the leaves turn red and red-brown before falling. H 25m (80ft), S 20m (65ft). Aspect Full sun or semi-shade. Hardiness ❁❁❁ Zones 3–9.

Q. suber
Cork oak

The distinguishing feature of this spreading, evergreen, North African tree is its thick, corky bark, the source of corks for wine bottles, for which purpose the trees were once widely planted in Portugal. The toothed leaves are dark green, up to 8cm (3in) long and covered with greyish hairs beneath. H and S 20m (65ft). Aspect Full sun or semi-shade. Hardiness ❁❁ Zones 8–9.

Q. x *turneri*
Turner's oak

This hybrid between *Q. ilex* and *Q. robur* is a fast-growing, spreading, deciduous tree, which may be semi-evergreen in mild areas. The dark grey to brown-grey bark becomes fissured with age. The dark green leaves, up to 25cm (10in) long, are shallowly lobed. H 20–30m (65–100ft), S 20–25m (65–80ft). Aspect Full sun or semi-shade. Hardiness ❁❁❁ Zones 7–9.

Q. velutina
Black oak

Originally from North America, this fast-growing, deciduous oak has very dark brown, almost black bark. The elliptic, deeply lobed, glossy leaves, up to 25cm (10in) long, are dark green, turning reddish-brown or yellow-brown in autumn. H 25–30m (80–100ft), S 25m (80ft). Aspect Full sun or semi-shade. Hardiness ❁❁❁ Zones 3–9.

Q. virginiana
Live oak

This spreading evergreen species is from the south-eastern USA. It is fast growing and has red-brown bark. The elliptic, round-tipped leaves, up to 12cm (5in) long, are glossy and dark green above and greyish beneath. It does well in dry, acidic soil. H and S 15m (50ft). Aspect Full sun or semi-shade. Hardiness ❁ Zones 8–9.

RHAMNUS
Buckthorn

There are about 125 species of deciduous and evergreen shrubs and trees in the genus, most of which are found in northern temperate regions. Most species are thorny, and both of the species described below can be used as hedges.
Cultivation Grow in moisture-retentive soil in sun. (Note that other species have different cultural requirements.)
Pruning Formative pruning should aim to encourage a single, short trunk and a balanced crown. Some species are best grown as multi-stemmed specimens. Occasional pruning may be required for the removal of any dead, dying, diseased or crossing branches.
Propagation Seed is the main method of propagation, and it should be collected when fresh. Sow the fresh seed into a container in an unheated glasshouse or cold frame until germination occurs.

R. cathartica
Common buckthorn

This dense, thorny shrub, native to Europe, north-west Africa and Asia, can be grown as a small tree. It has glossy, toothed, dark green leaves, 6–8cm (2½–3in) long, which turn golden-yellow in autumn. Tiny yellow-green flowers are borne in late spring and are followed by shiny, black berries in autumn. It is able to withstand a range of difficult conditions.

H 6m (20ft), S 5m (16ft). Aspect Full sun. Hardiness ❁❁❁ Zones 3–7.

R. frangula
Alder buckthorn

This species from Europe and northern Africa has red autumn colour and clusters of reddish-black berries in late summer and autumn. It has ovate, glossy green leaves, up to 8cm (3in) long, and greenish flowers in spring. It is as adaptable and tolerant as *R. cathartica*. H and S 5m (16ft). Aspect Full sun. Hardiness ❁❁❁ Zones 3–7.

ROBINIA

The small genus contains about eight species (some authorities give four, others 20) of deciduous trees and shrubs. These fast growing plants, native to the USA and Mexico, are grown for their pretty foliage, pea-like flowers and autumn colour. They tolerate atmospheric pollution.
Cultivation Grow in moisture-retentive but well-drained soil in full sun, although plants will also tolerate poorer, drier conditions. Protect from cold, drying winds.
Pruning Early formative pruning should aim to produce a clear trunk and a balanced crown. Occasional pruning is required for the removal of dead, dying, diseased or crossing branches.
Propagation Seed, winter grafting and summer budding are the main methods of propagation. Sow fresh seed into a container in an unheated glasshouse or cold frame

Rhamnus alaternus 'Argenteovariegata'

Robinia pseudoacacia 'Frisia'

until germination occurs. Winter grafting and summer budding are done using seedling robinias.

R. x ambigua 'Bella Rosea'
(syn. R. x ambigua 'Bella-rosea', R. x ambigua 'Bellarosea')
This strongly growing cultivar, developed from a hybrid between R. pseudoacacia and R. viscosa, is a small, elegant tree, bearing large racemes of pale pink, pea-like flowers in early summer. H 12m (40ft), S 7m (23ft).
Aspect Full sun.
Hardiness ❀❀❀ Zones 3–5.

R. x ambigua 'Idaho'
(syn. R. x ambigua 'Idahoensis', R. 'Idaho')
This cultivar is widely planted in the western states of the USA. It is similar to 'Bella Rosea' but has fragrant, lavender-pink flowers. H 12m (40ft), S 10m (33ft).
Aspect Full sun.
Hardiness ❀❀❀ (borderline) Zones 3–5.

R. x margaretta 'Pink Cascade'
(syn. R. x margaretta 'Casque Rouge', R. x slavinii 'Pink Cascade')
A fast-growing form, which develops into a large, suckering shrub or small tree, this bears masses of purple-pink, pea-like flowers. H and S 10m (33ft).
Aspect Full sun.
Hardiness ❀❀❀ Zones 3–5.

R. pseudoacacia
False acacia, black locust, locust
This suckering and thorny but broadly columnar tree has deeply furrowed bark. The feathery green, pinnate leaves, up to 30cm (12in) long, have up to 23 leaflets. In warm summers fragrant white flowers are borne in long racemes, followed by dark brown seedpods. H 25m (80ft), S 15m (50ft).
Named varieties The popular 'Frisia' has butter-yellow leaves in spring and summer. In warm areas the leaves fade to yellow-green.
'Pyramidalis' (syn. 'Fastigiata'), a fastigiate form with a conical habit and thornless branches, has smaller flowers than 'Frisia'.
Aspect Full sun.
Hardiness ❀❀❀ Zones 4–8.

Roystonia oleracea

R. x slavinii 'Hillieri'
This elegant small tree, which is best planted in a sheltered spot, is an excellent choice for a small garden. It has slightly arching branches and in early summer bears clusters of lilac-pink, slightly scented flowers. H 15m (50ft), S 10m (33ft).
Aspect Full sun.
Hardiness ❀❀❀ Zones 5–8.

R. x slavinii 'Purple Robe'
(syn. R. pseudoacacia 'Purple Robe')
This tree requires a sheltered position, where it will not be buffeted by strong winds. New growth is flushed with purple in spring, and clusters of violet-purple flowers are borne in summer. H 15m (50ft), S 10m (33ft).
Aspect Full sun.
Hardiness ❀❀❀ Zones 5–8.

ROYSTONEA
Royal palm
The genus contains ten to twelve species of fast-growing, single-stemmed palms, which are found throughout the Caribbean islands and neighbouring mainlands. The upright, usually smooth grey trunks may be swollen at the base or in the centre of mature plants. Small specimens can be grown in containers in conservatories.
Cultivation Outdoors, grow in fertile, moisture-retentive but well-drained soil in sun.
Pruning Like most palms, little pruning is required apart from the occasional cosmetic removal

of dead or dying leaves and spent flower clusters during early summer.
Propagation Seed is the easiest method of propagation and should be collected when fresh and sown into a container in a heated glasshouse in a humid environment at 29°C (84°F) until germination occurs.

R. oleracea
This species is widely grown in the tropics. It is a tall, slender plant with a narrow, silver trunk, the top quarter of which is green, although this is scarcely visible from the ground. The flattish, arching fronds, often up to 4m (12ft) long, consist of many narrow, dark green leaflets. H 40m (130ft), S 10m (33ft).
Aspect Full sun.
Hardiness (Min. 15°C/59°F) Zone 11.

R. regia
Cuban royal palm
A beautiful and graceful palm from Cuba, this has a silver-coloured trunk, of which the top

quarter is bright green. The long leaves, up to 5m (16ft) long, consist of numerous green leaflets arranged in several ranks, giving the fronds a spiky appearance. In summer panicles, up to 1m (3ft) long, of white flowers are borne, followed by large clusters of orange, marble-like fruits. H 30m (100ft), S 10m (33ft).
Aspect Full sun.
Hardiness (Min. 15°C/59°F) Zone 11.

SABAL
Palmetto
The 14 species of palm, which may be single-stemmed or stemless, are found in southern North America, Central America and the West Indies. They are tender, but in warm areas they make fine specimen trees. Small plants can be grown in containers and kept under glass.
Cultivation Outdoors, grow in fertile, moisture-retentive but well-drained soil in sun.
Pruning Pruning is only required to remove dead leaves and spent flower clusters during early summer.

Sabal mexicana

Salix babylonica

Propagation Seed is the easiest method of propagation and should be collected when fresh and be sown into a container in a heated glasshouse in a humid environment at 29°C (84°F) until germination occurs.

S. mexicana
(syn. *S. guatemalensis*, *S. texana*)
Texas palmetto
When young, this is a beautiful palm, but as it ages it can develop a sloping, sagging trunk and the stems of the lower branches tend to remain attached for a long period, giving an untidy appearance. The bright green or yellow-green leaves, up to 1m (3ft) long, are semicircular and deeply divided to about halfway. Long panicles of creamy-white flowers are borne above the foliage in late summer. H 18m (60ft), S 4m (12ft). Aspect Full sun. Hardiness (Min. 10–13°C/ 50–5°F) Zones 8–10.

S. minor
Dwarf palmetto, bush palmetto, scrub palmetto
The species is often found in swampy ground in the southern USA, where it grows as an under-storey plant, developing into thickets. The stems are usually prostrate, although clear-trunk specimens occasionally occur. The fan-shaped leaves, up to 1.5m (5ft) across, are blue-green and divided into numerous spiky lobes for about two-thirds of the leaf. In summer erect panicles, up to 1.8m (6ft) long, of cream flowers are produced and are followed by blackish fruits. H 1.8m (6ft), S 3m (10ft). Aspect Full sun. Hardiness (Min. 3–5°C/ 37–41°F) Zones 7–11.

S. palmetto
Cabbage palmetto, common blue palmetto
This palm, which is found in swampy ground in the southern states of the USA, has a rough, erect stem. The fan-shaped leaves, to 1.8m (6ft) across, are dark green and divided into pointed lobes with thread-like filaments between them. In summer there are panicles of cream flowers. H 30m (100ft), S 7m (23ft). Aspect Full sun to light shade. Hardiness (Min. 5–7°C/ 41–5°F) Zones 8–11.

SALIX
Willow, osier, sallow
The 300 or so species in this genus are mostly deciduous trees and shrubs, known especially for their catkins and their thirst for water. Larger species are suitable only for large gardens, where the vigorous, questing roots can't damage drains or foundations. Smaller species make attractive focal points, and shrubby species are ideal in mixed borders.
Cultivation Grow in moisture-retentive but well-drained soil in sun. They do not do well in chalky conditions. Willows are often pollarded.

Pruning Formative pruning should aim to produce a clear trunk and a balanced crown. Most willows can be pollarded and this should be done on a regular three-year cycle during winter. Occasional pruning is required to remove dead, dying, diseased or crossing branches.
Propagation Seed should be collected when fresh and sown into a container in an unheated glasshouse or cold frame until germination occurs. Softwood cuttings are taken during summer, dipped in a rooting hormone and placed in a humid environment until rooting occurs. Hardwood cuttings can be taken in winter and then be lifted and transplanted the following spring.

S. alba
White willow
This fast-growing, vigorous tree, native to Europe, northern Africa and Asia, is often found near rivers and in water meadows. It has semi-pendulous branches and pinkish-grey to grey-brown shoots. The catkins, male ones up to 5cm (2in) long, are yellow and appear in spring. The slender leaves, up to 10cm (4in) long, are covered with silvery hairs when young, giving the plant its characteristic silver-white appearance. H 20–25m (65–80ft), S 10–m (33ft).
Named varieties *S. alba* var. *vitellina* 'Britzensis' (scarlet willow, coral bark willow) has reddish-orange winter stems. The best colour appears on shoots less than two seasons old, so prune hard back in early spring in alternate years. Aspect Full sun. Hardiness ❀❀❀ Zones 2–8.

S. babylonica
Chinese weeping willow
This graceful tree from northern China often grows near rivers, where the long, pendent, green-brown shoots cascade towards the water. The narrow green leaves, up to 10cm (4in) long, are grey-green beneath. Silver-green catkins, male ones up to 5cm (2in) long, appear in spring. H and S 12m (40ft).
Named varieties *S. babylonica* var. *pekinensis* 'Tortuosa' (syn. *S. matsudana* 'Tortuosa'; dragon's claw willow) has a more upright habit. The twisted shoots create a striking silhouette in winter. H 15m (50ft), S 8m (26ft). Aspect Full sun. Hardiness ❀❀❀ Zones 6–8.

S. caprea
Goat willow, pussy willow, great sallow
Native to Europe and north-eastern Asia, this tree is grown for its attractive spring catkins: the female catkins are the pretty, silvery flowers (pussy willow) beloved of children and flower arrangers; the yellow-green male catkins are longer and borne early in the year, sometimes in midwinter. The leaves, up to 12cm (5in) long, are dark green above and greyish beneath. The bare winter stems are yellow-purple. It is too straggly for most gardens but provides fast-growing shelter in a new garden. Unlike most willows, this will tolerate dryish ground. H 8–10m (26–33ft), S 4–6m (14–20ft). Aspect Full sun. Hardiness ❀❀❀ Zones 4–8.

Salix daphnoides

S. daphnoides
Violet willow
This small, conical tree from Europe and Central Asia is upright at first, spreading with age. The elliptic leaves, up to 12cm (5in) long, are dark green above and blue-green beneath. The greyish catkins, up to 4cm (1½in) long, are borne in late winter to early spring on the bare, purplish branches, which in winter have a whitish bloom. The stems are even more colourful if they are cut hard back every two years. H 8m (26ft), S 5–6m (16–20ft). Aspect Full sun. Hardiness ❋❋❋ Zones 5–8.

S. x sepulcralis
Weeping willow
This large hybrid is similar to *S. babylonica*, although it has a slightly less weeping habit. Its catkins are similar to those of *S. alba*. H and S 20m (65ft). Named varieties *S. x sepulcralis* var. *chrysocoma* (syn. *S. alba* 'Tristis'; golden weeping willow) has strongly arching, golden-yellow stems. In summer the stems are clothed with narrow, bright green leaves, up to 12cm (5in) long.

'Erythroflexuosa' has twisted orange and yellow stems. Both can be grown as attractive pollards or coppiced trees. Aspect Full sun. Hardiness ❋❋❋ Zones 6–8.

SASSAFRAS
The three deciduous species in the genus have aromatic foliage. They are native to China, Taiwan and North America and are grown as specimen trees for their attractive habit, small spring flowers and good autumn colour. *Cultivation* Grow in moisture-retentive but well-drained, acidic soil in sun. Provide shelter from cold winds. Remove suckers as soon as they appear. *Pruning* Formative pruning should produce a clear trunk and a balanced crown. Prune occasionally to remove dead, dying, diseased or crossing branches. *Propagation* Seed and natural layers or suckers are the main methods of propagation. Sow fresh seed into a container in an unheated glasshouse or cold frame until

germination occurs. Sassafras will often produce natural layers or suckers that can be lifted and removed from the parent plant during late winter or early spring.

S. albidum
This medium-sized, often suckering tree from North America has an upright trunk with grey, fissured bark. The dark green leaves, up to 15cm (6in) long, have three deep lobes and turn yellow, orange and purple in autumn; the colours are best after hot summers. H 20–25m (65–80ft), S 10–15m (33–50ft). Aspect Full sun or semi-shade. Hardiness ❋❋❋ Zones 4–9.

SCHEFFLERA
This large genus contains some 700 species of evergreen trees, shrubs and climbers. They are mostly native to South-east Asia and the islands of the Pacific and are grown for their attractive, much-divided palmate leaves. They are tender plants, which are often grown as houseplants. *Cultivation* Outdoors, grow in fertile, moisture-retentive but well-drained soil in shade. Protect from cold, drying winds. *Pruning* Formative pruning should encourage a clear trunk and a balanced crown. Prune occasionally to remove dead, dying, diseased or crossing branches. *Propagation* Softwood cuttings to be taken during early summer and should be dipped in a rooting hormone and placed in a frost-free, humid environment until they root.

S. actinophylla
(syn. *Brassaia actinophylla*)
Australian ivy palm, octopus tree, umbrella tree
In its native New Guinea and north-eastern Australia this species can be invasive. It has an upright habit. The large, glossy, bright green leaves, up to 30cm (12in) across, have 7–16 oval leaflets and are borne in dense clusters, giving the stems a tufted appearance. In spring and summer panicles, up to 80cm (32in) long, of pink to red flowers are borne at the tips of the branches, followed by small clusters of red berries.

Schefflera arboricola

H 12m (40ft), S 6m (20ft). Aspect Light shade to full sun. Hardiness (Min. 13°C/55°F) Zones 9–12.

S. elegantissima
(syn. *Aralia elegantissima*, *Dizygotheca elegantissima*)
False aralia
Small specimens of this New Caledonian plant are popular as houseplants for the long, delicate leaflets. In the wild these erect trees have leaves up to 40cm (16in) long, each deeply divided into 7–11 narrow leaflets, dark green above and brown-green beneath, with white midribs. Umbels, up to 30cm (12in) long, of yellow-green flowers are borne in autumn and early winter and are followed by round black fruits. H 15m (50ft), S 3m (10ft). Aspect Light shade to full sun. Hardiness (Min. 13–15°C/55–9°F) Zones 9–12.

SCIADOPITYS
Japanese umbrella pine
The only species is the genus, which is native to Japan and is a generally slow-growing, evergreen conifer with a graceful habit and attractive foliage and cones. It can be grown as a specimen. *Cultivation* Grow in moisture-retentive but well-drained, neutral to acidic soil in sun. Train the leading stem to give an upright shape. *Pruning* Early formative pruning should aim to produce a clear trunk and a balanced crown, while

tipping the lateral branches of young trees will encourage a denser crown. *Propagation* Semi-ripe and softwood cuttings can be rooted during summer and should be dipped in a rooting hormone and placed in a humid environment until rooting occurs.

S. verticillata
This distinctive conifer has a strongly conical habit and slender, glossy, dark green leaves, yellow-green beneath and up to 12cm (5in) long, which are borne in whorls of 15–25 along the stems. The leaves are often fused in pairs. The bark is red-brown and peels in ribbons. Small male cones are borne in clusters, but the large female cones, up to 8cm (3in) long, are borne singly. H 20m (65ft), S 8m (26ft). Aspect Full sun or semi-shade. Hardiness ❋❋❋ Zones 5–7.

Sciadopitys verticillata

Sequoiadendron giganteum

SEQUOIA
Coast redwood, Californian redwood

The single species in the genus is a fast-growing, evergreen conifer, native to California and Oregon. These trees are among the tallest in the world. They do best in areas with moist, cool summers, when they can be used as handsome specimens. They tolerate pollution well.
Cultivation Grow in fertile, moisture-retentive but well-drained soil in sun or semi-shade. This is one of the few conifers that will re-shoot from old wood.
Pruning Early formative pruning should aim to produce a clear trunk and a balanced crown, while tipping the lateral branches of young trees will encourage a denser crown.

Propagation Seed is the easiest method of propagation. Sow fresh seed into a container in an unheated glasshouse or cold frame until germination occurs.

S. sempervirens
This columnar conifer has horizontal or slightly downturned branches and deeply ridged, red-brown bark. The dark green leaves, up to 2cm (½in) long, are borne in pairs, pointing forwards along the shoots. Cones, up to 4cm (1½in) long, ripen to brown. H 35m (115ft), S 10m (33ft).
Named varieties 'Cantab' is a fast-growing form with needles that are adpressed (flattened against the stem), light green when young and dark when older.
Aspect Full sun or semi-shade.
Hardiness ✱✱✱ Zones 7–9.

SEQUOIADENDRON
Sierra redwood, giant redwood, wellingtonia
The single species is an evergreen conifer from California, which makes a striking specimen, attaining heights of 80m (260ft) or more in the wild (less in gardens). It has a more columnar habit than the closely related *Sequoia sempervirens* and prefers a drier climate.
Cultivation Grow in fertile, moisture-retentive but well-drained soil.
Pruning Early formative pruning should aim to produce a clear trunk and a balanced crown, while tipping the lateral branches of young trees will encourage a denser crown.
Propagation Seed is the easiest method of propagation and should be collected when fresh and sown into a container in an unheated glasshouse or cold frame until germination occurs. Semi-ripe and softwood cuttings can be taken during summer and should be dipped in a rooting hormone and placed in a humid environment until rooting occurs.

S. giganteum
This fast-growing redwood is distinguished by its massive trunk, covered with thick, spongy red-brown bark. The long branches often sweep down to the ground. The tiny pointed leaves are scale-like and blue-green. H 30m (100ft), S 10m (33ft).
Named varieties 'Glaucum' is a bold narrowly conical form with intense blue-green foliage.
Aspect Full sun.
Hardiness ✱✱✱ Zones 6–8.

SOPHORA

The 50 or so species in the genus are evergreen and deciduous trees and shrubs. They have attractive leaves and fragrant flowers and can be successfully grown as specimen plants.
Cultivation Grow in well-drained soil in sun.
Pruning Early formative pruning should aim to produce a clear trunk and a balanced crown.
Propagation Seed, winter grafting and summer budding are the main methods of propagation. Seed

should be collected when fresh and sown into a container in an unheated glasshouse or cold frame until germination occurs. Winter grafting and summer budding can be carried out using seedling rowans or whitebeams.

S. japonica
Japanese pagoda tree
This graceful deciduous tree from China and Korea is not dissimilar to *Robinia pseudoacacia*, but it is thornless and smaller. The dark green leaves, up to 25cm (10in) long, are divided into up to 17 narrow leaflets, which turn yellow in autumn. In late summer to early autumn pea-like, fragrant, white flowers are borne in panicles. H 30m (100ft), S 20m (65ft).
Named varieties The cultivar 'Regent' is popular in the USA for its speed of growth, good summer and autumn foliage and ability to flower from a young age. 'Violacea' has white flowers, flushed with rose-violet, which are borne amid the green, fern-like foliage in early autumn.
Aspect Full sun or semi-shade.
Hardiness ✱✱✱ Zones 3–9.

SORBUS
Mountain ash
The genus contains about 100 species of deciduous trees and shrubs, which are found throughout the northern hemisphere. These are some of the finest ornamental trees for

Sequoia sempervirens

small gardens, providing an attractive habit together with flowers, variously coloured berries and good autumn foliage.

Cultivation Grow in fertile, moisture-retentive but well-drained soil in sun or light shade. Rowans prefer moister soil than whitebeams do.

Pruning Early formative pruning should aim to produce a clear trunk and a balanced crown. Fireblight can be a problem and any infected branches should be removed as soon as symptoms appear back to healthy tissue.

Propagation Seed, winter grafting and summer budding are the most common methods of propagation. Seed should be collected when fresh and sown into a container in a cold frame until germination occurs. Winter grafting and summer budding are done using seedling rowans or whitebeams.

S. alnifolia
Korean mountain ash, alder whitebeam
This medium-sized tree, native to eastern Asia, is broadly conical. It has toothed, dark green leaves, up to 10cm (4in) long, which turn yellow-orange and purple in autumn. Dense clusters, up to 8cm (3in) across, of small white flowers are borne in spring and are followed by pretty dark pink to red berries, up to 1cm (⅓in) across. H 20m (65ft), S 10m (33ft).

Sophora microphylla

Named varieties 'Skyline' has an upright habit and orange-yellow autumn colours.
Aspect Full sun or semi-shade.
Hardiness ❋❋❋ Zone 5.

S. aria
Whitebeam
A broadly columnar tree from Europe, this has toothed, glossy, dark green leaves, up to 12cm (5in) long, which are covered with silver-white hairs on the undersides and turn yellow in autumn. In late spring clusters, up to 8cm (3in) across, of white flowers are borne, and these are followed by dark red berries, up to 1cm (⅓in) across. H 15–20m (50–65ft), S 8–10m (26–33ft).
Aspect Full sun or semi-shade.
Hardiness ❋❋❋ Zone 5.

S. aucuparia
Common mountain ash, rowan
A small tree from Europe, this species has ferny, dark green leaves, 20cm (8in) long, which have 9–15 sharply toothed leaflets. The leaves turn red or yellowish in autumn. Clusters, up to 12cm (5in) across, of white flowers are borne in spring and are followed by orange-red berries. H 15m (50ft), S 7–8m (23–26ft).
Named varieties 'Cardinal Royal' is an upright form with masses of beautiful scarlet berries, which persist long into winter.
Aspect Full sun or semi-shade.
Hardiness ❋❋❋ Zones 3–6.

Sorbus aucuparia

S. cashmiriana
Kashmir rowan
This is a good tree or large shrub for a small garden. It is native to the western Himalayas, has a spreading habit and dark green, pinnate leaves, up to 20cm (8in) long and with 17–21 leaflets. In spring it bears clusters, up to 12cm (5in) across, of pink or white flowers, and these are followed by white berries. The berries remain on the tree long after the leaves have fallen. H 8m (26ft), S 5–7m (16–23ft).
Aspect Full sun or semi-shade.
Hardiness ❋❋❋ Zone 4.

S. commixta
(syn. S. discolor, S. reflexipetala)
Scarlet rowan
A broadly conical tree, this species from Japan and Korea has dark green, pinnate leaves, up to 20cm (8in) long and consisting of 17 leaflets. The leaves turn yellow-red and purple in autumn. In late spring the tree bears clusters, up to 15cm (6in) across, of creamy-white flowers, which are followed by bright orange-red berries. H 10m (33ft), S 5–7m (16–23ft).
Aspect Full sun or semi-shade.
Hardiness ❋❋❋ Zone 6.

S. folgneri
Chinese whitebeam
Native to China, this graceful if rather variable small garden tree

has toothed, dark green leaves, white beneath and up to 10cm (4in) long. White flowers are borne in dense clusters, to 10cm (4in) across, in spring and are followed by clusters of dark red or purple-red berries. H and S 8m (26ft).
Named varieties 'Lemon Drop' has orange-yellow berries and brownish-yellow autumn colour.
Aspect Full sun or semi-shade.
Hardiness ❋❋❋ Zone 6.

S. hupehensis
(syn. S. glabrescens)
Hubei rowan
This spectacular, small, round-headed tree from China has pinnate, blue-green leaves, up to 15cm (6in) long and with up to 15 leaflets. The leaves turn vivid red in autumn. In late spring pyramidal clusters, to 12cm (5in) across, of white flowers are borne and are followed by small white, occasionally pink-tinged, berries. H 8–12m (26–40ft), S 8m (26ft).
Named varieties 'Coral Fire' has reddish stems, scarlet berries and good autumn colour.
'Pink Pagoda' (syn. 'November Pink') has pink-tinged fruits, which slowly whiten in autumn before turning pink and persisting well into winter.
Aspect Full sun or semi-shade.
Hardiness ❋❋❋ Zone 6.

Sorbus vilmorinii

S. intermedia
Swedish whitebeam
A neat, round-headed tree, this whitebeam, which is native to north-western Europe, has toothed, glossy, dark green leaves, up to 12cm (5in) long, which are covered with grey-white hairs on the undersides. Dense clusters, up to 12cm (5in) across, of white flowers are borne in late spring and are followed by oval, bright red berries. H and S 12m (40ft).
Aspect Full sun or semi-shade.
Hardiness ❁❁❁ Zone 5.

S. 'Joseph Rock'
This widely planted tree has bright green, pinnate leaves, up to 15cm (6in) long, with 15–19 leaflets, which turn red, orange, purple and copper in autumn. White flowers are borne in clusters, up to 10cm (4in) across, in late spring, and these are followed by masses of yellow berries, which turn bright orange-yellow. It is susceptible to fireblight. H 10m (33ft), S 7m (23ft).
Aspect Full sun or semi-shade.
Hardiness ❁❁❁ Zones 3–6.

S. megalocarpa
A small garden tree or large shrub, this species from China has a spreading habit. The toothed, dark green leaves, up to 25cm (10in) long, are reddish as they emerge in spring and again in autumn. Clusters, up to 15cm (6in) across, of highly pungent, creamy-white flowers are borne in early spring and are followed in late summer by edible, yellow-brown fruits. H 8m (26ft), S 10m (33ft).
Aspect Semi-shade.
Hardiness ❁❁❁ Zone 6.

S. 'Sunshine'
This small cultivar has dark green, pinnate leaves, each with 14–18 leaflets, which turn vivid orange and yellow in autumn. Large clusters of golden-yellow berries follow the white flowers which appear in spring. H 10m (33ft), S 7m (23ft).
Aspect Full sun or semi-shade.
Hardiness ❁❁❁ Zones 3–6.

S. thibetica
A broadly conical tree from south-western China, this has dark green leaves, up to 12cm (5in) long, which are covered with white hairs when they first emerge, remaining hairy on the undersides. White flowers are borne in clusters, up to 6cm (2½in) across, in late spring and are followed by greenish berries. H 20m (65ft), S 15m (50ft).
Named varieties 'John Mitchell', an attractive small tree, has large green leaves, silvery on the underside. Small, creamy-white flowers are followed by clusters of large, orange-yellow berries. H and S 15m (50ft).
Aspect Full sun or semi-shade.
Hardiness ❁❁❁ Zone 5.

S. vilmorinii
Vilmorin's rowan
This outstandingly beautiful small garden tree, which is native to south-western China, has low, spreading branches. The glossy, dark green, pinnate leaves, up to 15cm (6in) long, have 11–31 leaflets. Creamy-white flowers are borne in clusters, up to 10cm (4in) across, from late spring to early summer and are followed by dark red fruits. H and S 5–8m (16–26ft).
Aspect Full sun or semi-shade.
Hardiness ❁❁❁ Zone 5.

S. 'Wilfred Fox'
This upright tree has glossy, dark green leaves, up to 12cm (5in) long, which are covered with white hairs beneath. The white flowers, borne in clusters, up to 10cm (4in) across, in late spring, are followed by red-flushed, yellowish berries. H 12–15m (40–50ft), S 10–12m (33–40ft).
Aspect Full sun or semi-shade.
Hardiness ❁❁❁ Zone 5.

SPATHODEA
African tulip tree
The single species in the genus is a usually evergreen tree from tropical Africa. It is tender and needs to be grown under glass where the temperature falls below 13°C (55°F). In warm areas it can be grown as a specimen tree.
Cultivation Grow in fertile, moisture-retentive soil in full sun.
Pruning Formative pruning should produce a clear trunk and a balanced crown. Prune dead, diseased or crossed branches.
Propagation Sow fresh seed in a pot at 18–24°C (64–75°F) in spring, or air-layer in summer.

S. campanulata
The fast-growing species is grown for its bright red, azalea-like flowers, which are borne in large clusters in spring and autumn. The glossy, dark green, pinnate leaves, up to 45cm (18in) long, have 9–19 leaflets, arranged in pairs down a central stem. The quick growth produces brittle branches, which are easily damaged. H 25m (80ft), S 18m (60ft).
Aspect Full sun.
Hardiness (Min. 13–15°C/55–9°F) Zones 10–12.

STAPHYLEA
Bladdernut
There are 11 species of deciduous shrubs and small trees in the genus, which are found in temperate areas of the northern hemisphere. They can be used in shrub borders and woodland gardens.
Cultivation Grow in moisture-retentive but well-drained soil in sun or semi-shade.
Pruning Early formative pruning should aim to produce a clear trunk and a balanced crown. Occasional pruning is required for the removal of dead, dying, diseased or crossing branches.
Propagation Collect fresh seed and sow in a pot in an unheated glasshouse or cold frame. Softwood cuttings are taken during summer and placed in a humid environment until rooting occurs. Bladdernuts will often produce natural layers or suckers that can be lifted and removed from the parent plant during late winter or early spring.

Spathodea campanulata

Staphylea trifolia

Stewartia pseudocamellia

S. holocarpa
Chinese bladdernut

This spreading shrub or small tree has blue-green leaves with three leaflets, up to 10cm (4in) long. In late spring white to pink bell-shaped flowers, up to 15mm (½in) long, are borne in clusters and are followed by greenish fruits, up to 5cm (2in) long. H 10m (33ft), S 6m (20ft).
Named varieties 'Rosea' is a large, shrub-like plant, which can be easily trained to grow as a small standard tree. In spring it has beautiful dangling clusters of pale pink flowers. Its blue-green leaves are tinged with bronze in spring and pale yellow in autumn.
Aspect Full sun or semi-shade.
Hardiness ❀❀❀ Zone 6.

STEWARTIA
(syn. Stuartia)

The 15–20 species in the genus are related to *Camellia*. They are deciduous and evergreen trees and shrubs from eastern Asia and the south-eastern USA, grown for their attractive foliage and flowers. They make good specimen trees.
Cultivation Grow in fertile, moisture-retentive but well-drained, neutral to acidic soil in full sun or semi-shade.
Pruning Formative pruning should aim to produce a clear trunk and a balanced crown. Prune occasionally to remove dead, dying, diseased or crossing branches.
Propagation Collect fresh seed and sow in a pot in an unheated glasshouse or cold frame. Take softwood cuttings in summer.

Winter grafting on to seedlings is practised on those that are hard to root.

S. malacodendron
Silky camellia

This small, deciduous tree makes a lovely garden tree. The glossy, dark green, ovate leaves are up to 10cm (4in) long, toothed and covered with hairs on the undersides; they turn orange-yellow in autumn. In midsummer white flowers, streaked and centred with purple, up to 10cm (4in) across, are borne along the stems. H 6–7m (20–23ft), S 6m (20ft).
Aspect Semi-shade.
Hardiness ❀❀ Zones 6–9.

S. monadelpha
Tall stewartia

This deciduous tree has a broadly columnar habit, which spreads with age, and attractive grey and red-orange, peeling bark. The dark green, ovate leaves, up to 10cm (4in) long, are glossy and toothed, turning orange and red in autumn. Yellow-centred, white flowers, up to 4cm (1½in) across, are borne in summer. H 25m (80ft), S 20m (65ft).
Aspect Semi-shade.
Hardiness ❀❀❀ Zones 5–8

S. pseudocamellia
Japanese stewartia

This small, deciduous tree from Japan has a tight, upright habit. In autumn the toothed, dark green leaves turn russet-orange and the winter bark is a brownish silver and green. In summer white,

yellow-centred flowers, up to 6cm (2½in) across, are produced in abundance. H 20m (65ft), S 8–10m (26–33ft).
Named varieties The semi-weeping form 'Cascade' has long, arching shoots.

Plants in Koreana Group (syn. *S. koreana*, *S. pseudocamellia* var. *koreana*; Korean stewartia) are grown for their large flowers, which open wide in late summer. They have an upright habit and silver, green and brown bark. In autumn the dark green leaves turn orange-yellow.
Aspect Semi-shade.
Hardiness ❀❀❀ Zones 5–8.

S. serrata

This small deciduous tree has orange-brown bark and reddish shoots. The leaves, up to 8cm (3in) long, turn orange-yellow in autumn. In early summer purple-tinged, white flowers, up to 6cm (2½in) across and with yellow centres, are borne singly on branches. H 4m (12ft), S 3m (10ft).
Aspect Semi-shade.
Hardiness ❀❀ Zone 6.

S. sinensis
(syn. S. gemmata)
Chinese stewartia

This small deciduous tree has peeling reddish-brown bark. The dark green leaves, up to 10cm (4in) long, turn crimson in autumn. Fragrant white flowers, to 5cm (2in) across, are borne singly in midsummer. H 20m (65ft), S 5m (16ft).
Aspect Full sun or semi-shade.
Hardiness ❀❀❀ Zones 5–7.

S. 'Skyrocket'
(syn. S. x henryae)

This fast-growing hybrid between *S. monadelpha* and *S. pseudocamellia* has flaking bark. The dark green leaves turn orange-yellow in autumn, and yellow-centred, white flowers are borne in midsummer. H 25m (80ft), S 8m (26ft).
Aspect Semi-shade.
Hardiness ❀❀❀ Zones 5–8.

STYRAX
Snowbell, silverballs

This genus comprises 100 or so species of evergreen and deciduous shrubs and trees grown

for their lovely spring and summer flowers. They do best in a woodland setting.
Cultivation Grow in fertile, moisture-retentive but well-drained, neutral to acidic soil in sun or semi-shade.
Pruning Formative pruning should produce a clear trunk and a balanced crown. Prune occasionally to remove dead, dying, diseased or crossing branches.
Propagation Sow fresh seed in a pot in an unheated glasshouse or cold frame until germination occurs. Softwood cuttings are taken during summer. Winter grafting on to seedling snowbell trees can also be done.

S. japonicus
Japanese snowbell

This small, deciduous garden tree has wide-spreading branches with drooping tips. The glossy green leaves, up to 10cm (4in) long, turn yellow or red in autumn. In early summer clusters of white, yellow-centred flowers hang from the undersides of the branches. H 10m (33ft), S 8m (26ft).
Named varieties Benibana Group 'Pink Chimes' has an upright habit and pink flowers.

'Crystal' is an upright, vigorous form with dark purple-green foliage and white flowers, faintly tinted purple.

'Emerald Pagoda' has large white, fragrant flowers, an attractive vase-shaped habit and good heat tolerance.
Aspect Full sun or semi-shade.
Hardiness ❀❀❀ Zones 5–8.

Styrax japonicus

SYZYGIUM

There are about 500 species of evergreen trees and shrubs in the genus. They are closely related to myrtles and have aromatic foliage. The most widely grown member of the genus is *S. aromaticum* (clove). They are tender plants, mostly native to tropical areas of South-east Asia and Australasia, where they can be grown in mixed borders or, in cold areas, in containers under glass.

Cultivation Outdoors, grow in moisture-retentive but well-drained soil in sun or semi-shade.

Pruning Early formative pruning should aim to encourage a clear trunk and a balanced crown. Occasional pruning is required for the removal of dead, dying, diseased, or crossing branches.

Propagation Sow fresh seed in a pot in a heated glasshouse in a frost-free and humid environment. Low branches can also be layered.

Taxodium distichum

S. pycnanthum
Wild rose

This dainty, highly ornamental tree from Java, Sumatra and Borneo has glossy green leaves and dense clusters of pink flowers in spring and occasionally also in autumn. The flowers are followed by pale pink or purple fruits. H 15m (50ft), S 10m (33ft).
Aspect Full sun.
Hardiness ❀ Zones 10–12.

TABEBUIA

This genus of evergreen and deciduous trees includes about 100 species, which are found in the West Indies and in Central and South America. They are grown for their attractive foliage and the clusters of bell-shaped flowers that appear on mature trees. They are tender plants, suitable for specimen trees or for growing in a mixed border in mild areas or in containers under glass.

Cultivation Outdoors, grow in fertile, moisture-retentive but well-drained soil in sun.

Pruning Formative pruning should aim to encourage a clear trunk and a balanced crown. Occasional pruning is required for the removal of dead, dying, diseased, or crossing branches.

Propagation Sow fresh seed into a container in a heated glasshouse until germination occurs.

T. chrysantha

This fast growing, generally deciduous tree from Central America is widely grown in the tropics. The palmate green leaves, up to 18cm (7in) long, are mid-green and covered with hairs beneath. In spring and throughout the season large clusters of yellow, azalea-like flowers are produced. H 30m (100ft), S 20m (65ft).
Aspect Full sun.
Hardiness (Min. 8°C/46°F) Zones 10–12.

T. heterophylla
White cedar, pink trumpet flower

This wonderful, fast-growing landscape tree from Cuba and Puerto Rico is well adapted to dry soils. The flowers, up to 8cm (3in) long, can vary in colour from rosy-pink to pale pink or white, but all have a pink throat. Flowering usually follows rain, followed by a period of drought, at which point the tapered, glossy green leaves fall and the flowers open. H 15m (50ft), S 8m (26ft).
Aspect Full sun.
Hardiness (Min. 10–15°C/ 50–9°F) Zones 10–12.

T. impetignosa

This species from Central and South America is the least drought-tolerant species in the genus, needing moist, fertile soil to do prosper. In spring it produces a spectacular display of flowers. The dense clusters of spectacular, trumpet-shaped dark pink flowers are borne before the leaves and continue until the leaves emerge. H 10m (33ft), S 8m (26ft).
Aspect Full sun.
Hardiness (Min. 8°C/46°F) Zones 9–11.

Syzygium aromaticum

T. rosea
(syn. *T. pentaphylla*)
Pink poui, pink tecoma, rosy trumpet tree

This vigorous tree, which is native to Central America, has pink, yellow-throated flowers, produced in great numbers in spring on almost leafless branches. The lower branches are often shed, leaving a clear trunk. H 25m (80ft), S 10m (33ft).
Aspect Full sun.
Hardiness (Min. 10–15°C/ 50–9°F) Zones 10–12.

TAXODIUM
Bald cypress

The genus contains two to three species of deciduous or semi-evergreen coniferous trees from the USA and Central America. When grown in wet ground they produce pneumatophores (hollow tubes known as 'knees'), which allow the exchange of oxygen and carbon dioxide in times of flooding or when the roots are below water level. They make handsome specimen trees.

Cultivation Grow in moist, acidic soil in sun or semi-shade.

Pruning Formative pruning should aim to produce a clear trunk and a balanced crown, while tipping the lateral branches of young trees will encourage a denser crown. Occasional pruning may be required to remove dead, dying, diseased or crossing branches.

Propagation Seed is the easiest method of propagation. Collect it when it is fresh and sow into a container in an unheated glasshouse or cold frame until germination occurs. Softwood cuttings can be taken during summer and should be dipped in a rooting hormone and placed in a humid environment until rooting occurs.

T. distichum
Swamp cypress

This slow- to medium-growing tree is native to the south-eastern USA. It is found growing in wet ground near, on or even in rivers and swamps. The sturdy trunk is wide and fluted at the base in order to withstand the force of moving water. Young trees are conical, and they develop flat tops with age. The pale green, needle-like foliage turns rusty brown in autumn before falling. H 20–40m (65–130ft), S 6–9m (20–30ft).
Named varieties The naturally occurring form *T. distichum* var. *imbricarium* (syn. *T. ascendens*) (pond cypress) is one of the most widely seen trees in the South Georgia swamps and Florida Everglades. A slow-growing tree when grown in water, it has narrow, needle-like, slightly twisted foliage. When it is growing in water the tree produces pneumatophores, but in ordinary soil these are rarer. The tops of the trees become flatter with age. H 20m (65ft), S 9m (30ft).

Taxus baccata

T. distichum var. *imbricatum* 'Nutans' has a conical habit and twisted stems, and the foliage weeps slightly on the branches.
Aspect Full sun.
Hardiness ❋❋❋ Zones 4–11.

TAXUS

There are ten species of evergreen coniferous shrubs and trees in the genus, mainly from northern temperate areas. They are fairly slow growing, but are highly adaptable plants, suitable for use as small, under-storey garden trees, as informal screens or formal hedges or as specimens.

They are unusual among conifers in that they will re-grow from old wood, which makes them popular for topiary. Most are spreading trees or large shrubs, although some forms have a strongly upright habit, and others have been developed for their bronze-coloured foliage.

They have male and female flowers in spring, usually on different trees, and the female flowers develop a single, fleshy, brightly coloured fruit, which contains a poisonous seed. The foliage is poisonous to animals, apart from deer. The leaves, borne in two opposite ranks, are long and narrow, dark green above and with two light green bands beneath.
Cultivation Grow in fertile, well-drained soil in sun or shade.
Pruning Formative pruning should produce a clear trunk and a balanced crown, while tipping the lateral branches of young trees will encourage a denser crown. Occasional pruning is required to remove dead, dying, diseased or crossing branches.
Propagation Seed should be collected when fresh and be sown into a container in an unheated glasshouse or cold frame until germination occurs. Semi-ripe cuttings can be taken in late summer and early autumn. The base of the cutting should be dipped in a rooting hormone and placed in a humid environment in a glasshouse until the cuttings root.

T. baccata
Common yew, English yew

This is one of the three conifers native to the UK, where it

naturally occurs on chalky, alkaline soil. It is a broadly spreading tree with ascending branches, and the gnarled trunk is covered with shredding, dark red-brown bark, which may become hollow on old trees. The foliage is very dark green, and the berries are red. H 20m (65ft), S 10m (33ft).
Named varieties Many garden-worthy forms have been developed from the species. The female form 'Adpressa' has short, stumpy needles, which are pressed flat to the stems. It is a small tree or spreading shrub, with bright red berries in autumn. H 6m (20ft), S 4m (12ft).

'Adpressa Variegata' is a non-fruiting male form with the same tightly pressed foliage and habit as 'Adpressa', but the new leaves have bright yellow margins, which age to old gold.

Plants in Aurea Group have golden-yellow or gold-edged foliage. Their yellow colouration is brightest in spring and fades by the time the needles are two years old. Members of this group eventually develop into small but broadly spreading trees.

'Dovastoniana' (West Felton yew) is a broadly spreading or vase-shaped tree with long, horizontal branches, dressed with hanging foliage. Although a fruitless male form exists, the distinctive fruiting female form is more commonly grown.

Young specimens of the female 'Fastigiata' (syn. 'Hibernica'; Irish yew) have a narrow, tightly columnar habit, and although they spread a little as they age, they remain columnar and densely leaved. The foliage is black-green, and the berries are red. H 10m (33ft), S 6m (20ft).

'Lutea' (syn. 'Fructu Lutea') is grown for its unusual, pale yellow berries. It is ultimately a spreading tree.

'Washingtonii' is a freely fruiting, spreading, female form with slightly upright branches clothed with bright yellow foliage, which fades to green-yellow. When winter temperatures are sufficiently cold the foliage turns a delightful bronze-yellow.
Aspect Full sun or semi-shade.
Hardiness ❋❋❋ Zones 5–7.

Taxus baccata 'Fastigiata'

T. chinensis
Chinese yew

The species is less widely planted than the common yew (*T. baccata*). It is an elegant if slow-growing tree. The glossy needles, which are larger than those of other yews, are greenish-yellow, and it produces abundant, red, fleshy fruits. H 12m (40ft), S 10m (33ft).
Aspect Full sun or semi-shade.
Hardiness ❋❋❋ Zones 5–7.

T. cuspidata
Japanese yew

The species is native to north-eastern China and Japan. It is hardier than *T. baccata* and can be planted where that species would not survive. It is a medium-sized tree with greenish-yellow foliage and bright red fruits. H 15m (50ft), S 8m (26ft).
Aspect Full sun or semi-shade.
Hardiness ❋❋❋ Zones 4–7.

T. x media

This hybrid of *T. baccata* and *T. cuspidata* arose in Massachusetts in 1903 and is now widely planted in place of *T. baccata* in colder parts of the USA, for which purpose a number of named forms have been developed. These exhibit similar habits and needle colour to the cultivars of *T. baccata*, although some forms develop curiously twisted branches. It is intermediate between both parents, with dark green foliage in two ranks, H and S 20–25m (65–80ft). Aspect Full sun or semi-shade. Hardiness ❁❁❁ Zones 4–7.

TECOMA

There are about 12 species of evergreen trees and shrubs in the genus, and they are native to southern Africa and to the southern USA and Central and South America. They are grown for their large, colourful flowers and attractive foliage. They are not hardy and in cold areas can be grown in large containers under glass. In mild areas they can be grown as specimens.
Cultivation Outdoors, grow in fertile, moisture-retentive but well-drained soil in sun.
Pruning Formative pruning should aim to encourage a clear trunk and a balanced crown. Occasional pruning is required for the removal of dead, dying, diseased or crossing branches.

Thuja plicata

Propagation Seed should be collected when fresh and sown into a container in a heated glasshouse in a frost-free and humid environment until germination occurs.

T. stans
(syn. *Bignonia stans,*
Stenolobium stans)
Yellow elder, trumpet bush,
yellow bells
A beautiful, small tree or large, multi-stemmed shrub, this species from the southern USA to Argentina, produces bright yellow, trumpet-shaped flowers in dense clusters over a long period from late winter to summer. The pinnate leaves, up to 35cm (14in) long, are bright green and have 5–13 leaflets. The flowers are followed by cylindrical seedpods. H 8–9m (26–30ft), S 3–5m (10–16ft). Aspect Full sun.
Hardiness (Min. 7–10°C/45–50°F) Zones 10–12.

THUJA
Arborvitae
The six species in the genus are coniferous evergreen trees native to eastern Asia and North America. They have a conical or broadly columnar habit and small, overlapping leaves. They make handsome specimens and can also be used in hedges.
Cultivation Grow in fertile, moisture-retentive but well-drained soil in sun. Protect young plants from cold, drying winds.
Pruning Formative pruning should produce a clear trunk and a balanced crown, while tipping the lateral branches of young trees will encourage a denser crown.
Propagation Seed is the easiest method of propagation. It should be collected when fresh and sown into a container in an unheated glasshouse or cold frame until germination occurs. Semi-ripe and softwood cuttings can be taken during summer and should be dipped in a rooting hormone and placed in a humid environment until rooting occurs.

T. koraiensis
(syn. *Thujopsis koraiensis*)
Korean arborvitae
This small tree from China and Korea has a conical habit and flattened, fern-like leaves, which are bright green above and silvery beneath. When the leaves are crushed they emit a pungent aroma. The bark is reddish-brown. H 10m (33ft), S 3–5m (10–16ft).
Aspect Full sun or semi-shade.
Hardiness ❁❁❁ Zones 5–7.

T. plicata
Western red cedar
A tall, beautiful conifer, this fast-growing species from western North America has strongly weeping and billowing lower branches and reddish, shredding bark. The flattened, scale-like leaves are mid- to dark green and smell of pineapple when crushed. H 25–35m (80–115ft), S 10m (33ft).
Named varieties A huge number of selections have been made from the species, and these vary from dwarf forms to those with brightly coloured foliage.

Tecoma stans

'Atrovirens', probably the most widely grown form in Europe, is often used for hedging because it is fast-growing and has dense, glossy, dark green foliage.

'Fastigiata' is a slow-growing, narrow form with tightly upright branches and green foliage that weeps at the tips.

'Green Giant' is widely grown in the USA as a screening or hedging plant because it is quick-growing and heat tolerant. The foliage occasionally turns bronze in winter.
Aspect Full sun or semi-shade.
Hardiness ❁❁❁ Zones 4–7.

THUJOPSIS
Hiba
The only species in the genus is a slow-growing evergreen conifer from Japan. It is closely related to *Thuja* but has larger leaves. These trees make good specimens.
Cultivation Grow in fertile, moisture-retentive but well-drained soil in sun. Protect plants from cold, drying winds.
Pruning Formative pruning should aim to produce a clear trunk and a balanced crown, while tipping the lateral branches of young trees encourages a denser crown.
Propagation Seed is the easiest method of propagation. It should be collected when fresh and be sown into a container in an unheated glasshouse or cold frame until germination occurs. Semi-ripe and softwood cuttings can be taken during summer and should be dipped in a rooting hormone and placed in a humid environment until rooting occurs.

T. dolabrata

This broadly conical tree has shredding, reddish-brown bark. The scale-like leaves are borne in dense sprays and are dark green above and marked with silver-white beneath. H 20m (65ft), S 6–10ft (20–33ft).
Named varieties The cultivar 'Aurea' is a large shrub or small tree with stunning yellow-green foliage, strongest in spring and dulling with age.
Aspect Full sun or semi-shade.
Hardiness ❀❀❀ Zones 5–7.

TILIA
Lime, linden

There are about 45 species of deciduous trees in the genus. They come from Europe, Asia and North America, where they are found in woodlands, and are grown for their fragrant flowers and attractive foliage. They are traditionally used in landscape avenues or as specimen trees, although they can also be pleached and pollarded.
Cultivation Grow in moisture-retentive but well-drained soil in sun or semi-shade.
Pruning Early formative pruning should aim to produce a clear trunk and a balanced crown. Trunk suckers are common on many lime trees and should be removed during late spring or early summer.
Propagation Seed and budding are the main methods of propagation. Seed should be collected when fresh and be sown into a container in an unheated

Tilia cordata

glasshouse or cold frame until germination occurs. Summer budding on to seed-grown limes is commonly practised. Trunk suckers can also be rooted if a cage frame is built around the trunk and the cages filled with compost during spring. The cage is removed a year later in winter and the rooted suckers are removed.

T. cordata
Small-leaved lime

This broadly conical tree from Europe has small, heart-shaped leaves, up to 8cm (3in) long, which are glossy, dark green above and blue-green below. In late summer it bears clusters of scented, cream-white flowers with the typical lance-shaped, grey-green bract. It is not as tolerant of heat as some species. H 25–30m (80–100ft), S 15–20m (50–65ft).
Named varieties 'Corinthian' is a compact, pyramidal form, with dark green, but smaller leaves.

The fast-growing 'Greenspire' is one of the most widely grown of the cultivars. It develops into a straight-trunked tree, with an open, oval crown, dark green foliage and orange shoots. H 15m (50ft), S 7m (23ft).

'Rancho' is a free-flowering form with smaller than average leaves and an upswept habit. H 15m (50ft), S 8m (26ft).

Best grown as a pollard, 'Winter Orange' has red buds and orange shoots. It is particularly attractive when it is in flower and in autumn.
Aspect Full sun or semi-shade.
Hardiness ❀❀❀ Zones 4–7.

T. x europaea
(syn. T. intermedia, T. x vulgaris)
Common lime, European lime

This widely grown hybrid between T. cordata and T. platyphyllos often produces suckers.. The dark green leaves, up to 10cm (4in) long, are heart-shaped and pale green beneath; they turn yellow in autumn. In summer clusters of pale yellow flowers are produced. H 35m (115ft), S 15m (50ft).
Named varieties 'Goldcrown' is a beautiful cultivar with leaves that are yellow when they first emerge, fading to yellow-green in summer.

Thujopsis dolabrata

'Pallida' (Kaiser linden) is a form with ascending branches and broadly conical crown. The stems are reddish-brown.
Aspect Full sun or semi-shade.
Hardiness ❀❀❀ Zones 3–7.

T. platyphyllos
Broad-leaved lime, large-leaved lime

This stately tree, which is native to Europe and is often planted in parks, develops a broadly conical crown. The trunk is covered with suckering shoots. The dark green leaves, 8–15cm (3–6in) long, are covered with dense hairs on the underside and turn yellow in autumn. Clusters of fragrant, pale yellow flowers are borne in late summer. H 30m (100ft), S 15–20m (50–65ft).
Named varieties 'Aurea' has attractive bright yellow shoots, turning olive-green as they mature.

'Fastigiata' (syn. 'Erecta') is an initially strongly upright form that becomes more open with age. H 13m (43ft).

'Prince's Street', a widely grown street tree, has an upright habit and reddish shoots.
Aspect Full sun or semi-shade.
Hardiness ❀❀❀ Zones 4–6.

T. tomentosa
European white lime, silver lime

This lovely tree from south-eastern Europe and south-western

Asia has a broadly conical habit. The dark green leaves, up to 10cm (4in) long, are covered with silvery hairs on the undersides. In summer fragrant white flowers are borne in clusters. H 25–30m (80–100ft), S 20m (65ft).
Named varieties The conical 'Brabant' is widely planted as a street tree. Its dark green leaves turn yellow in autumn.

'Green Mountain' is a fast-growing cultivar with dark green leaves, which are silvery beneath. It has reliable autumn colour, good drought and heat tolerance and a conical habit.

The beautiful 'Petiolaris' develops a clear central leader, and the strongly weeping branches, covered with dark green leaves, silver beneath, hang like curtains. The fragrant white flowers are borne in late summer. H 30m, S 20m (65ft).
Aspect Full sun or semi-shade.
Hardiness ❀❀❀ Zones 4–7.

TRACHYCARPUS

There are six species of evergreen palm trees in the genus. They are single-stemmed or clustering plants from tropical Asia and are grown for their divided, fan-shaped leaves and flower clusters.
Cultivation Outdoors, grow in fertile, well-drained soil in sun or light shade. Protect from cold, drying winds.

Trachycarpus fortunei

Pruning Like most palms, little pruning is required apart from the cosmetic removal of dead leaves and spent flower clusters during early summer.
Propagation Seed is the easiest method of propagation. It should be collected when fresh and be sown into a container in a heated glasshouse in a humid environment at 29°C (84°F) until germination occurs.

T. fortunei
(syn. *Chamaerops excelsa*, *T. excelsa*)
Chusan palm, windmill palm
This popular species is of unknown origin. It is probably the hardiest of the palms, and can be grown in mild maritime regions or sheltered gardens in cooler areas, as long as it is not exposed to cold winds or frost. It develops a single, unbranched trunk, covered with brown fibre and the remains of dead stems, which should be removed to keep the trunk neat.
   The dark green leaves, up to 75cm (30in) long, are fan-shaped and deeply cut into numerous sharply pointed leaflets. The leaves are arranged spirally around the main trunk. In early summer pendent panicles of yellow flowers, up to 60cm (24in) long, are borne just below the leaves from the trunk, and are followed by small brown fruits. H 12m (40ft), S 2.4m (8ft).
Aspect Full sun or semi-shade.
Hardiness ✻✻ Zones 7–11.

T. wagnerianus
This slow-growing species has a fatter and squatter trunk than *T. fortunei*, and the leaves grow up to 45cm (18in) long. They are white-green when they first emerge. Although the species was discovered in Japan, it is not native to the region and is known only through having been cultivated in Japan and China. H 7–9m (23–30ft), S 2.4m (8ft).
Aspect Full sun or semi-shade.
Hardiness ✻✻ Zones 7–11.

TSUGA
Hemlock
The 10–11 species in the genus are evergreen coniferous trees from the forests of eastern Asia and North America. They are grown for their elegant habit and make fine specimen trees.
Cultivation Grow in fertile, moisture-retentive but well-drained, acidic to slightly alkaline soil in sun or semi-shade. In poor soils protect plants from cold, drying winds.
Pruning Formative pruning should aim to produce a clear trunk and a balanced crown, while tipping the lateral branches of young trees to encourage a denser crown.
Propagation Seed should be collected when fresh and be sown into a container in an unheated glasshouse or cold frame until germination occurs. Semi-ripe and softwood cutting can be taken during summer and should be dipped in a rooting hormone and placed in a humid environment until rooting occurs. Selected forms are winter grafted on to seedling-raised rootstocks.

T. canadensis
Eastern hemlock
This spreading conifer from eastern North America is an excellent tree for a shady position, and it can also be used as an under-storey tree. It has arching new growth, and dark green, small needles with silvery-white undersides. The needles are arranged in two ranks at opposite sides of the stems. It is a fast-growing tree, often grown for its timber. It makes a beautiful hedge. H 25m (80ft), S 10m (33ft).

Named varieties 'Golden Splendor' is a fast-growing, narrow form with yellow foliage that is less prone to sun scorch than some golden conifers. The new growth is bright yellow, which turns yellow-green as it ages.
   'Pendula' is a slow-growing, strongly arching, small tree, often trained up a short trunk before being allowed to weep. H 4m (12ft), S 8m (26ft).
Aspect Full sun or semi-shade.
Hardiness ✻✻✻ Zones 3–7.

T. mertensiana
Mountain hemlock, blue hemlock
This columnar to conical tree from western North America is one of the most ornamental of the genus. It has purple to red-brown bark and spiky, grey-green or blue-grey foliage. H 15m (50ft), S 6m (20ft).
Aspect Full sun or semi-shade.
Hardiness ✻✻✻ Zones 5–6.

ULMUS
Elm
The genus contains 45 species of deciduous or semi-evergreen trees and a few shrubs. They are native to northern temperate areas and are grown for their habit and attractive foliage. Until the outbreak of Dutch elm disease (DED) in the 1930s, followed by a second outbreak in the 1970s, elms were widely planted as city, street, hedgerow and parkland trees in Europe and the USA. DED, a fungal disease spread by beetles, is usually fatal and, for this reason, elms are not suitable for long-term planting as

Tsuga mertensiana

specimen trees, although they are still grown in areas free of the disease. Some elms have been found to show varying degrees of resistance, including *U. parvifolia* and its cultivars, *U. pumila* and *U. 'Sapporo Autumn Gold'*. Some other cultivars that are believed to be resistant to DED are noted below.
Cultivation Grow in well-drained soil in sun or semi-shade.
Pruning Early formative pruning should aim to produce a clear trunk and a balanced crown. Some elms produce tight branch angles and these should be removed when the tree is young.
Propagation Seed and summer budding are the main methods of propagation. Seed should be collected when it is fresh and be sown into a container in an unheated glasshouse or cold frame until germination occurs. Summer budding can be done using seed-grown elms.

U. 'Accolade'
This vase-shaped tree, a hybrid between two Asiatic species, *U. japonica* and *U. wilsoniana*, has glossy green foliage that turns yellow in autumn. It has good resistance to DED. H 18m (60ft), S 12m (40ft).
Aspect Full sun.
Hardiness ✻✻✻ Zone 3.

U. americana
American white elm
A graceful, spreading tree from the eastern USA, the species is often multi-stemmed with large, V-shaped trunks covered with silver bark. The dark green leaves, up to 15cm (6in) long, are heavily toothed and turn butter yellow in autumn. It is still widespread in the USA, although it is not resistant to DED. H 25m (80ft), S 20m (65ft).
Named varieties The cultivar 'American Liberty' has an upright habit; it shows good resistance to DED.
   In tests 'Valley Forge', which has good autumn colour, has been shown to have the greatest resistance to DED of all American elms.
Aspect Full sun.
Hardiness ✻✻✻ Zones 3–9.

U. x hollandica
Dutch elm
This naturally occurring hybrid, probably between *U. glabra* (wych elm) and *U. minor* (European field elm), appears wherever the parents meet. It is a broadly columnar tree, with toothed, dark green leaves, up to 12cm (5in) long, which turn yellow in autumn. Small red flowers are borne in spring, followed by winged fruits. H 30–35m (100–115ft), S 20–25m (65–80ft).
Named varieties The cultivar 'Christine Buisman' has a tight vase shape and has shown good disease resistance.

'Dampieri Aurea' (syn. 'Wredei') is a narrowly conical tree with beautiful yellow leaves up to 6cm (2½in) long, and with some resistance to DED. H 10m (33ft), S 1m (3ft).
Aspect Full sun.
Hardiness ❈❈❈ Zones 3–9.

U. 'New Horizon'
This hardy hybrid elm, arising from *U. japonica* and *U. pumila*, is a vigorous tree with dark green foliage, an upright habit and vivid autumn colour. It has good resistance to DED. H 18m (60ft), S 10m (33ft).
Aspect Full sun.
Hardiness ❈❈❈ Zone 3.

U. parvifolia
Chinese elm
This spreading tree has glossy, dark green leaves, up to 6cm (2½in) long, which can turn orange-yellow in autumn, but which often persist into winter.

Ulmus

The grey-brown bark flakes to reveal the light brown underbark. The species does not appear to be affected by DED. H 15–18m (50–60ft), S 12–15m (40–50ft).
Named varieties 'Allee' has an upright, vase-shaped habit. The flaking bark is green-grey, silver-green and orange-brown. The leaves turn yellow in autumn. H 20–25m (65–80ft), S 20m (65ft).

'Athena' has a rounded habit with green foliage and exfoliating bark, grey-silver-green and brown.

The US form 'Golden Ray' has leaves that are gold-coloured in summer, turning yellow in autumn.
Aspect Full sun.
Hardiness ❈❈❈ Zone 4.

U. 'Patriot'
This narrow form, derived from *U. 'Urban'* and *U. wilsoniana*, has good autumn colour and high resistance to DED. H 18m (60ft), S 12m (40ft).
Aspect Full sun.
Hardiness ❈❈❈ Zone 3.

U. pumila
Siberian elm
This rather variable tree has toothed, dark green leaves, up to 10cm (4in) long, which are covered with hairs beneath. Small red flowers are borne in spring and are followed by winged fruits. H 30m (100ft), S 12m (40ft).
Aspect Full sun.
Hardiness ❈❈❈ Zone 3.

U. 'Sapporo Autumn Gold'
This hardy and fast-growing cultivar, a hybrid between *U. pumila* and *U. japonica*, is a broadly conical tree with upright branches. The glossy leaves, up to 8cm (3in) long, are tinged with red in spring, turning dark green and then yellow-green in autumn. H 18m (60ft), S 12m (40ft).
Aspect Full sun.
Hardiness ❈❈❈ Zone 3.

U. 'Urban'
The parents of this hardy, drought-resistant form include *U. x hollandica* var. *vegeta*, *U. minor* and *U. pumila*. It has a spreading habit and dark green leaves. H 18m (60ft), S 12m (40ft).
Aspect Full sun.
Hardiness ❈❈❈ Zone 3.

WASHINGTONIA
Fan palm
There are two species of single-stemmed palms in the genus. They are native to dry areas in the southern USA and northern Mexico.
Cultivation Outdoors, grow in fertile, well-drained soil in full sun.
Pruning Little pruning is required apart from the removal of dead leaves and spent flower clusters.
Propagation Sow fresh seed into a container in a heated glasshouse in a humid environment at 29°C (84°F) until germination occurs.

W. filifera
Desert fan palm
This is a medium to large palm tree with 2m (6ft) wide and long leaves that have a spiky petiole. The clusters of stunning white flowers are up to 5m long and drupe from the foliage. H 20m (70ft), S 6m (20ft).
Aspect Full sun.
Hardiness ❈ Zones 8–11.

W. robusta
Thread palm
A fast-growing, slender palm, this has sharply toothed leaf stalks, and less fibre hanging from the leaves. The trunk is quite tapered at the base and the palm-like foliage grows to 1m wide and long (3ft x 3ft). The flowers are creamy-white. H 25m (80ft), S 5m (15ft).
Aspect Full sun.
Hardiness ❈ Zones 9–11.

ZELKOVA
The genus contains five or six species of deciduous trees, which are grown for their habit and foliage. The genus is closely related to *Ulmus*. Zelkovas may be distinguished by their round fruits.
Cultivation Grow in fertile, moisture-retentive, well-drained soil in sun or semi-shade. Protect plants from cold, drying winds.
Pruning Early formative pruning should aim to produce a clear trunk and a balanced crown. Occasional pruning is required for the removal of dead, dying, diseased or crossing branches.
Propagation Fresh seed should be sown into a container outside in an unheated glasshouse or cold

Zelkova carpinifolia

frame until germination occurs. Summer budding on to seed-grown zelkovas is also quite commonly practised.

Z. serrata
(syn. Z. keaki)
Japanese zelkova
This spreading, fast-growing tree, from Korea, Taiwan and Japan, has upswept branches, which create a rounded crown. The bark is grey, flaking to reveal orange underbark. The narrow, ovate leaves, up to 12cm (5in) long, are toothed, dark green, turning yellow, orange and red in autumn. H 30m (100ft), S 18m (60ft).
Named varieties 'Autumn Glow' is smaller than the species and has a compact habit and stunning purple leaves in autumn.

The vigorous and fast-growing 'Green Vase' has dark green leaves that turn orange-yellow and bronze-red in autumn.

'Green Veil' is often grown as a graft on the species to make an unusual weeping standard tree.

The fast-growing, pollution-tolerant and apparently disease-resistant 'Village Green' has orange-yellow and purple-red autumn colour.
Aspect Full sun.
Hardiness ❈❈❈ Zones 5–8.

Index

African tulip tree (*Spathodea*) 86
alder (*Alnus*) 15
alder buckthorn (*Rhamnus frangula*) 80
Allegheny serviceberry
(*Amelanchier laevis*) 16
almond (*Prunus dulcis*) 74–5
American aspen
(*Populus tremuloides*) 70
American beech (*Fagus grandifolia*) 42
American holly (*Ilex opaca*) 47
American hornbeam
(*Carpinus caroliniana*) 24
American persimmon
(*Diospyros virginiana*) 39
American smoke tree (*Cotinus obovatus*
(syn. *C. americanus*,
Rhus cotinoides)) 35
American sweet chestnut
(*Castanea dentata*) 25
American white elm
(*Ulmus americana*) 92
amur cork tree
(*Phellodendron amurense*) 64
apple (*Malus sylvestris* var. *domestica*)
58–9
apricot (*Prunus armeniaca*) 72–3
arborvitae (*Thuja*) 90
ash (*Fraxinus*) 44
Atlantic cedar (*Cedrus atlantica*
(syn. *C. libani* subsp. *atlantica*)) 27
Australian fan palm
(*Livistona australis*) 53
Australian ivy palm (*Schefflera
actinophylla* (syn. *Brassaea
actinophylla*)) 83

bald cypress (*Taxodium*) 88–9
banana shrub (*Michelia*) 61
banyan (*Ficus benghalensis*) 42
bay (*Laurus nobilis*) 51
bead tree (*Melia azedarach*) 60
beech (*Fagus*) 42
Bhutan pine (*Pinus wallichiana*) 67
big-cone pine (*Pinus coulteri*) 66
birch (*Betula*) 19–20
bitternut (*Carya cordiformis*) 24
black birch (*Betula lenta*) 20
black jack oak (*Quercus marilandica*) 79
black mulberry (*Morus nigra*) 62
black oak (*Quercus velutina*) 80
black poplar (*Populus nigra*) 70
black sapote (*Diospyros digyna*
(syn. *D. ebanaster*)) 38
black walnut (*Juglans nigra*) 48
black wattle (*Acacia auriculaeformis*) 7
blackwood wattle
(*Acacia melanoxylon*) 7
bladdernut (*Staphylea*) 86
bottlebrush (*Callistemon*) 22
box elder (*Acer negundo*) 10
breadfruit (*Artocarpus*) 18
Brewer's spruce (*Picea breweriana*) 65
bristlecone fir (*Abies bracteata*) 6
broad-leaved lime
(*Tilia platyphyllos*) 91

buckthorn (*Rhamnus*) 80
bull bay (*Magnolia grandiflora*) 55
Burmese fishtail palm (*Caryota mitis*) 25

cabbage palmetto (*Sabal palmetto*) 82
Campbell's magnolia
(*Magnolia campbellii*) 55
Canadian poplar
(*Populus* X *canadensis*) 69
Canary Island date palm
(*Phoenix canariensis*) 64
candlenut (*Aleurites moluccana*) 15
Caucasian spruce (*Picea orientalis*) 65
Caucasian wing nut
(*Pterocarya fraxinifolia*) 76
cedar of Lebanon (*Cedrus libani*) 27
cherry birch (*Betula lenta*) 20
cherry plum (*Prunus cerasifera*) 72
chestnut-leaved oak
(*Quercus castaneifolia*) 78
Chilean fire bush
(*Embothrium coccineum*) 39
Chinese bladdernut
(*Staphylea holocarpa*) 87
Chinese elm (*Ulmus parvifolia*) 93
Chinese evergreen oak
(*Quercus myrsinifolia*) 79
Chinese fan palm
(*Livistona chinensis*) 53
Chinese fir (*Cunninghamia*) 36
Chinese honey locust
(*Gleditsia sinensis*) 45
Chinese juniper
(*Juniperus chinensis*) 48
Chinese magnolia (*Magnolia* X
soulangeana) 56
Chinese mastic (*Pistacia chinensis*) 67
Chinese necklace poplar (*Populus
lasiocarpa*) 70
Chinese privet (*Ligustrum lucidum*) 52
Chinese red birch
(*Betula albosinensis*) 19
Chinese redbud (*Cercis chinensis*) 28
Chinese stewartia (*Stewartia sinensis*
(syn. *S. gemmata*)) 87
Chinese tulip tree
(*Liriodendron chinense*) 53
Chinese weeping willow
(*Salix babylonica*) 82
Chinese whitebeam
(*Sorbus folgneri*) 85

Chinese yellow wood
(*Cladrastis sinensis*) 32
Chinese yew (*Taxus chinensis*) 89
chulta (*Dillenia indica*) 38
Chusan palm (*Trachycarpus fortunei* (syn.
Chamaerops excelsa, *T. excelsa*)) 92
cider gum (*Eucalyptus gunnii*) 40–1
citron (*Citrus medica*) 31
clementine (*Citrus reticulata*) 31
coast banksia (*Banksia integricola*) 18
coast redwood (*Sequoia sempervirens*) 84
cockspur thorn (*Crataegus crus-galli*) 35
coigue (*Nothofagus dombeyi*) 62
Colorado spruce (*Picea pungens*) 65
common alder (*Alder glutinosa*) 15
common apple (*Malus sylvestris* var.
domestica) 58
common ash (*Fraxinus excelsior*) 44
common beech (*Fagus sylvatica*) 42
common buckthorn
(*Rhamnus cathartica*) 80
common frangipani
(*Plumeria rubra*) 68
common guava (*Psidium guajava*) 75–6
common hawthorn
(*Crataegus monogyna*) 35
common hornbeam
(*Carpinus betulus*) 24
common lime (*Tilia* X *europaea* (syn.
T. intermedia, *T.* X *vulgaris*)) 91
common mountain ash
(*Sorbus aucuparia*) 85
common oak (*Quercus robur* (syn. *Q.
pedunculate*)) 80
common pohutakawa (*Metrosideros
excelsus* (syn. *M. tomentosa*)) 61
common walnut (*Juglans regia*) 48
common yew (*Taxus baccata*) 89
Cootamundra wattle
(*Acacia baileyana*) 7
coral bark maple (*Acer palmatum*
'Sango-kaku') 10
cork oak (*Quercus suber*) 80
Cornelian cherry (*Cornus mas*) 34
crab apple (*Malus*) 56–7
crimson bottlebrush
(*Callistemon citrinus*) 22
Cuban royal palm (*Roystonea regia*) 81
cypress (*Cupressus*) 37

daimio oak (*Quercus dentata*) 78
damson (*Prunus insititia*) 74
date palm (*Phoenix dactylifera*) 64
date plum (*Diospyros lotus*) 38–9
dawn redwood (*Metasequoia*) 60
deodar (*Cedrus deodara*) 27
dogwood (*Cornus*) 32–3
Douglas fir (*Pseudotsuga menziesii*) 75
Dutch elm (*Ulmus* X *hollandica*) 93
dwarf fan palm (*Chamaerops*) 30
dwarf palmetto (*Sabal minor*) 82

Eastern hemlock (*Tsuga canadensis*) 92
Eastern redbud (*Cercis canadensis*) 28
Eastern white pine (*Pinus strobus*) 66

Malus pumila

ebony (*Diospyros ebenum*) 38
elm (*Ulmus*) 92
empress tree
(*Paulownia tomentosa*) 64
English holly (*Ilex aquifolium*) 46–7
Erman's birch (*Betula ermanii*) 20
European larch (*Larix decidua*) 50–1
European olive (*Olea europaea*) 63
European silver fir (*Abies alba*) 6
European white lime
(*Tilia tomentosa*) 91

fall orchid tree
(*Bauhinia purpurea*) 19
false acacia (*Robinia pseudoacacia*) 81
false aralia (*Schefflera elegantissima*
(syn. *Aralia elegantissima*,
Dizygotheca elegantissima)) 83
false koa (*Acacia confusa*) 7
fan palm (*Washingtonia*) 93
fiddle-leaf fig (*Ficus lyrata*) 43
field maple (*Acer campestre*) 8
fig (*Ficus*) 42
firewood banksia
(*Banksia menziesii*) 18
fishtail palm (*Caryota*) 24–5
flowering dogwood
(*Cornus florida*) 33
fountain palm (*Livistona*) 53
frangipani (*Plumeria*) 68
Freeman's maple (*Acer* X *freemanii*) 9
full moon maple (*Acer japonicum*) 9

Georgia oak (*Quercus georgiana*) 79
giant American wonder lemon
(*Citrus* 'Ponderosa' (syn.
C. limon 'Ponderosa')) 31
goat willow (*Salix caprea*) 82
golden deodar
(*Cedrus deodara* 'Aurea') 27
golden larch (*Pseudolarix*) 75
golden oak (*Quercus alnifolia*) 78
golden rain (*Laburnum*) 49
golden rain tree
(*Koelreuteria paniculata*) 49
golden shower tree
(*Cassia fistula*) 25
grapefruit (*Citrus* X *paradisi*) 31
great white cherry
(*Prunus* 'Taihaku') 72
Grecian strawberry tree
(*Arbutus andrachne*) 17

Ailanthus altissima

green bottlebrush
(*Callistemon viridiflorus*) 23
grey alder (*Alnus incana*) 16
guava (*Psidium*) 75–6

half-barked gum
(*Eucalyptus confertifolia*) 40
hardiness 96
hardiness zones 96
hawthorn (*Crataegus*) 35
hemlock (*Tsuga*) 92
hersii maple (*Acer grosseri* var. *hersii*
(syn. *A. davidii* subsp. *grosseri*,
A. grosseri, A. hersii)) 9
hiba (*Thujopsis*) 90
hickory (*Carya*) 24
highclere holly (*Ilex* **X** *altaclerensis*) 46
Himalayan birch (*Betula utilis* var.
jacquemontii) 20–1
Himalayan larch (*Larix griffithii*) 51
Himalayan maple (*Acer sterculiaceum*
(syn. *A. villosum*) 12–13
Himalayan weeping juniper
(*Juniperus recurva*) 48
Hinoki cypress (*Chamaecyparis obtusa*)
29
holly (*Ilex*) 46–7
holm oak (*Quercus ilex*) 79
honey locust (*Gleditsia triacanthos*) 45
Hong Kong orchid tree
(*Bauhinia* **X** *blakeana*) 19
hornbeam (*Carpinus*) 23
horse chestnut (*Aesculus*) 13
Hubei rowan (*Sorbus hupehensis*
(syn. *S. glabrescens*)) 85
Hungarian oak (*Quercus frainetto*
(syn. *Q. conferta*)) 78–9

incense cedar (*Calocedrus decurrens*
(syn. *Heyderia decurrens*,
Libocedrus decurrens)) 23
India rubber tree (*Ficus elastica*) 42–3
Indian bean tree
(*Catalpa bignonioides*) 26
Indian horse chestnut
(*Aesculus indica*) 13
Italian alder (*Alnus cordata*) 15
Italian cypress
(*Cupressus sempervirens*) 37

Japanese big-leaf magnolia (*Magnolia
obovata* (syn. *M. hypoleuca*)) 56
Japanese blue oak (*Quercus glauca*) 79
Japanese cedar
(*Cryptomeria japonica*) 36
Japanese crab apple
(*Malus floribunda*) 57
Japanese fir (*Abies firma*) 6
Japanese horse chestnut
(*Aesculus turbinate*) 14
Japanese larch (*Larix kaempferi* (syn. *L.
leptolepis*)) 51
Japanese maple (*Acer palmatum*) 10
Japanese pagoda tree
(*Sophora japonica*) 84

Japanese persimmon
(*Diospyros kaki*) 38
Japanese red maple
(*Acer pycnanthum*) 11
Japanese red pine (*Pinus densiflora*) 66
Japanese snowbell (*Styrax japonicus*) 87
Japanese stewartia
(*Stewartia pseudocamellia*) 87
Japanese walnut
(*Juglans ailanthifolia*) 48
Japanese yew (*Taxus cuspidata*) 89
Japanese zelkova (*Zelkova serrata*
(syn. *Z. keaki*)) 93
Judas tree (*Cercis siliquastrum*) 28
juneberry (*Amelanchier*) 16
juniper (*Juniperus*) 48

Kashmir cypress (*Cupressus cashmeriana*
(syn. *C. torulosa* 'Cashmeriana') 37
Kashmir rowan
(*Sorbus cashmiriana*) 85
katsura tree (*Cercidiphyllum japonicum*)
27
kauri pine (*Agathis australis*) 14
kohuhu (*Pittosporum tenuifolium*) 67
Korean mountain ash
(*Sorbus alnifolia*) 85
kousa dogwood (*Cornus kousa*) 33
kumquat (*Fortunella*) 43
kusamaki (*Podocarpus macrophyllus*) 69

lacebark pine (*Pinus bungeana*) 66
larch (*Larix*) 50–1
Lawson cypress (*Chamaecyparis
lawsoniana*) 29
lemon (*Citrus limon*) 31
lemonwood (*Pittosporum eugenioides*) 67
Leyland cypress (**X** *Cupressocyparis
leylandii*) 36–7
lime (*Citrus aurantiifolia*) 30–1
lime, linden (*Tilia*) 91
live oak (*Quercus virginiana*) 80
Loebner's magnolia
(*Magnolia* **X** *loebneri*) 56
London plane (*Platanus* **X** *hispanica*
(syn. *P.* **X** *acerifolia*)) 68
loquat (*Eriobotrya japonica*) 39–40
loquat oak (*Quercus rhysophylla*) 80
Lucombe oak (*Quercus* **X** *hispanica*) 79

maidenhair tree (*Ginkgo biloba*) 44–5
manna ash (*Fraxinus ornus*) 44
maple (*Acer*) 4, 7
Mexican flame bush
(*Calliandra tweedii*) 22
Mexican weeping pine
(*Pinus patula*) 66
Mexican white pine
(*Pinus ayacahuite*) 65
Meyer's lemon (*Citrus* 'Meyer'
(syn. *C. limon* 'Meyer', *C.* **X** *meyeri*
'Meyeri')) 31
midland hawthorn (*Crataegus laevigata*
(syn. *C. oxyacantha*)) 35
mimosa (*Acacia dealbata*) 7

monkey puzzle (*Araucaria araucana*
(syn. *A. imbricata*)) 17
Monterey cypress
(*Cupressus macrocarpa*) 37
Moreton Bay fig
(*Ficus macrophylla*) 43
Mount Wellington peppermint
(*Eucalyptus coccifera*) 40
mountain ash (*Sorbus*) 84–5
mountain ebony (*Bauhinia*) 18–19
mountain gum
(*Eucalyptus dalrympleana*) 40
mountain hemlock
(*Tsuga mertensiana*) 92
mountain snowdrop tree (*Halesia
monticola*) 46
mulberry (*Morus*) 61–2
myrtle (*Myrtus*) 62

narrow-leaved ash
(*Fraxinus angustifolia*) 44
narrow-leaved black peppermint
(*Eucalyptus nicholii*) 41
noble palm (*Bismarckia nobilis*) 21
Nootka cypress
(*Chamaecyparis nootkatensis*) 29
Norfolk Island pine (*Araucaria
heterophylla* (syn. *A. excelsa*)) 17
northern rata (*Metrosideros robusta*) 61
Norway maple (*Acer platanoides*) 10–11
Norway spruce (*Picea abies*) 65

oak (*Quercus*) 78
olive spp. (*Olea*) 62–3
Oregon maple (*Acer macrophyllum*) 10
oriental beech (*Fagus orientalis*) 42
oriental plane (*Platanus orientalis*) 68
Oven's wattle (*Acacia pravissima*) 7

Pacific dogwood (*Cornis nuttallii*) 34
palas (*Licuala*) 51
palmetto (*Sabal*) 81–2
Panama flame tree
(*Brownea macrophylla*) 21
paper birch (*Betula papyrifera*) 20
paperbark maple (*Acer griseum*) 9
Patagonian cypress (*Fitzroya
cupressoides* (syn. *F. patagonia*)) 43
pecan (*Carya illinoinensis*) 24
Père David's maple
(*Acer davidii*) 9–10
Persian ironwood (*Parrotia*) 63
pin oak (*Quercus palustris*) 79
pindo palm (*Buta capitata*) 22
pine (*Pinus*) 65
pink poui (*Tabebuia rosea*
(syn. *T. pentaphylla*)) 88
pink shower tree
(*Cassia javanica*) 25
pistachio (*Pistacia*) 67
plane (*Platanus*) 68
plum (*Prunus domestica*) 74
plum-fruited yew (*Prumnopitys andina*
(syn. *P. elegans, Podocarpus andinus*))
71

podocarp (*Podocarpus*) 68
pohutakawa (*Metrosideros*) 60–1
pomegranate (*Punica*) 76
poor man's orchid
(*Bauhinia variegata*) 19
poplar (*Populus*) 19
privet (*Ligustrum*) 52

quaking aspen (*Populus tremuloides*) 70
Queensland kauri
(*Agathis robusta*) 14

rata (*Metrosideros*) 60–1
red horse chestnut
(*Aesculus* **X** *carnea*) 13
red maple (*Acer rubrum*) 11
red mulberry (*Morus rubra*) 62
red oak (*Quercus rubra*
(syn. *Q. borealis*)) 80
red-flowering gum
(*Eucalyptus ficifolia*) 40
Roblé (*Nothofagus obliqua*) 62
round kumquat (*Fortunella japonica*
(syn. *Citrus japonica*,
C. madurensis)) 43
royal palm (*Roystonea*) 81
ruffled fan palm (*Licuala grandis*
(syn. *Pritchardia grandis*)) 51

Santa Lucia fir (*Abies bracteata*) 6
Sargent cherry (*Prunus sargentii*) 72
saw banksia (*Banksia serrata*) 18
sawara cypress
(*Chamaecyparis pisifera*) 29
sawtooth oak (*Quercus acutissima*) 78
scarlet banksia (*Banksia coccinea*) 18
scarlet oak (*Quercus coccinea*) 78
Scotch laburnum
(*Laburnum alpinum*) 49
Scots pine (*Pinus sylvestris*) 66
sessile oak (*Quercus petraea* (syn.
Q. sessiflora)) 79
shagbark hickory (*Carya ovata*) 24
shingle oak (*Quercus imbricaria*) 79
shower tree (*Cassia*) 25
Siberian elm (*Ulmus pumila*) 93
Sicily fir (*Abies nebrodensis*) 6
Sierra redwood (*Sequoiadendron
giganteum*) 84
silk trees (*Albizia*) 15
silky camellia (*Stewartia*) 87

Laburnum anagyroides

silky oak (*Grevillea robusta*) 45
silver birch (*Betula pendula*) 20
silver fir (*Abies*) 6
silver gum (*Eucalyptus cordata*) 40
small-leaved lime (*Tilia cordata*) 91
smoke tree (*Cotinus*) 34-5
snakebark maple (*Acer pensylvanicum*) 10
snow gum (*Eucalyptus pauciflora*) 41
snowbell (*Styrax*) 87
snowdrop tree (*Halesia*) 46
sorrel tree (*Oxydendron*) 63
sour cherry (*Prunus cerasus*) 73-4
southern beech (*Nothofagus*) 62
Spanish fir (*Abies pinsapo*) 6
Spanish oak (*Quercus falcata*) 78
spider flower (*Grevillea*) 45
spruce (*Picea*) 64-5
star magnolia (*Magnolia stellata*) 56
strawberry guava (*Psidium littorale*) 76
strawberry tree (*Arbutus*) 17
striped maple (*Acer pensylvanicum*) 10
sunrise horse chestnut (*Aesculus* X
    neglecta 'Erythroblastos') 14
swamp cypress (*Taxodium disticum*) 89
swamp white oak (*Quercus bicolor*) 78
Swedish whitebeam
    Sorbus intermedia) 86

sweet cherry (*Prunus avium*) 73
sweet chestnut (*Castanea sativa*) 26
sweet gum (*Liquidambar styraciflua*)
    52-3
sweet orange (*Citrus sinensis*) 32
sycamore (*Acer pseudoplatanus*) 11
Sydney golden wattle
    (*Acacia longifolia*) 7

table dogwood (*Cornus controversa*) 33
tall stewartia (*Stewartia monadelpha*) 87
tamarack (*Larix laricina*) 51
Tasmanian yellow gum
    (*Eucalyptus johnstonii*) 41
Texan palmetto (*Sabal mexicana* (syn.
    S. guatemalensis, S. texana))
    81, 82
totara (*Podocarpus totara*) 69
tree lily (*Portlandia grandiflora*) 70
trident maple (*Acer buergerianum*) 7
tulip tree (*Liriodendron tulipifera*) 53
tupelo (*Nyssa sylvatica*) 62
Turkey oak (*Quercus cerris*) 78
Turner's oak (*Quercus* X *turneri*) 80

ugli fruit (*Citrus* X *tangelo*) 32
ulmo (*Eucryphia cordifolia*) 41

Vilmorin's rowan
    (*Sorbus vilmorinii*) 86
violet willow (*Salix daphnoides*) 83

walnut (*Juglans*) 48
wattle (*Acacia*) 6-7
weeping bottlebrush
    (*Callistemon viminalis*) 23
weeping fig (*Ficus benjamina*) 42
weeping willow (*Salix* X *sepulcralis*) 83
wellingtonia (*Sequoiadendron*
    giganteum) 84
western red cedar
    (*Thuja plicata*) 90
white ash (*Fraxinus americana*) 44
white cedar (*Tabebuia*
    heterophylla) 88
white mulberry (*Morus alba*) 61
white oak (*Quercus alba*) 78
white willow (*Salix alba*) 82
whitebeam (*Sorbus aria*) 85
wild rose (*Syzygium pycanthum*) 88
willow (*Salix*) 82
willow bottlebrush
    (*Callistemon salignus*) 22-3
willow oak (*Quercus phellos* (syn.
    Q. pumila)) 79

Cedrus atlantica

willow-leaf podocarp (*Podocarpus*
    salignus (syn. *P. chilinus*)) 69
wing nut (*Pterocarya*) 76

yellow birch (*Betula alleghaniensis*
    (syn. *B. lutea*)) 19
yellow catalpa
    (*Catalpa ovata*) 26
yellow elder (*Tecoma stans*) 90
yellow haw (*Crataegus flava*) 35
yellow wood (*Cladrastis kentukea*
    (syn. *C. lutea*)) 32
yellow-wood (*Podocarpus*) 68
yew (*Taxus*) 89-90

US plant hardiness zones

Plant entries in this book have been given zone numbers, and these zones relate to their hardiness. The zonal system used, shown below, was developed by the Agricultural Research Service of the U.S. Department of Agriculture. According to this system, there are 11 zones, based on the average annual minimum temperature in a particular geographical zone. When a range of zones is given for a plant, the smaller number indicates the northernmost zone in which a plant can survive the winter, and the higher number gives the most southerly area in which it will perform consistently. This system is only a rough indicator, as many factors other than temperature also play an important part where hardiness is concerned. These factors include altitude, wind exposure, proximity to water, soil type, the presence of snow or existence of shade, night temperature, and the amount of water received by a plant. These kinds of factors can easily alter a plant's hardiness by as much as two zones.

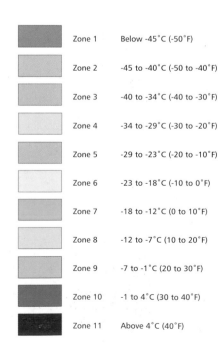

Zone 1	Below -45°C (-50°F)
Zone 2	-45 to -40°C (-50 to -40°F)
Zone 3	-40 to -34°C (-40 to -30°F)
Zone 4	-34 to -29°C (-30 to -20°F)
Zone 5	-29 to -23°C (-20 to -10°F)
Zone 6	-23 to -18°C (-10 to 0°F)
Zone 7	-18 to -12°C (0 to 10°F)
Zone 8	-12 to -7°C (10 to 20°F)
Zone 9	-7 to -1°C (20 to 30°F)
Zone 10	-1 to 4°C (30 to 40°F)
Zone 11	Above 4°C (40°F)